THE DIABETIC'S

FOOD EXCHANGE HANDBOOK

Compiled and Written by
Clara G. Schneider, M.S., R.D., L.D.

With a Foreword by
Charles R. Shuman, M.D.

RUNNING PRESS
Philadelphia • Pennsylvania

Canadian representatives: General Publishing Co., Ltd., 30 Lesmill Road, Don Mills, Ontario M3B 2T6.

International representatives: Worldwide Media Services, Inc., 115 East Twenty-third Street, New York, New York 10010.

9 8 7 6 5 4 3 2 1

Digit on the right indicates the number of this printing.

Library of Congress Cataloging-in-Publication Number 88-43387

Schneider, Clara G.
The diabetic's brand name food exchange handbook / compiled and written by Clara G. Schneider; with a foreword by Charles R. Shuman.—2nd ed.
p. cm.
Rev. ed. of: The diabetic's brand-name food exchange handbook / Andrea Barrett. © 1984.
Includes index.
ISBN 0-89471-596-8
1. Diabetes—Diet therapy. 2. Food—Tables. 3. Brand name products. 4. Food exchange lists.
I. Barrett, Andrea. Diabetic's brand-name food exchange handbook. II. Title.
RC662.S36 1991
616.4'620654—dc20

ISBN 0-89471-596-8

Cover design by Toby Schmidt
Typography: CG Palacio with ITC American Typewriter Light by Commcor Communications Corporation, Philadelphia, PA. Printed by Berryville Graphics, Berryville, VA.

This book may be ordered by mail from the publisher. Please add $2.50 for postage and handling.
But try your bookstore first!
Running Press Book Publishers
125 South Twenty-second Street
Philadelphia, Pennsylvania 19103

ACKNOWLEDGMENTS

Many thanks to the American Dietetic Association and the American Diabetes Association for their helpful assistance in providing materials and guidance when needed, and to the many manufacturers for providing information and taking time to answer questions and send additional material when requested.

Thanks to my husband Philip, our children Amy and Stephen, and our nephew Christoph for moral support, to Jina Watts for pitching in when needed, and to Barbara Herbst for her friendship.

A NOTE TO READERS

This book is written to be used with the information contained in the booklet, *Exchange Lists for Meal Planning,* copyright © 1986 by The American Diabetes Association, Inc., and The American Dietetic Association.

The Diabetic's Brand-Name Food Exchange Handbook is not intended to be used without a calorie prescription and counseling by a physician or a registered dietitian.

Clara G. Schneider, M.S., R.D., L.D., is a nutrition consultant and a freelance writer. She has served on the Board of Directors for the District of Columbia Dietetic Association for more than six years, and she has published articles in *Diabetes Self-Management* and in publications for the American Institute for Cancer Research. As a consultant, she has evaluated materials for the National Association of WIC (Women, Infants, and Children) Directors, the American Home Economics Association, and "The Office Nurse."

She presently serves as a nutritionist for Head Start programs in the Washington, D.C., area, consults in nursing homes, and advises private clients on nutrition. She and her husband and their children, Amy and Stephen, live in Arlington, Virginia.

Charles R. Shuman, M.D., a specialist in the field of diabetes, served as Chief of the Section of Metabolism at Temple University Hospital from 1952 to 1978 and is now Professor of Medicine at Temple University School of Medicine. A former member of the editorial board of the journal *Diabetes Care,* he has served two terms on the National Board of Directors of the American Diabetes Association, Inc.

CONTENTS

Foreword

DIABETES—AN OVERVIEW

The number of diabetic patients continues to increase around the world. In the United States, 600,000 new patients are found to have developed the disease each year. Considerable research is being conducted to learn more about the causes of this disease and to develop new methods to improve its treatment. Progress has been made in treating Type I diabetes with immunosuppressive agents, and pancreatic transplants have been successful in other cases. For the vast majority of diabetic patients, however, proper management of diet continues to be a fundamental method of treatment.

In 1979, the National Diabetes Data Group, an international work group sponsored by the National Institutes of Health, developed a practical classification of diabetes mellitus and other categories of glucose intolerance. Diabetes was subdivided into three different types, based primarily on the underlying causes of the disease.

Type I—insulin-dependent diabetes mellitus (IDDM)—is caused by a gradual destruction of the insulin-producing tissue (the beta cells of the pancreatic islets). In patients with this form of diabetes, comprising about 15 percent of the diabetic population, the immune system launches an attack against the beta cells because of a previous injury to them by viral infection or other toxic agents. Type I diabetes occurs most often in young patients and is related to genetic factors involving the body's immune system. There is usually a rapid onset of symptoms, which can progress to diabetic ketosis if the condition is not recognized and treated with insulin.

Type II—non-insulin-dependent diabetes (NIDDM)—occurs in 80 percent of the diabetic population, and has a genetic basis unrelated to the immune system. It is seen most frequently in adults, but may also occur in young members of families affected by this type of diabetes. Obesity is an important factor, affecting 60 percent to 90 percent of these patients. Excessive caloric intake, resulting in weight gain, leads to persistent hyperglycemia; weight loss improves the condition.

Two major factors are recognized in the origin and development of diabetes. The first involves a deficiency in glucose-stimulated insulin release from the pancreas; the second is a reduced response to insulin in tissues such as muscle, liver, and fat. Patients with Type II diabetes may have few or no symptoms for many years, but during periods of weight gain, stress, or infection they may develop the same hyperglycemia and symptoms seen in those with Type I diabetes.

Other types—secondary diabetes—occur rarely, in association with certain endocrine disorders, following disease involving the pancreas, or with a variety of genetic syndromes.

Efforts to improve the treatment of diabetes have given patients as well as physicians new and effective methods for controlling blood sugar levels. One important innovation is home blood-glucose monitoring, which enables diabetics to monitor their insulin doses and dietary intake for the most effective regulation of blood-sugar levels.

An understanding of the nutritional aspects of diabetes is crucial to its management. Diet therapy can help prevent or delay the cardiovascular, renal, retinal, and neurological complications of diabetes. The Committee on Nutrition of the American Diabetes Association advocates a balanced intake of carbohydrate, fat, and protein food sources in meal planning. The Committee recommends regular, uniform meals to ensure a consistent availability of the nutritional elements required to maintain normal function of all tissues. A diabetic's diet should be designed to accommodate the individual's eating habits, with appropriate modifications to satisfy nutritional needs and to avoid excessive amounts of refined sugars and saturated fats.

Traditional dietary management of diabetes is based on the arrangement of foods into groups. In 1950, the American Diabetes Association, The American Dietetic Association, and the U.S. Public Health System devised the *Food Exchange System*, using six lists of food. This system permits diabetics to select a wide variety of foods, each of equivalent caloric value, from the specific lists. Portions are determined by household measurements. Diets are individualized for each patient, who receives careful instruction and counseling from a physician, dietitian, and diabetes teaching nurse so as to select the proper foods for his or her daily schedule.

Using this system, the total intake of calories and the distribution of food can be kept reasonably consistent with more flexibility and more eating pleasure. This book has been prepared with these important objectives in mind.

Charles R. Shuman, M.D.
Professor of Medicine
Temple University School of Medicine
Philadelphia, PA

Introduction

USING THIS BOOK

A diabetic's meals can be varied and enjoyable as well as healthy. In the pages that follow, you'll find information in concise listings that will add scope to your diet. This information will be useful in professional counseling with your dietitian and physician and in resolving your own questions about how to enjoy a healthier diet.

Life would be easier for diabetics if manufacturers of brand-name products published exchanges and sodium values in a concise, easy-to-read format. Diabetics could then fit the products into their diets and expand their menu choices. Filling that need by providing this information for a sampling of products is the purpose of this book.

Treating Diabetes through Diet

Diet therapy has been used to treat diabetes for a very long time, and many combinations of foods were used before insulin was introduced, in 1921, by Frederick G. Banting and Charles H. Best.

In 1950 the exchange diet was introduced, together with precalculated meal plans, by The American Diabetes Association and the diabetes branch of the United States Public Health Service.[1] That original diet has been modified several times, most recently in 1986.

The 1986 diabetic exchange system is considered by The American

1. S.J. Brink, *Pediatric and Adolescent Diabetes Mellitus* (Chicago: Yearbook Medical Publishers Inc., 1987), 274.

Diabetes Association, Inc., and The American Dietetic Association as the model diabetic diet.[2] This book is based on the 1986 recommendations.

The Newest Exchange List for Meal Planning

New recommendations contained in the 1986 version of exchange lists for meal planning include:

1. Reordering the list to emphasize a diet high in carbohydrates and low in fat.
2. Adding symbols to note high-fiber foods (more than two grams fiber per serving) and high-sodium foods (more than 400 milligrams sodium per exchange).
3. Changing the nutrient content of three exchanges: the starch/bread exchange, the fruit exchange, and the skim milk exchange.
4. Expanding other lists (free foods, combination foods, foods for occasional use).
5. Revising the text of the booklet to make it more useful to diabetic patients.[3]

The information in this book complements these recommendations.

Sodium

Because about 40 percent or 50 percent of all diabetics in the U.S. have hypertension, information about sodium is of critical importance.

Hypertension affects a diabetic just as it does a non-diabetic—and it also can upset the body's blood-sugar level and aggravate diabetic complications. When untreated in a diabetic, hypertension can speed the onset of atherosclerosis and kidney disease. It also can aggravate circulation problems in the feet and legs, and weaken blood vessels in the eyes.[4] This can contribute to diabetic retinopathy, the leading cause of newly diagnosed blindness in the U.S.[5]

2. The American Diabetes Association, The American Dietetic Association *Nutrition Guide for Professionals* (Alexandria, VA: The American Diabetes Association, and Chicago: The American Dietetic Association, 1988), vii.
3. ibid., 25.
4. L.G. Lipson, "Diabetes and Hypertension" in *Diabetes Forecast* (May–June 1985), 53–54, 74, 76.
5. National High Blood Pressure Education Program, *Hypertension in Diabetes* (1987).

Hypertension can be controlled. The usual treatment includes weight loss, sodium restriction, exercise, and medications.[6] If there is a weight problem, a registered dietitian can calculate the caloric level of the exchange diet to help the patient lose weight. The sodium level of a diabetic's diet should be prescribed by a physician, especially if hypertension is present. The amount of sodium recommended by The American Heart Association and The American Diabetes Association is not more than 3,000 milligrams per day.[7] One teaspoon of table salt (sodium chloride) contains about 2,000 milligrams of sodium.

The sodium values listed in this book were provided by manufacturers. Values are given in milligrams and listed in the product exchange charts. It should be recognized that sodium values given by manufacturers must be calculated according to the Code of Federal Regulations, but these laws allow for rounding of values. According to federal law, nutrition labeling for sodium must be expressed as follows: "Sodium content shall be expressed as 0 (zero) when the serving (portion) contains less than 5 milligrams of sodium, to the nearest 5-milligram increment when the serving portion contains 5 to 140 milligrams of sodium, and to the nearest 10-milligram increment when the serving (portion) contains greater than 10 milligrams of sodium."[8]

Fiber

High-fiber foods are encouraged by The American Diabetes Association and The American Dietetic Association. Unfortunately, not many manufacturers provide information about the fiber content of their products. A registered dietitian can help plan your diet to include high-fiber foods.

Nutrient Content of the Exchange Lists

In 1986, the nutrient content of three exchange lists was revised by The American Diabetes Association and The American Dietetic Association to more accurately reflect the content of usual food portions.

The starch/bread exchange was changed to 80 calories, 15 grams of carbohydrate, 3 grams of protein, and a trace of fat. (The 1976 bread exchange was listed as 70 calories, 15 grams carbohydrate, and 2 grams protein.)

6. Lipson, 53–54, 74, 76.
7. *Nutrition Guide for Professionals*, 47.
8. U.S. Government Printing Office, *Code of Federal Regulations, Parts 100–169* (Washington, D.C., 1987), 21.

The fruit exchange was changed to 60 calories and 15 grams of carbohydrate. (The 1976 version was 40 calories and 10 grams of carbohydrate.)

The skim milk exchange represents the third change in nutrient content. It is now 90 calories, 12 grams of carbohydrate, 8 grams of protein, and a trace of fat. (In 1976, one skim milk exchange had only 80 calories.)[9]

For a complete list of the 1986 exchange values, see "Exchange Lists," page 181.

Calculating the Exchange Values in this Book

The exchange values in this book are based on one serving size of each food. Remember to measure the food and note the serving size. Any information not available for a column is noted by the symbol (N/A).

The exchanges in this book are rounded to the half exchange; it doesn't seem practical for a diabetic to deal in values less than these.

The number of calories (kcal) in carbohydrate, fat, and protein is normally calculated as 4 calories per gram of carbohydrate, 9 calories per gram of pure fat, and 4 calories per gram of pure protein.[10] In an ideal situation, it's possible to multiply the grams of carbohydrate, fat, and protein in any food by these numbers to find out the number of calories per serving.

For example, let's calculate the exchange values for "LeSueur Peas, Onions and Carrots in Butter Sauce" (page 60). The quantity for one serving is one-half cup. There are 11 grams of carbohydrate, 4 grams of protein, and 3 grams of fat in this product. If you subtract one-half starch exchange from the values (7.5 grams of carbohydrate, 1.5 grams of protein, and a trace of fat) it would leave 3.5 grams of carbohydrate, 2.5 grams of protein, and 3 grams of fat. That is approximately equal to 1 vegetable exchange and one-half fat exchange. The net calculation would be one-half starch, 1 vegetable, and one-half fat exchange.

Most values in this book come close to the ideal, but remember that the exchanges in this book are rounded to the one-half exchange.

9. *Nutrition Guide for Professionals*, 25.
10. C. H. Robinson and M. R. Lawier, *Normal and Therapeutic Nutrition, 15th edition* (New York, Macmillan Publishing Co., 1977), 93.

Rounding also takes place at the manufacturing level. According to federal law, if a manufacturer includes nutrition information on its label, the amount of carbohydrate, protein, and fat must be expressed to the nearest gram (except that when a serving contains less than one gram, label could say "contains less than one gram"). Manufacturers' listings for calories must follow federal guidelines: calories per serving must be expressed to the nearest 2-calorie increment for servings up to and including 20 calories. Amounts of more than 20 calories and up to 50 calories must be calculated to the nearest 5-calorie increment, and amounts above 50 must be calculated to the nearest 10-calorie increment. Caloric content may be calculated on the basis of 4 calories per gram for protein, 4 calories per gram for carbohydrate, 9 calories per gram for fat (unless the use of these values gives a caloric value different from one obtained by using the more accurate values determined by using the Atwater method described in USDA Handbook 74, 1955).[11]

Rounding also has been done in calculating the caloric values of The American Diabetes Association and The American Dietetic Association's *Exchange Lists for Meal Planning*. When the values for carbohydrate, protein, and fat are calculated at 4, 4, and 9 calories per gram for the data shown on page 181, the following caloric values are derived (Column A). These differ slightly from some of the calorie levels listed by The American Diabetes Association and The American Dietetic Association (Column B) in *Exchange Lists for Meal Planning*.

Exchange	A Calories	B Exchange calories
Starch/Bread	72	80
Meat—Lean	55	55
—Medium-Fat	73	75
—High-Fat	100	100
Vegetable	28	25
Fruit	60	60
Milk —Skim	80	90
—Low-Fat	125	120
—Whole	152	150
Fat	45	45

11. *Code of Federal Regulations*, 19.

Rounding seems to affect products with many bread exchanges more than any other foods. Any questions you may have about this subject should be discussed with a dietitian.

Abbreviations

Exchanges are listed in this book as follows:

Exchange	Abbreviation
Starch/Bread	S
Leat Meat	LMt
Medium Fat Meat	MFMt
High Fat Meat	HFMt
Vegetables	V
Fruits	Fr
Skim Milk	SMk
Low Fat Milk	LFMk
Whole Milk	WMk
Fat	Fat

In addition, in listing portions, these measurements are used:

Measurement	Abbreviation
fluid ounce (volume)	fl. oz.
gram	g
kilocalories	kcal
less than	<
milligram	mg
milliliter	ml
more than	>
not applicable	(N/A)
ounce (weight)	oz.
package	pkg.
packet	pkt.
pint	pt.
pound	lb.
quart	qt.
tablespoon	tbsp.
tsp.	tsp.

Free Foods

A "free food" is any food or drink with less than 20 calories per serving.[12] Some free foods have a specific serving size and some do not. For ones that do, 2 to 3 servings are allowed per day (spread throughout the day).

To be on the safe side, discuss all free foods with a dietitian.

Combination Foods

Combination foods are those that fit into more than one food exchange list. In analyzing combination foods for this book, grams of carbohydrate, protein, and fat were calculated. When available, ingredient listings were studied and telephone calls were placed to manufacturers. Rounding could alter some of the calculations given for these foods, but it should not have a major effect.

Foods for Occasional Use

Foods that contain concentrated sources of carbohydrates are allowed in a diabetic's diet as long as blood-glucose values are controlled. Servings should be small, and all foods should be discussed with a dietitian for use in a food plan. Foods with concentrated sources of carbohydrates are listed with the symbol (*) in this book.

12. The American Diabetes Association, The American Dietetic Association, *Exchange Lists for Meal Planning* (Alexandria, VA, The American Diabetes Association, and Chicago, IL, The American Dietetic Association, 1986), 22.

1

SOUPS & STEWS

Soups and stews are nutritious foods that need little preparation. Nothing tastes better on cold wintry days when you want a quick meal.

When you measure soup, be sure to add the recommended amount of milk or water. Remember that one serving of soup can be quite high in sodium. Using low-sodium soup will make a big difference.

Talk to your dietitian about soups that have free exchanges. Ask about the number of free servings allowed per day, taking sodium content into consideration. Soups that have about 20 calories per serving should be limited to two or three servings spread throughout the day.

Food	Portion	Exchanges	Calories	Sodium (mg)
Soups & Stews				
Asparagus, Cream of				
Campbell's Condensed, prepared w/water	(8 oz.)	½ S, ½ V, 1 Fat	90	840
Campbell's Creamy Natural Condensed, prepared w/whole milk	(8 oz.)	½ S, ½ WMk, 1 Fat	170	710
Bean (*See also* Lentil)				
Campbell's Chunky, ready to serve (individual-size can)				
Ham 'n' Butter Bean	(10¾ oz.)	2 S, 1 MFMt, 1 Fat	280	1180
Old Fashioned Bean w/Ham	(11 oz.)	2½ S, 1 MFMt, ½ Fat	290	1110
Campbell's Chunky, Old Fashioned Bean w/Ham, ready to serve	(9⅝ oz. of 19-oz. can)	2 S, 1 LMt, 1 Fat	260	960
Campbell's Condensed, prepared w/water (8 oz.)				
Bean w/Bacon		1½ S, ½ Fat	150	860
Black Bean		1 S, ½ LMt	110	950
Campbell's Semi-Condensed, Chunky Old Fashioned Bean w/Ham, for one	(11 oz.)	2 S, 1½ Fat	220	1340
Beef				
Campbell's Chunky, ready to serve (individual-size can)				
Beef	(10¾ oz.)	1½ S, 1 MFMt	190	1080
Chili Beef	(11 oz.)	2½ S, 2 LMt	290	1150
Sirloin Burger	(10¾ oz.)	1½ S, 1 LMt, 1 Fat	220	1270
Steak & Potato	(10¾ oz.)	1½ S, 1 MFMt, ½ V	200	1110
Stroganoff-Style Beef	(10¾ oz.)	1½ S, 1 MFMt, 1 V, 2 Fat	300	1290
Campbell's Chunky, ready to serve (19-oz. can)				
Beef	(9½ oz.)	1 S, 1 V, 1 MFMt	170	950
Chili Beef	(9¾ oz.)	2 S, 1 V, 1½ LMt	260	1000
Old Fashioned Vegetable Beef	(9½ oz.)	1 S, 1 MFMt	160	1000
Sirloin Burger	(9½ oz.)	1 S, 1 V, 1 HFMt	200	1100
Steak 'n' Potato	(9½ oz.)	1½ S, 1 LMt	170	980
Campbell's Condensed, prepared w/water (8 oz.)				
Beef		1 S, 1 V, ½ Fat	80	840
Beef Noodle		½ S, ½ MFMt	70	860
Beef Noodle Homestyle		½ S, 1 LMt	80	800
Beefy Mushroom		1 V, ½ LMt	60	960
Chili Beef		1 S, ½ HFMt	130	900
Consomme (Beef), gelatin added		½ LMt	25	770
Meatball Alphabet		½ S, ½ V, ½ HFMt	100	950

Food	Portion	Exchanges	Calories	Sodium (mg)
Noodles & Ground Beef		½ S, ½ HFMt	90	820
Vegetable Beef		2 V, ½ Fat	70	820
Campbell's Home Cookin', Vegetable Beef, ready to serve	(10¾ oz.)	1 S, 1 LMt, ½ V	150	1110
Campbell's Low Sodium, ready to serve (10¾ oz.)				
Chunky Beef & Mushroom		1½ S, 1 HFMt	210	65
Chunky Vegetable Beef		1 S, 1 V, 1 MFMt	170	60
Campbell's Semi-Condensed, Barley Vegetable Beef & Bacon, for one	(11 oz.)	1 S, ½ MFMt, 1 V, ½ Fat	160	1440
Fresh Chef, Beef w/Garden Vegetables	(7¼ oz.)	2 V, 1 LMt	110	670
Weight Watchers, Vegetable w/Beef Stock	(10½ oz.)	1 S, ½ Fat	90	1370
Borscht				
Manischewitz (8 fl. oz.)				
*w/Beets**		½ S, ½ Fr	80	660
Low Calorie		free	20	725
Broccoli, Cream of				
Campbell's Creamy Natural Condensed, prepared w/whole milk	(8 oz.)	½ WMk, 1½ V, ½ Fat	140	570
Fresh Chef	(7 oz.)	½ S, 4 Fat	230	730
Broth & Bouillon				
Campbell's Condensed Broth, prepared w/water (8 oz.)				
Beef		free	16	820
Chicken		½ V, ½ Fat	35	750
Scotch		½ S, ½ MFMt	80	870
Campbell's Low Sodium, Chicken Broth, ready to serve	(10½ oz.)	½ V, ½ Fat	40	70
College Inn Broth (1 cup)				
Beef		free	18	1280
Chicken		½ Fat	35	1320
Herb-Ox Instant Broth (1 pkt.)				
Beef Flavor, Low Sodium		free	12	10
Vegetable Flavor		free	12	840
Lite-Line Low Sodium Instant Bouillon (1 tsp.)				
Beef Flavor w/Other Natural Flavor		free	12	5
Chicken Flavor		free	12	5
Swanson Canned Broth (7¼ oz.)				
Beef		free	20	750
Chicken		½ Fat	30	910

*Contains concentrated sources of carbohydrates

Food	Portion	Exchanges	Calories	Sodium (mg)
Broth & Bouillon, cont.				
Weight Watchers Broth (1 pkt.)				
Beef		free	8	930
Chicken		free	8	990
Wyler's Instant Bouillon				
Beef Flavor w/Other Natural Flavor	(1 tsp. or 1 cube)	free	6	930
Chicken Flavor	(1 cube)	free	8	900
Onion Flavor	(1 tsp.)	free	10	670
Vegetable Flavor	(1 tsp.)	free	6	910
Cauliflower, Campbell's Creamy Natural Condensed, prepared w/whole milk	(8 oz.)	½ S, ½ WMk, 2 Fat	200	850
Celery, Cream of, Campbell's Condensed, prepared w/water	(8 oz.)	½ S, 1½ Fat	100	860
Cheese				
Campbell's Condensed, prepared w/water (8 oz.)				
Cheddar		½ S, ½ MFMt, 1 Fat	130	750
Nacho		½ V, ½ MFMt, 1 Fat	100	680
Campbell's Quality Dry Mix, Cheddar	(8 oz.)	½ S, 1 V, ½ MFMt, 1½ Fat	160	820
Chicken				
Campbell's Chunky, ready to serve (individual-size can)				
Chicken Noodle w/Mushroom	(10¾ oz.)	1½ S, ½ MFMt, 1 Fat	200	1140
Creamy Chicken Mushroom	(10½ oz.)	½ S, 1 V, 1 MFMt, 4 Fat	320	1420
Old Fashioned Chicken	(10¾ oz.)	1½ S, 1 MFMt	180	1190
Campbell's Chunky, ready to serve (19-oz. can)				
Chicken Noodle	(9½ oz.)	1 S, 1 V, 1 MFMt	180	1010
Chicken Rice	(9½ oz.)	1 S, 1 LMt	140	1050
Chicken Vegetable	(9½ oz.)	1 S, ½ V, 1 MFMt	170	1100
Creamy Chicken Mushroom	(9⅜ oz.)	½ S, ½ V, 1 LMt, 4 Fat	280	1260
Old Fashioned Chicken	(9½ oz.)	1 S, 1 MFMt	150	1040
Campbell's Condensed, prepared w/water (8 oz.)				
Chicken Alphabet		½ S, ½ V, ½ Fat	70	850
Chicken Broth & Noodles		½ S, ½ Fat	60	870
Chicken Broth & Rice		½ S	50	850
Chicken 'n' Dumplings		½ S, ½ MFMt	80	980
Chicken Gumbo		½ S, ½ Fat	60	900
Chicken Noodle		½ S, ½ Fat	70	910

Food	Portion	Exchanges	Calories	Sodium (mg)
Chicken Noodle Homestyle		½ S, ½ Fat	70	920
Chicken Noodle O's		½ S, ½ Fat	70	840
Chicken w/Rice		½ S, ½ Fat	60	820
Chicken & Stars		½ S, ½ Fat	60	870
Chicken Vegetable		½ S, ½ Fat	70	880
Cream of Chicken		½ S, ½ LMt, 1 Fat	110	850
Creamy Chicken Mushroom		½ S, ½ LMt, 1 Fat	120	940
Campbell's Home Cookin', Chicken w/Noodles, ready to serve	(10¾ oz.)	½ S, 1½ LMt, 1 V	140	1020
Campbell's Low Sodium, ready to serve (10¾ oz.)				
Chicken w/Noodles		1 S, 1½ LMt	160	85
Chunky Chicken Vegetable		1 S, 1 V, 1½ MFMt, ½ Fat	240	95
Campbell's Quality Dry Mix (8 oz.)				
Chicken Noodle		1 S, ½ LMt	100	780
Chicken Rice		1 S, ½ Fat	90	810
Campbell's Semi-Condensed, for one (11 oz.)				
Full Flavored Chicken Vegetable		2½ V, 1½ Fat	120	1500
Golden Chicken & Noodles		½ S, ½ HFMt, 1 V	120	1450
Fresh Chef, Chicken w/Garden Vegetables	(7¼ oz.)	2 V, 1 LMt	110	600
Lipton (8 fl. oz.)				
Chicken Noodle		1 S, ½ Fat	80	800
Hearty Chicken Noodle		1 S	80	680
Weight Watchers, Chicken Noodle	(10½ oz.)	½ S, ½ V, ½ LMt	80	1230
Chowder				
Campbell's Chunky, ready to serve (10¾ oz. individual-size can)				
Clam Chowder, Manhattan Style		1 S, 1 V, ½ MFMt, ½ Fat	160	1230
Clam Chowder, New England Style		1½ S, ½ V, ½ LMt, 3 Fat	290	1180
Fisherman Chowder		1½ S, 1 MFMt, 1½ Fat	260	1320
Campbell's Chunky, ready to serve (½ of 19-oz. can)				
Clam Chowder, Manhattan Style		1 S, 1 V, ½ HFMt	150	1080
Clam Chowder, New England Style		1½ S, ½ MFMt, 2½ Fat	250	1040
Fisherman Chowder		1½ S, 1 LMt, 2 Fat	230	1160
Campbell's Condensed (8 oz.)				
Clam Chowder, Manhattan Style, prepared w/water		½ S, ½ V, ½ Fat	70	840
Clam Chowder, New England Style, prepared w/whole milk		½ S, ½ WMk, 1 Fat	150	930
Campbell's Semi-Condensed, for one (11 oz.)				
Clam Chowder, New England Style, prepared w/water		1 S, ½ HFMt	130	1360

Food	Portion	Exchanges	Calories	Sodium (mg)
Chowder, cont.				
Clam Chowder, New England Style, prepared w/whole milk		1 S, ½ HFMt, ½ WMk	190	1410
Fresh Chef, New England Clam Chowder	(7¼ oz.)	1 S, 2 Fat	160	1020
Gorton's New England Clam Chowder, prepared w/whole milk	(¼ can)	½ WMk, ½ S, ½ LMt	140	740
Snow's Condensed, before adding milk	(3¾ oz.)			
Manhattan Clam Chowder		½ MFMt, 1 V	70	630
New England Clam Chowder		½ S, ½ MFMt	70	620
New England Corn Chowder		1 S, ½ Fat	80	590
New England Fish Chowder		½ LMt, ½ S	60	560
New England Seafood Chowder		½ LMt, ½ S	60	640
Stouffer's New England Clam Chowder	(8 oz.)	½ S, ½ LMt, ½ WMk, 1 Fat	200	790
Lentil, Campbell's Home Cookin', ready to serve	(10¾ oz.)	2 S, ½ LMt	170	940
Minestrone				
Campbell's Chunky, ready to serve	(½ of 19 oz. can)	1½ S, ½ V, ½ Fat	160	860
Campbell's Condensed, prepared w/water	(8 oz.)	½ S, 1 V, ½ Fat	80	910
Campbell's Home Cookin', ready to serve	(10¾ oz.)	1 S, 1½ V, ½ Fat	140	1200
Lipton Hearty	(8 fl. oz.)	1 S, ½ Fat	100	700
Manischewitz Mix	(6 fl. oz.)	½ S, ½ V	50	160
Mushroom				
Campbell's Chunky, Creamy Mushroom, ready to serve	(10½ oz. individual-size can)	½ S, ½ MFMt, 4 Fat	260	1280
Campbell's Chunky, Creamy Mushroom, ready to serve	(½ of 19-oz. can)	½ S, 1 V, 4 Fat	240	1140
Campbell's Condensed, prepared w/water	(8 oz.)			
Cream of Mushroom		½ S, 1½ Fat	100	820
Golden Mushroom		½ S, ½ V, ½ Fat	80	880
Campbell's Low Sodium, Cream of Mushroom, ready to serve	(10½ oz.)	1 S, 3 Fat	200	55
Campbell's Semi-Condensed, Savory Cream of Mushroom, for one	(11 oz.)	½ S, 1 V, 2½ Fat	180	1500
Fresh Chef, Country Mushroom Bisque	(7 oz.)	1 S, 4 Fat	240	650
Weight Watchers, Cream of Mushroom	(10½ oz.)	1 S, ½ Fat	90	1250

Food	Portion	Exchanges	Calories	Sodium (mg)
Noodle				
Campbell's Condensed, Curly Noodle, prepared w/water	(8 oz.)	½ S, ½ MFMt	70	960
Campbell's Quality Dry Mix, Noodle	(8 oz.)	1 S, ½ V, ½ Fat	110	730
Onion				
Campbell's Condensed, French Onion, prepared w/water	(8 oz.)	½ S, ½ Fat	60	920
Campbell's Low Sodium, French Onion, ready to serve	(10½ oz.)	1 V, 1 Fat	80	50
Campbell's Quality Dry Mix (8 oz.)				
Onion		½ S	50	730
Onion Mushroom		½ S	50	700
Lipton, Onion Soup & Recipe Mix	(8 fl. oz.)	½ S	35	640
Oriental				
Campbell's Condensed, Won Ton, prepared w/water	(8 oz.)	½ S	40	880
La Choy Chicken Won Ton	(1 pkg.)	1 S, ½ LMt	50	2100
Oyster Stew, Campbell's Condensed, prepared w/whole milk	(8 oz.)	½ WMk, ½ MFMt, ½ V, ½ Fat	150	900
Pea				
Campbell's Chunky, Split Pea 'n' Ham, ready to serve	(10¾ oz. individual-size can)	2 S, 1 MFMt	230	1070
Campbell's Chunky, Split Pea w/Ham, ready to serve	(½ of 19-oz. can)	2 S, ½ MFMt, ½ Fat	210	940
Campbell's Condensed, prepared w/water (8 oz.)				
Green Pea		1½ S, ½ MFMt	160	830
Split Pea w/Ham & Bacon		1½ S, ½ HFMt	160	790
Campbell's Home Cookin' Split Pea w/Ham, ready to serve	(10¾ oz.)	2 S, 1 LMt	210	1180
Campbell's Low Sodium, Split Pea, ready to serve	(10¾ oz.)	2½ S, ½ HFMt	240	25
Manischewitz, Split Pea Mix	(6 fl. oz.)	½ S	45	320
Stouffer's, Split Pea w/Ham	(8¼ oz.)	2 S, 1 LMt	200	1130
Potato, Cream of				
Campbell's Condensed, prepared w/whole milk	(8 oz.)	½ S, ½ WMk	110	910
Campbell's Creamy Natural Condensed, prepared w/whole milk	(8 oz.)	½ S, ½ WMk, 1½ Fat	190	510

Food	Portion	Exchanges	Calories	Sodium (mg)
Spinach, Cream of				
Campbell's Creamy Natural Condensed, prepared w/whole milk	(8 oz.)	½ WMk, 1 V, 1 Fat	160	700
Stouffer's	(8 oz.)	½ S, ½ V, ½ WMk, 2 Fat	220	1020
Shrimp, Cream of, Campbell's Condensed*, prepared w/whole milk	(8 oz.)	½ S, ½ WMk, 1 Fat	160	850
Tomato				
Campbell's Condensed, prepared w/water (8 oz.)				
Tomato		1 S	90	660
*Tomato Bisque**		1 S, ½ Fr, ½ Fat	120	820
Tomato Rice, Old Fashioned		1 S, ½ Fat	110	760
Campbell's Condensed, prepared w/whole milk (8 oz.)				
Cream of Tomato, Homestyle		1 S, ½ WMk, ½ Fat	180	880
Tomato		1 S, ½ WMk	160	710
Campbell's Low Sodium, Tomato w/Tomato Pieces, ready to serve	(10½ oz.)	1 S, 1 Fr, 1 Fat	180	40
Campbell's Semi-Condensed, Tomato Royale, for one	(11 oz.)	1 S, 1 Fr, 1 Fat	180	1080
Fresh Chef, Tomato Bisque	(7 oz.)	1 S, 1½ Fat	150	630
Lipton (8 fl. oz.)				
Hearty Cream of Tomato & Rice		1½ S	130	1050
Hearty Tomato Vegetable Noodle		1 S	80	680
Turkey				
Campbell's Chunky, Turkey Vegetable, ready to serve	(9⅜ oz. of 19 oz.)	½ S, 1½ V, 1 MFMt	150	1060
Campbell's Condensed, prepared w/water (8 oz.)				
Turkey Noodle		½ S, ½ MFMt	70	870
Turkey Vegetable		½ S, ½ Fat	70	800
Weight Watchers, Turkey Vegetable	(10½ oz.)	2 V, ½ Fat	70	1020
Vegetable				
Campbell's Chunky, ready to serve (10¾ oz. individual-size can)				
Old Fashioned Vegetable		1 S, 1 V, 1 MFMt	180	1130
Vegetable		1 S, 1½ V, ½ Fat	140	1100
Campbell's Chunky, ready to serve (½ of 19-oz. can)				
Mediterranean Vegetable		1½ S, 1 Fat	160	1020
Vegetable		1 S, 1 V, ½ Fat	130	970
Campbell's Condensed, prepared w/water (8 oz.)				
Old Fashioned Vegetable		1½ V, ½ Fat	60	890
Pepper Pot		½ S, ½ HFMt	90	960

*Contains concentrated sources of carbohydrates

Food	Portion	Exchanges	Calories	Sodium (mg)
Vegetable		½ S, 1 V, ½ Fat	90	800
Vegetarian Vegetable		1 S, ½ Fat	90	800
Campbell's Home Cookin', Country Vegetable, ready to serve	(10¾ oz.)	1 S, 1 V, ½ Fat	120	1130
Campbell's Semi-Condensed, Old World Vegetable, for one	(11 oz.)	½ S, 2 V, 1 Fat	130	1470
Manischewitz, Vegetable Mix	(6 fl. oz.)	½ S, ½ V	50	85
Weight Watchers, Vegetarian Vegetable	(10½ oz.)	1 S, ½ V, ½ Fat	100	1250

2

COMBINATION MAIN DISHES

Frozen, refrigerated, and canned main dishes can be helpful in planning a diet because the meal has already been measured by its manufacturer. For a diabetic on a weight-loss plan, this can be very helpful.

Look at sodium values in these dishes, because some choices in this category are high in sodium, while others are moderate. To make an evaluation, add up all the sodium consumed in one meal.

Sometimes you'll see a fruit exchange listed for a main dish even though there is no fruit in the dinner. This is because the meal contains concentrated sources of carbohydrate. Ask your dietitian for advice.

Food	Portion	Exchanges	Calories	Sodium (mg)
■ American-Style				
Beef				
Carnation				
Beef Stew	(7½ oz. of 15-oz. can)	1 S, 1 MFMt, ½ V	160	(N/A)
Beef Stew	(8 oz. of 24-oz. can)	1 S, 1 MFMt, ½ V	170	(N/A)
Sloppy Joe Barbeque Sauce w/Beef	(⅓ cup of 15¼-oz. can)	½ HFMt, 1½ V, ½ Fat	110	190
Dinty Moore (7½ oz.)				
Beef Stew		1 S, 1½ MFMt	180	939
Sliced Potatoes 'n' Beef		1½ S, ½ V, 1 HFMt, 1 Fat	250	(N/A)
Hamburger Helper				
Beef Noodle	(⅕ pkg.)	1½ S, 2 MFMt, 1 Fat	320	1050
Beef Romanoff	(⅕ pkg.)	2 S, 2 MFMt, 1 Fat	350	1150
Cheeseburger Macaroni	(⅕ pkg.)	2 S, 2 MFMt, 1½ Fat	360	1030
Hamburger Hash	(⅕ pkg.)	1½ S, 2 MFMt, 1 Fat	320	1020
Hamburger Stew	(⅕ pkg.)	1 S, 2 V, 1½ MFMt, 1 Fat	300	1010
Meat Loaf	(⅕ pkg.)	1S, 3½ MFMt, ½ Fat	360	710
Potatoes au Gratin	(⅕ pkg.)	1½ S, 2 MFMt, 1 Fat	320	910
Potato Stroganoff	(⅕ pkg.)	1½ S, 2 MFMt, 1 Fat	320	900
Sloppy Joe Bake	(⅙ pkg.)	1½ S, 1½ MFMt, 2 V, 1½ Fat	340	1090
Hormel (7½ oz.)				
Beef Goulash		1 S, 2 MFMt, ½ Fat	230	(N/A)
Noodles 'n' Beef		1 S, 1 MFMt, 2 Fat	230	974
Hungry-Man Dinners (1 complete dinner)				
*Chopped Beef Steak**	(16¾ oz.)	1½ S, 1 Fr, 4 MFMt, 3 Fat	640	1600
Salisbury Steak	(18¼ oz.)	1 S, 1 Fr, 1 V, 5 MFMt, 3 Fat	680	1730
*Sliced Beef**	(15½ oz.)	2 S, 1 Fr, 4½ LMt	450	1060
Western Style	(17½ oz.)	3½ S, 1 Fr, 4½ MFMt, 2 Fat	740	1730
Hungry-Man Entrees, Salisbury Steak	(1 complete entree)	2 S, 4½ MFMt, 3 Fat	610	1310
Hungry-Man Pot Pies, Beef	(1 pie)	4 S, 2 V, 1½ MFMt, 5 Fat	680	1500
Le Menu Dinners (1 complete dinner)				
Beef Sirloin Tips		2½ S, 1 V, 3 MFMt, 1 Fat	410	820
Beef Stroganoff		2½ S, 1 V, 3 MFMt, 2 Fat	450	1100
Chopped Sirloin Beef		2 S, 1 V, 2 MFMt, 2 Fat	410	1020
Pepper Steak		2 S, 1½ V, 2½ MFMt	380	1100
Yankee Pot Roast		1½ S, 1 V, 3 MFMt	360	780
Le Menu Entrees, Beef Burgundy	(1 complete entree)	1 V, 3 MFMt, 2 Fat	330	660

*Contains concentrated sources of carbohydrates

Food	Portion	Exchanges	Calories	Sodium (mg)
Le Menu Light Style Dinners (1 complete dinner)				
*Beef à l'Orange**		1 S, ½ Fr, 1½ V, 2½ LMt	290	580
Salisbury Steak		1 S, 1 V, 2 LMt	220	830
Mary Kitchen (7½ oz.)				
Corned Beef Hash		1 S, 2½ HFMt, 1 Fat	360	1368
Roast Beef Hash		1 S, 1 V, 2 MFMt, 2½ Fat	360	1156
Stouffer's Dinner Supreme				
Beef Tips Bourguignonne	(12⅜ oz.)	1 S, 1 V, 3 LMt, 1 Fat	360	1390
Salisbury Steak w/Gravy & Mushrooms	(13½ oz.)	1½ S, 1 V, 3 MFMt, ½ Fat	380	1090
Stouffer's Entrees				
Beef Pie	(10 oz.)	2 S, 1 V, 2 HFMt, 4 Fat	560	1300
Beef Stew	(10 oz.)	1 S, 1 V, 2½ MFMt, ½ Fat	310	1460
Beef Stroganoff w/Parsley Noodles	(9¾ oz.)	2 S, 2½ LMt, 2½ Fat	410	1180
Creamed Chipped Beef	(5½ oz.)	½ S, 1 LMt, ½ LFMk, 2 Fat	240	890
Roast Beef Hash	(5¾ oz.)	1 S, 2 MFMt, 1 Fat	250	710
Salisbury Steaks w/Onion Gravy	(6 oz.)	½ S, 2½ MFMt	230	1120
Short Ribs of Beef w/Vegetable Gravy	(5¾ oz.)	½ V, 3 MFMt, 1 Fat	280	510
Steak & Mushroom Pie	(10 oz.)	2 S, ½ V, 2 MFMt, 2½ Fat	430	1220
Stuffed Green Peppers w/Beef in Tomato Sauce	(7¾ oz.)	1 S, ½ V, 1 MFMt, 1 Fat	220	870
Swedish Meatballs in Gravy w/Parsley Noodles	(11 oz.)	2½ S, 2½ MFMt, 2½ Fat	470	1460
Stouffer's Lean Cuisine				
Beef & Pork Cannelloni w/Mornay Sauce	(9⅝ oz.)	1 S, ½ V, ½ SMk, 2 MFMt	270	940
Meatball Stew	(10 oz.)	1 S, 1 V, 2½ LMt, ½ Fat	250	1120
Salisbury Steak w/Italian-Style Sauce & Vegetables	(9½ oz.)	½ S, 1 V, 3 LMt, 1 Fat	270	700
Stuffed Cabbage w/Meat in Tomato Sauce	(10¾ oz.)	1 S, 1 V, 1½ LMt, 1 Fat	220	930
Swanson Chunky Pies				
Beef	(1 pie)	3 S, 1½ V, 1 MFMt, 4½ Fat	550	920
Swanson Entrees (1 complete dinner)				
Salisbury Steak	(10 oz.)	½ S, 3 MFMt, 3½ Fat	410	970
Swedish Meatballs	(9¼ oz.)	1 S, 2½ MFMt, 3½ Fat	420	710
Swanson 4-Compartment Dinners (1 complete dinner)				
*Beef**		1½ S, 1 Fr, 3½ LMt	360	860

*Contains concentrated sources of carbohydrates

Food	Portion	Exchanges	Calories	Sodium (mg)
*Beef in Barbeque Sauce**		2 S, 1 Fr, 1 V, 3 MFMt	460	890
*Chopped Sirloin Beef**		1 S, ½ Fr, 1½ V, 2 MFMt, 2 Fat	370	850
Meat Loaf		1½ S, 1 Fr, 1 V, 1½ MFMt, 3 Fat	430	1030
*Salisbury Steak**		2 S, 1 Fr, 2 MFMt, 1½ Fat	410	880
Swiss Steak		1½ S, 1 Fr, 2½ LMt, 1 Fat	350	700
Western-Style		2 S, 1 Fr, 2 MFMt, 2 Fat	450	1010
Swanson Pot Pies				
Beef	(1 pie)	2 S, 2 V, ½ MFMt, 3½ Fat	410	760
Weight Watchers				
Beef Salisbury Steak Romana w/Rotini Noodles	(8¾ oz.)	1½ S, 2 V, 2 MFMt,	320	1030
Beef Stroganoff w/Parsley Noodles	(9 oz.)	1½ S, 1 V, 2½ MFMt, ½ Fat	340	930
Chopped Beef Steak in Green Pepper & Mushroom Sauce w/Carrots & Green Beans	(9 oz.)	½ S, 1½ V, 2½ MFMt	270	1000
Cheese & Crepes				
Stouffer's Entrees				
Cheese Souffle	(7⅝ oz.)	1 S, 3 MFMt, 4 Fat	480	1210
Spinach Crepes w/Cheddar Cheese Sauce	(9½ oz.)	1½ S, 1 V, 1½ HFMt, 3 Fat	420	1100
Welsh Rarebit	(½ of a 10-oz. pkg)	½ S, 1 HFMt, ½ LFMk, 3½ Fat	360	700
Chili				
Carnation (7½ oz.)				
No Beans		2 V, 2 MFMt, 4 Fat	390	(N/A)
w/Beans		1 S, 1 MFMt, 2 V, 1½ Fat	270	810
Hamburger Helper				
No Beans	(¼ pkg.)	2 S, 1 V, 2½ MFMt, ½ Fat	400	1670
w/Beans	(¼ pkg.)	1 S, 2 V, 2 MFMt, 1½ Fat	350	1760
w/Beans; Hot	(¼ pkg.)	1 S, 2 V, 2½ MFMt, 1 Fat	350	1310
Tomato	(⅕ pkg.)	1½ S, ½ V, 2 MFMt, ½ Fat	330	1360
Hormel Individual (7½-oz. can)				
No Beans		½ S, 1 V, 2½ HFMt, 1½ Fat	360	961
w/Beans		1½ S, 1 HFMt	280	1134
w/Beans; Hot		1½ S, 2 HFMt	300	1086
Stouffer's, *w/Beans*	(8¾ oz.)	1 S, 1½ V, 2½ MFMt	280	1190
Eggs & Breakfast Dishes				
Eggs, Swanson's Great Start Breakfasts				
Omelets w/Cheese Sauce & Ham	(7 oz.)	1 S, 2 MFMt, 4 Fat	400	1160

*Contains concentrated sources of carbohydrates

Food	Portion	Exchanges	Calories	Sodium (mg)
Eggs & Breakfast Dishes, cont.				
Scrambled Eggs & Sausage w/Hashed Brown Potatoes	(6¼ oz.)	1 S, 1½ MFMt, 5½ Fat	430	780
Spanish-Style Omelet	(7¾ oz.)	1 S, 1 MFMt, 2½ Fat	250	810
Egg Substitutes, Fleischmann's				
Egg Beaters Cholesterol-free Egg Product	(¼ cup)	½ LMt	25	80
Cheez Egg Product w/Imitation Cheese	(½ cup)	2 LMt	130	440
French Toast, Swanson's Great Starts Breakfast (6½ oz.)				
Cinnamon Swirl		2½ S, 1 LMt, 5 Fat	480	670
w/Sausages		2½ S, 1 MFMt, 4 Fat	460	640
Pancakes, Swanson's Great Starts Breakfast				
*Pancakes & Blueberry Sauce**	(7 oz.)	2½ S, 2 Fr, 2 Fat	410	800
*Pancakes & Sausage**	(6 oz.)	2½ S, ½ Fr, 1 MFMt, 4 Fat	470	890
*Pancakes w/Strawberries**	(7 oz.)	3 S, 2 Fr, 2 Fat	430	940
Sandwiches, Swanson Great Starts Breakfast (1 sandwich)				
Biscuit & Sausage	(4¾ oz.)	2½ S, 1 HFMt, 3 Fat	410	1370
Egg, Canadian Bacon, & Cheese/Muffin	(4½ oz.)	1½ S, 1½ MFMt, 1½ Fat	310	860
Sausage, Egg, & Cheese/Biscuit	(6¼ oz.)	2½ S, 1½ MFMt, 5 Fat	520	1640
Fish & Seafood				
Fresh Chef Salads, Seafood Pasta	(4¼ oz.)	1 S, 3½ Fat	240	540
Gorton's, Fishniks 'n' Chips	(⅓ pkg.)	3 S, 1 MFMt, 4 Fat	450	460
Gorton's Light Recipe (1 pkg.)				
Baked Stuffed Scrod		½ S, 3½ LMt, ½ Fat	260	490
Baked Stuffed Shrimp		2½ S, 1 MFMt, 2 Fat	340	950
Crab au Gratin		1 S, ½ V, 2½ MFMt	280	810
Filet of Haddock w/Lemon Butter Sauce		½ S, 3½ LMt	240	570
Filet of Sole w/Lemon Butter Sauce		½ S, 3½ LMt, ½ Fat	250	730
Shrimp & Pasta Medley		2 S, 2 MFMt, 1½ Fat	370	550
Shrimp Scampi		1 S, 2 MFMt, 3 Fat	350	420
Stuffed Crabs Imperial		2 S, 1½ MFMt, 2½ Fat	360	670
Stuffed Flounder		1 S, 2½ MFMt	260	880
Hungry Man Dinners, Fish 'n' Chips	(1 complete dinner)	4 S, 1 Fr, 3 MFMt, 4½ Fat	780	1400

*Contains concentrated sources of carbohydrates

Food	Portion	Exchanges	Calories	Sodium (mg)
LeMenu Dinners, Stuffed Flounder	(1 complete dinner)	1½ S, 1 V, 2 MFMt, 1½ Fat	350	970
Le Menu Light Style Dinner, Flounder vin Blanc	(1 complete dinner)	1 S, 2 V, 1½ LMt	220	640
Mrs. Paul's Light Seafood Entrees				
Fish au Gratin	(10 oz.)	1½ S, 3½ LMt	290	1130
Fish Dijon	(9½ oz.)	½ S, ½ V, 3 MFMt	280	650
Fish Florentine	(9 oz.)	½ S, 1 V, 3 LMt	210	700
Fish Mornay	(10 oz.)	1 S, ½ V, 2½ MFMt	280	700
Fish & Pasta	(9 oz.)	1½ S, 2 LMt, ½ Fat	230	870
Fish & Pasta Florentine	(9½ oz.)	1 S, 1 V, 2 MFMt	240	710
Shrimp Cajun Style	(10½ oz.)	1½ S, 1½ V, ½ MFMt	200	550
Shrimp & Clams w/Linguini	(10 oz.)	2½ S, 1 V, ½ MFMt, ½ Fat	280	680
Shrimp Primavera	(11 oz.)	2 S, 1 V, 1LMt	240	970
Tuna Pasta Casserole	(11 oz.)	2 S, ½ V, 2½ LMt	290	990
Mrs. Paul's Prepared Breaded Seafood, Combination Platter	(9 oz.)	3½ S, 1½ MFMt, 4½ Fat	590	1220
Stouffer's Dinner Supreme				
Flounder w/Dill Cream Sauce	(11⅝ oz.)	1½ S, 1 V, 2½ MFMt, 1 Fat	370	1020
Flounder w/Roasted Red Pepper Sauce	(12 oz.)	1½ S, 1 V, 3 MFMt, ½ Fat	360	980
Stouffer's Entrees				
Lobster Newburg	(6½ oz.)	1½ LMt, ½ LFMk, 4½ Fat	360	840
Scallops & Shrimp Mariner w/Rice	(10¼ oz.)	2 S, 1½ MFMt, ½ LFMk, 2 Fat	390	850
Tuna Noodle Casserole	(5¾ oz.)	1 S, ½ V, 1 MFMt, ½ Fat	190	680
Stouffer's Lean Cuisine				
Filet of Fish Divan	(12⅜ oz.)	½ S, 1 V, ½ SMk, 3 LMt	270	700
Filet of Fish Florentine	(9 oz.)	1 V, ½ SMk, 3 LMt	240	700
Filet of Fish Jardiniere w/Souffleed Potatoes	(11¼ oz.)	1 S, ½ V, 3½ LMt	280	840
Swanson Entrees, Fish 'n' Fries	(1 complete dinner)	3 S, 1 MFMt, 3 Fat	420	780
Swanson 4-Compartment Dinners (1 complete dinner)				
*Fish 'n' Chips**	(10 oz.)	2½ S, 1 Fr, 1½ MFMt, 2½ Fat	500	930
Fish Nugget	(9½ oz.)	2½ S, 1½ V, 1 LMt, 3 Fat	420	860

*Contains concentrated sources of carbohydrates

Food	Portion	Exchanges	Calories	Sodium (mg)
Fish & Seafood, cont.				
Tuna Helper				
au Gratin	(1/5 pkg.)	2 S, 1½ MFMt, 1 Fat	300	1110
Cheesy Noodles 'n' Tuna.	(1/5 pkg.)	2 S, 1 MFMt, ½ Fat	250	910
Cold Salad	(1/5 pkg.)	2 S, 1 MFMt, 5 Fat	440	1020
Creamy Mushroom	(1/5 pkg.)	2 S, 1 MFMt, ½ Fat	250	800
Creamy Noodles 'n' Tuna	(1/5 pkg.)	2 S, 1 MFMt, 1 Fat	270	910
Tuna Pot Pie	(1/6 pkg.)	2 S, 1 MFMt, 4½ Fat	430	1040
Tuna Tetrazzini	(1/5 pkg.)	1½ S, 2 MFMt	270	860
Weight Watchers				
Fillet of Fish au Gratin w/Broccoli	(9¼ oz.)	½ S, 1 V, ½ SMk, 1 Fat	220	370
Oven Fried Fish w/Vegetable Medley	(6 13/16 oz.)	1½ V, ½ LMt, 1 Fat	220	370
Stuffed Sole w/Newburg Sauce	(10½ oz.)	1½ S, 1 V, ½ SMk, ½ LMt, 1 Fat	270	1090
Pork				
Carnation, Sloppy Joe Barbeque Sauce w/Pork	(1/3 cup)	½ HFMt, 1 V, 1 Fat	120	(N/A)
Fresh Chef Salads, Ham & Cheddar Cheese	(4½ oz.)	½ S, 1½ MFMt, 4 Fat	330	850
Hormel (7½ oz.)				
au Gratin Potatoes 'n' Bacon		1½ S, 1 HFMt, 1 Fat	230	942
Beans 'n' Bacon		2½ S, 1 HFMt, 1 Fat	340	330
Beans 'n' Ham		2 S, ½ V, 1½ MFMt, 2½ Fat	370	1182
Beans 'n' Wieners		2 S, 1 HFMt, 1 Fat	290	1342
Le Menu Dinners				
Ham Steak	(1 complete dinner)	2 S, 1 V, 1½ MFMt, ½ Fat	310	1410
Stouffer's Entrees				
Ham & Asparagus Bake	(9½ oz.)	1½ S, 1 V, 1 MFMt, ½ LFMk, 5½ Fat	510	890
Ham & Asparagus Crepes	(6¼ oz.)	1½ S, ½ V, 1 MFMt, 2½ Fat	310	750
Ham & Swiss Cheese Crepes w/Cream Sauce	(7½ oz.)	1½ S, 2½ MFMt, 2½ Fat	410	980
Swanson 3-Compartment Dinners				
*Beans & Franks**	(1 complete dinner)	1½ S, 2 Fr, 1 HFMt, 2½ Fat	440	900

*Contains concentrated sources of carbohydrates

Food	Portion	Exchanges	Calories	Sodium (mg)
Swanson 4-Compartment Dinners* (1 complete dinner)				
Loin of Pork		1 S, 1 Fr, 2½ LMt, 1 Fat	310	770
Beans & Franks		3 S, 1½ Fr, ½ MFMt, 3 Fat	500	1020
Poultry				
Chicken Helper (⅕ pkg.)				
Chicken & Dumplings		2½ S, 3½ MFMt, 1½ Fat	530	1320
Chicken Tetrazzini		2½ S, 1 MFMt, 1½ Fat	340	870
Crispy Chicken & Biscuits		3 S, 4 MFMt, 4 Fat	710	1240
Crispy Chicken & Seasoned Rice		3 S, 4 MFMt, 3½ Fat	680	1490
Potato & Gravy		3 S, 3½ MFMt, 2½ Fat	600	1000
Stuffing		2 S, 4 MFMt, 2½ Fat	570	1600
Teriyaki Chicken		2 S, ½ V, 3½ MFMt, 1 Fat	480	1010
Green Giant Frozen Entrees, Chicken & Broccoli	(1 pkg.)	1 S, 2½ V, 2 MFMt, 1 Fat	340	890
Hungry-Man Dinners (1 complete dinner)				
*Boneless Chicken**	(17¾ oz.)	4 S, 1 Fr, 3½ LMt, 3 Fat	700	1480
Chicken Nuggets	(16 oz.)	3½ S, 1 Fr, 2 MFMt, 3 Fat	600	680
*Chicken Parmigiana**	(20 oz.)	2 S, 1 Fr, 1 V, 4 MFMt, 6 Fat	810	2090
*Fried Chicken, Dark Portions**	(14½ oz.)	4 S, 1 Fr, 3½ MFMt, 5½ Fat	860	1660
*Fried Chicken, White Portions**	(15½ oz.)	4½ S, 1 Fr, 3 MFMt, 6 Fat	870	2150
*Turkey**	(17 oz.)	3 S, 1 Fr, 4 LMt, 1 Fat	550	1810
Hungry-Man Pot Pies (1 pie)				
Chicken		4 S, 1 V, 1½ MFMt, 6½ Fat	730	1550
Turkey		4 S, 1½ V, 1½ MFMt, 6 Fat	690	1600
Swanson Hungry-Man Entrees (1 complete entree)				
Fried Chicken, Breast Portions	(11¾ oz.)	3 S, 3½ MFMt, 4 Fat	680	1760
Fried Chicken, Dark Portions	(11 oz.)	3 S, 3 MFMt, 4 Fat	630	1380
Turkey	(13¼ oz.)	2½ S, 3 LMt, 1 Fat	390	1650
Poultry Combinations				
Le Menu Dinners (1 complete dinner)				
Breast of Chicken	(10 oz.)	1 S, 1½ V, 3 LMt	260	650
Breast of Chicken Parmigiana	(11½ oz.)	1½ S, 1 V, 3 MFMt, ½ Fat	400	900
Chicken à la King	(10¼ oz.)	1½ S, 1 V, 2 MFMt, 1 Fat	330	810
Chicken Cordon Bleu	(11 oz.)	3 S, 1 V, 1½ MFMt, 2½ Fat	460	870
Chicken Florentine	(12½ oz.)	2 S, 2 V, 2½ MFMt, 2½ Fat	480	910

*Contains concentrated sources of carbohydrates

Food	Portion	Exchanges	Calories	Sodium (mg)
Poultry Combinations, cont.				
Sliced Breast of Turkey w/Mushrooms	(11¼ oz.)	2 S, 1 V, 3 MFMt, 1½ Fat	460	1110
Le Menu Entrees (1 complete entree)				
Chicken Kiev	(8 oz.)	1½ S, 2 MFMt, 6 Fat	530	780
Le Menu Light Style Dinners (1 complete dinner)				
Chicken Cacciatore	(10 oz.)	1 S, 2½ V, 2 LMt, ½ Fat	270	640
Chicken Cannelloni	(10¼ oz.)	1½ S, 3 V, ½ LMt, ½ Fat	250	600
Glazed Chicken Breast	(10 oz.)	1 S, 1 V, 3 LMt	270	740
Herb Roasted Chicken	(9¼ oz.)	1 S, 1 V, 2 LMt	220	610
Turkey Divan	(10 oz.)	1½ S, 1 V, 2 LMt, ½ Fat	280	820
Stouffer's Dinner Supreme				
Baked Chicken Breast w/Gravy	(11 oz.)	1½ S, 1½ V, 3 LMt	330	660
Chicken Florentine	(11 oz.)	1½ S, 2 V, 3½ LMt, 1½ Fat	430	930
Chicken in Supreme Sauce	(11⅜ oz.)	1½ S, 1 V, 4 LMt	360	990
Stouffer's Entrees				
Chicken à la King w/Rice	(9½ oz.)	2 S, 1½ LMt, ½ LFMk, 1½ Fat	320	840
Chicken Crepes w/Mushroom Sauce	(8¼ oz.)	1 S, 3 LMt, ½ LFMk, 2 Fat	370	930
Chicken Divan	(8½ oz.)	1½ V, 2½ LMt, ½ LFMk, 2½ Fat	350	850
Chicken Paprikash w/Egg Noodles	(10½ oz.)	2 S, 4 LMt, ½ Fat	390	1250
Chicken Pie	(10 oz.)	2 S, 1 V, 2 MFMt, 5 Fat	530	1210
Chicken Stuffed Pasta Shells w/Cheese Sauce	(9 oz.)	1½ S, 3½ MFMt, 1½ Fat	420	810
Creamed Chicken	(6½ oz.)	2 MFMt, ½ LFMk, 2½ Fat	320	700
Escalloped Chicken & Noodles	(5¾ oz.)	1 S, 1½ MFMt, 1½ Fat	260	720
Turkey Casserole w/Gravy & Dressing	(9¾ oz.)	1½ S, 1 V, 2½ MFMt, 1 Fat	380	1250
Turkey Pie	(10 oz.)	2 S, 1 V, 2 MFMt, 5 Fat	540	1260
Turkey Tetrazzini	(6 oz.)	1 S, 1½ MFMt, 1 Fat	230	650
Stouffer's Lean Cuisine				
Breast of Chicken Marsala w/Vegetables	(8½ oz.)	½ S, 1 V, 3 LMt, 1 Fat	190	980
Chicken à l'Orange w/Almond Rice	(8 oz.)	1½ S, ½ Fr, 3 LMt	270	400
Chicken Cacciatore w/Vermicelli	(10⅞ oz.)	1½ S, ½ V, 2½ LMt, ½ Fat	280	950

Food	Portion	Exchanges	Calories	Sodium (mg)
Glazed Chicken w/Vegetable Rice	(8½ oz.)	1½ S, 3 LMt	270	710
Turkey Dijon	(9½ oz.)	1 S, 1 V, 3 LMt	280	820
Swanson, canned				
Chicken & Dumplings	(7½ oz.)	1 S, 1 V, 1 MFMt, 1 Fat	220	960
Chicken à la King	(5¼ oz.)	½ S, 1 MFMt, ½ V, 1½ Fat	180	690
Chicken Stew	(7⅝ oz.)	1 S, 1 MFMt, ½ Fat	170	960
Swanson Chicken Duet Entrees (6 oz.)				
Creamy Broccoli		½ S, 2 V, 2 MFMt, 1½ Fat	310	630
Creamy Green Beans		½ S, 3 V, 2 MFMt, 1½ Fat	330	600
Saucy Tomato		½ S, 3 V, 2 MFMt, 1½ Fat	340	600
Savory Wild Rice		1½ S, 2 MFMt, ½ Fat	290	610
Swanson Duet Gourmet Nuggets (3 oz.)				
Chicken		1 S, 1½ MFMt, 1 Fat	220	410
Ham & Cheese		1 S, 1½ MFMt, 1 Fat	220	410
Pizza-Style		1 S, 1 MFMt, 1 Fat	210	440
Spinach & Herb		1 S, 1 MFMt, 1½ Fat	230	420
Swanson Chunky Pies (1 pie)				
Chicken		3 S, 1½ V, 1 MFMt, 5½ Fat	580	850
Turkey		2½ S, 1½ V, 1½ MFMt, 4½ Fat	540	960
Swanson Dipsters (3 oz.)				
*Barbecue**		½ S, ½ Fr, 1½ MFMt, ½ Fat	220	300
*Chicken**		½ S, ½ Fr, 1½ MFMt, ½ Fat	220	390
*Coconola**		½ S, ½ Fr, 1½ MFMt, 1½ Fat	240	140
*Herb**		½ S, ½ Fr, 1½ MFMt, 1 Fat	220	410
Italian-Style		½ S, 1½ MFMt, 1½ Fat	230	390
Swanson Entrees (1 complete entree)				
Chicken Nibbles		1 S, 1 LMt, 3 Fat	260	450
Fried Chicken		1 S, 1½ MFMt, 2½ Fat	300	630
Turkey		1½ S, 2 MFMt	270	1030
Swanson 4-Compartment Dinners (1 complete dinner)				
*Chicken in Barbeque Sauce**		2 S, 1 Fr, 1½ V, 3 LMt, 1 Fat	450	1040
*Chicken, Dark Meat in Barbeque Sauce**		2½ S, 1 Fr, 3 LMt, 1 Fat	450	1040
Chicken Drumlet Dinner		1½ S, 1 Fr, 1 V, 3 MFMt, 3½ Fat	570	730
*Chicken Drumlets**		1½ S, 1 Fr, 3 MFMt, 3 Fat	540	990

*Contains concentrated sources of carbohydrates

Food	Portion	Exchanges	Calories	Sodium (mg)
Poultry Combinations, cont.				
*Chicken Nuggets Platter**		1½ S, 1 Fr, 2 MFMt, 3 Fat	460	710
*Fried Chicken, Barbecue Flavor**		3 S, 1 Fr, 2½ MFMt, 2½ Fat	580	1300
*Fried Chicken, Dark Meat**		2½ S, 1 Fr, 2 MFMt, 3½ Fat	560	1100
*Fried Chicken, White Meat**		3 S, 1 Fr, 2 MFMt, 3 Fat	560	1380
*Sweet 'n' Sour Chicken**		2 S, 1 Fr, 1 V, 2 MFMt	390	480
*Turkey**		2 S, 1 Fr, 2 MFMt	350	1110
Swanson Pot Pies (1 pie)				
Chicken		2 S, 1 V, ½ MFMt, 4½ Fat	420	820
Turkey		2 S, 1 V, 1 MFMt, 3½ Fat	410	780
Swanson 3-Compartment Dinners, Fried Chicken Platter	(1 complete dinner)	2 S, 1 V, ½ HFMt, 2 Fat	340	850
Weaver (3.5 oz.)				
Chicken à la King		½ S, 1 LMt	109	293
Chicken au Gratin		1 S, 1 LMt, ½ Fat	137	430
Scalloped Chicken		½ S, 1 LMt, 1 Fat	130	381
Weight Watchers				
Breaded Chicken Patty Parmigiana w/Vegetable Medley	(8¹⁄₁₆ oz.)	½ S, 1½ V, 2 LMt	280	810
Chicken à la King	(9 oz.)	½ S, ½ V, ½ SMk, 2½ LMt	220	960
Chicken Nuggets, Breaded Chicken Patties	(4 nuggets)	½ S, 1½ LMt, 1½ Fat	180	340
*Imperial Chicken Tenders & Mushrooms in Sauce w/Rice & Broccoli**	(9¼ oz.)	1 S, 1 V, 2½ LMt	220	940
Southern Fried Chicken Patty w/Vegetable Medley	(6½ oz.)	½ S, 1 V, 2 LMt, 2 Fat	270	610
Stuffed Turkey Breast w/Gravy & Vegetable Medley	(8⁷⁄₁₆ oz.)	1 S, 1½ V, 2 LMt, 1 Fat	260	870
Veal				
Le Menu Dinners, Veal Parmigiana	(1 complete dinner)	1½ S, 2 V, 2½ LMt, 2 Fat	400	930
Le Menu Light Style Dinners Veal Marsala	(1 complete dinner)	1½ S, 1 V, 2 LMt	260	800
Stouffer's Lean Cuisine Veal Primavera	(9⅛ oz.)	1 S, 1 V, 2½ LMt	250	790
Swanson Entrees, Veal Parmigiana	(1 complete dinner)	1½ S, 1 MFMt, 2 Fat	280	880
Swanson 4-Compartment Dinners, Veal Parmigiana	(1 complete dinner)	1½ S, 1 Fr, 1 V, 2 MFMt, 2½ Fat	450	1100

*Contains concentrated sources of carbohydrates

Food	Portion	Exchanges	Calories	Sodium (mg)
Swanson Hungry-Man Dinners, Veal Parmigiana	(1 complete dinner)	2½ S, 1 Fr, 1 V, 2½ MFMt, 3½ Fat	630	1750
Weight Watchers Veal Patty Parmigiana w/Vegetable Medley	(8 7/16 oz.)	½ S, ½ V, 3 LMt	220	780

■ Mexican-Style

Food	Portion	Exchanges	Calories	Sodium (mg)
Burritos				
Van De Kamp Mexican Classic Entrees				
Crispy Fried Burrito	(6 oz.)	2½ S, ½ MFMt, 2½ Fat	365	825
Guacamole Packet	(1½ oz.)	1 Fat	45	85
Sirloin Burrito Grande	(11 oz.)	2½ S, 1½ V, 2 MFMt, 1 Fat	440	1120
Weight Watchers (5 oz.)				
Beefsteak		2 S, ½ V, 1 MFMt, 1½ Fat	310	730
Chicken		2 S, 1½ LMt, 1 Fat	280	650
Enchiladas				
Swanson 4-Compartment Dinners, Beef Enchiladas*	(1 complete dinner)	2 S, 1 Fr, 1 MFMt, 4 Fat	480	1130
Van De Kamp Mexican Classic Entrees (5½ oz.)				
Cheese Enchilada Ranchero		1 S, 1 V, 1 MFMt, 2 Fat	250	540
Chicken Enchiladas Suiza		1 S, 1 V, 1 MFMt, 1 Fat	220	590
Shredded Beef Enchilada		1 S, 1 MFMt, 1 Fat	180	930
Van De Kamp Mexican Holiday Enchiladas				
Beef	(7½ oz.)	1 S, 1 V, 1 MFMt, 2 Fat	250	1200
Beef Dinner	(12 oz.)	2½ S, 1½ V, 1½ MFMt, 1½ Fat	390	2175
Cheese	(7½ oz.)	1½ S, 1 MFMt, 2 Fat	270	965
Cheese Dinner	(12 oz.)	2½ S, 1½ V, 1½ MFMt, 2½ Fat	450	1665
Chicken	(7½ oz.)	1½ S, 1½ MFMt, ½ Fat	250	1105
4 Beef	(8½ oz.)	2 S, 1½ MFMt, 1½ Fat	340	1480
4 Cheese	(8½ oz.)	2 S, 1½ MFMt, 2½ Fat	370	1175
Mexican-Style Dinner	(11½ oz.)	2½ S, 1½ V, 1½ MFMt, 2½ Fat	420	1040
Weight Watchers				
Beef Enchilada Ranchero	(9⅛ oz.)	1½ S, 1 V, 2 MFMt, ½ Fat	310	1230
Cheese Enchilada Ranchero	(8⅞ oz.)	1 S, 1½ V, 1½ HFMt, 2 Fat	350	950
Chicken Enchilada Suiza	(9 5/16 oz.)	1½ S, ½ SMk, 2 LMt, 2 Fat	350	950
4-Compartment Dinner, Combination (1 complete dinner)	(14¼ oz.)	3 S, 1 V, 5 Fat	500	1390

*Contains concentrated sources of carbohydrates

Food	Portion	Exchanges	Calories	Sodium (mg)
Hungry-Man Dinner*	(1 complete dinner)	4½ S, 1 Fr, 1 V, 1½ MFMt, 6½ Fat	820	2080
Taco, Hamburger Helper				
Tacobake	(1/6 pkg.)	1½ S, 1½ V, 1½ MFMt, 1 Fat	320	960
Tamales				
Hamburger Helper				
Tamale Pie Mix	(1/5 pkg.)	2 S, 2 V, 1½ MFMt, 1½ Fat	380	940
Hormel				
Beef Tamales	(7½ oz.)	1 S, 1 HFMt, 2 Fat	270	1140
Taquitos, Van De Kamp Mexican Classic Entrees				
Shredded Beef	(8 oz.)	2½ S, 1½ V, ½ MFMt, 4½ Fat	490	990
Tostada, Van De Kamp Mexican Classic Entrees, Beef Tostada Supreme	(8½ oz.)	2 S, 2 V, 2 MFMt, 4 Fat	530	900

■ Oriental-Style

Food	Portion	Exchanges	Calories	Sodium (mg)
Beef, Beef Pepper, & Pepper Steak				
Chun King Divider Pak Entrees, Beef Pepper Oriental	(7 oz.)	½ S, ½ V, ½ LMt, ½ Fat	110	880
Chun King Stir-Fry Entrees				
Canned	(6 oz.)	½ S, ½ V, 2 MFMt, 1 Fat	250	1000
La Choy, Beef Pepper Oriental Dinner	(1 pkg.)	2½ S, ½ MFMt, 1 V	250	1985
La Choy Bi-Packs, Beef Pepper Oriental	(¾ cup prepared)	2 V, ½ LMt	80	950
La Choy Entrees, Beef Pepper Oriental canned	(¾ cup)	1 LMt, 1½ V	90	1060
La Choy Entrees, Beef Pepper Oriental frozen	(⅔ cup)	½ LMt, 2 V	80	820
Stouffer's Entrees, Green Pepper Steak w/Rice	(10½ oz.)	2 S, 1½ V, 2 LMt, 1 Fat	340	1470
Stouffer's Lean Cuisine, Oriental Beef w/Vegetables & Rice	(8⅝ oz.)	1½ S, 1½ V, 2 LMt, ½ Fat	270	1090
Chicken				
Le Menu Entrees, Oriental Chicken*	(1 complete entree)	1 S, ½ Fr, 1½ V, 2 LMt	260	780
Stouffer's Entrees, Cashew Chicken in Sauce w/Rice	(9½ oz.)	2 S, 3½ MFMt	410	1240
Chop Suey, Stouffer's Entrees, Beef w/Rice	(12 oz.)	2 S, 1½ V, 1½ MFMt, 1 Fat	360	1590

*Contains concentrated sources of carbohydrates

Food	Portion	Exchanges	Calories	Sodium (mg)
Chow Mein				
Chun King Divider Pak Entrees, canned				
Beef	(7 oz.)	½ S, ½ V, 1 LMt	100	560
Beef	(8 oz.)	½ S, 1 V, 1 LMt	110	640
Chicken	(7 oz.)	½ S, ½ V, 1 LMt	110	820
Chicken	(8 oz.)	½ S, 1 V, ½ LMt, ½ Fat	120	940
Pork	(7 oz.)	½ S, ½ V, 1 MFMt	120	500
Shrimp	(7 oz.)	½ S, 1 V, ½ LMt	100	260
Chun King Stir-Fry Entrees, canned				
w/Beef	(6 oz.)	½ S, ½ V, 2 MFMt, 2 Fat	290	540
w/Chicken	(6 oz.)	½ S, ½ V, 2½ LMt, ½ Fat	220	540
General Mills Oriental Classics	(¼ pkg.)	2 S, 2½ V, 1 LMt	260	1130
La Choy (1 pkg.)				
Chicken Dinner		2 S, 2 V, ½ HFMt	260	1740
Shrimp Dinner		2½ S, 1 V	220	1740
La Choy Bi-Packs (¾ cup)				
Beef		½ LMt, 2 V	70	840
Chicken		½ MFMt, 2 V	80	970
Pork		½ HFMt, 1 V	80	950
Shrimp		½ LMt, 2 V	70	860
Vegetable		1 V, ½ Fat	50	640
La Choy Chow Meins, canned (¾ cup)				
Beef		1 V, ½ LMt	60	890
Chicken		1 V, 1 LMt	70	800
Meatless		1 V	35	780
Shrimp		1 V, ½ LMt	45	820
La Choy Entrees, frozen (⅔ cup)				
Chicken		½ MFMt, 2 V	90	720
Shrimp		½ LMt, 2 V	70	820
Le Menu Light Style Dinners Chicken	(1 complete dinner)	2 S, ½ V, 2 LMt	260	790
Stouffer's Entrees, Chicken w/o Noodles	(8 oz.)	½ S, 1 V, 1 LMt, ½ Fat	140	1170
Stouffer's Lean Cuisine, Chicken w/Rice	(11¼ oz.)	2 S, 1 V, 1 LMt, ½ Fat	250	1160
Egg Foo Young, Chun King Stir-Fry Entrees	(5 oz.)	½ S, 1 HFMt	140	520
Egg Rolls				
La Choy				
Chicken	(3 egg rolls of 15)	½ S, 1 V, ½ Fat	90	185
Lobster	(1 egg roll of 5)	1½ S, ½ V, 1 Fat	180	485

Food	Portion	Exchanges	Calories	Sodium (mg)
Egg Rolls, cont.				
Lobster	(3 egg rolls of 15)	½ S, 1 V, ½ Fat	80	240
Meat & Shrimp	(3 egg rolls of 15)	½ S, ½ V, ½ Fat	80	220
Meat & Shrimp	(6 egg rolls of 30)	1 S, ½ Fat	100	250
Shrimp	(1 egg roll of 2 or 5)	1½ S, ½ HFMt	160	575
Shrimp	(3 egg rolls of 15)	½ S, 1 V, ½ Fat	80	210
Fried Rice				
General Mills Oriental Classics, Stir-Fried Rice	(¼ pkg.)	2½ S, ½ V, 4 LMt	430	1370
La Choy Entrees, Fried Rice w/Meat	(¾ cup)	1½ S, ½ Fat	140	885
Hamburger Helper, Rice Oriental*	(⅕ pkg.)	2 S, ½ Fr, 2 MFMt, ½ Fat	340	1120
Shrimp & Scallops				
Mrs. Paul's Light Seafood Entrees, Shrimp Oriental	(11 oz.)	3 S, ½ MFMt, ½ Fat	280	880
Stouffer's Lean Cuisine				
Oriental Scallops & Vegetables w/Rice	(11 oz.)	2 S, 1 V, 1 LMt	220	1200
Shrimp & Chicken w/Noodles	(10⅛ oz.)	1½ S, 2½ LMt	270	1010
Sukiyaki				
Chun King Stir-Fry Entrees, canned	(6 oz.)	½ S, ½ V, 2 MFMt, 1 Fat	260	400
La Choy Bi-Packs	(¾ cup)	2 V, ½ LMt	79	740
Sweet & Sour				
La Choy Chicken	(⅔ cup)	2 S, ½ V, ½ LMt	190	1005
Le Menu Dinners Chicken*	(1 complete dinner)	1½ S, 1 Fr, 1 V, 2 MFMt, 2½ Fat	460	950
Weight Watchers, Chicken Tenders	(10³⁄₁₆ oz.)	2 S, 1 V, ½ Fr, 1 LMt	250	590
Teriyaki				
General Mills Oriental Classics	(¼ pkg.)	2½ S, 2 V, 2 LMt	360	830
La Choy Bi-Packs Chicken	(¾ cup)	½ MFMt, 2 V	85	850
Stouffer's Dinner Supreme Beef*	(11⅜ oz.)	1½ S, ½ Fr, 3 LMt, 1 Fat	370	1040
Stouffer's Entrees, Beef in sauce w/Rice & Vegetables*	(9¾ oz.)	2 S, 2 LMt, ½ Fr, ½ Fat	330	1260

*Contains concentrated sources of carbohydrates

3

MEATS, LUNCH MEATS, POULTRY, FISH, & SEAFOOD

It's surprising how lean some commercial poultry products have become. They can be excellent sources of meat for your diet. Do be sure to note whether an item is to be weighed before or after cooking when measuring a food, because this affects the number of exchanges.

Some lunch meats also are very lean, but others have a lot of fat. Sodium varies widely among lunch meats, but is generally on the high side. Remember that many lunch meats and convenience products contain preservatives and additives. Ask your dietitian about these, what they do, and if they are harmful or beneficial.

Some fish products are good lean meat sources. These contain omega-3 fatty acids that may help reduce cholesterol. Batter-dipped fish products vary in the amount of fat added. When choosing these products, consider how much fish you're getting compared to the breading (starch). Fish fillets are lean meats that contain no extra fat or breading. You can use meat exchanges for these products to free up starch exchanges for other foods which you might enjoy choosing to round out a meal.

Consider all factors in choosing a protein source—including the amount of sodium each product contains.

Food	Portion	Exchanges	Calories	Sodium (mg)
■ Meats, Lunch Meats, & Sandwich Spreads				
Bacon & Breakfast Strips, Oscar Mayer				
Bacon	(1 slice)	1 Fat	35	120
Bacon	(1/8″ slice)	½ HFMt, ½ Fat	70	225
Bacon Bits	(1 tbsp.)	½ LMt	20	180
Bacon, Canadian-Style Lean Cold Cuts 93% fat-free	(1 slice)	1 LMt	35	390
Bacon, Center Cut	(1 slice)	½ Fat	25	95
Breakfast Strips, Beef "Lean 'n' Tasty"	(1 slice)	½ HFMt	45	190
Breakfast Strips, Pork "Lean 'n' Tasty"	(1 slice)	½ HFMt	50	190
Bar B Q Loaf, Oscar Mayer Lean Cold Cuts, 90% fat-free	(1 slice)	½ MFMt	50	345
Beef (*See also* Corned Beef)				
Buddig	(1½ oz.)	1 LMt	60	645
Oscar Mayer Lean Cold Cuts				
Italian Style, 97% fat-free	(1 slice)	½ LMt	20	210
Smoked, 97% fat-free	(3 slices)	1 LMt	45	555
Bologna				
Oscar Mayer, Bologna	(1 slice)	½ HFMt, 1 Fat	90	300
Beef	(1 slice)	½ HFMt, 1 Fat	90	300
Beef Lebanon	(1 slice)	1 LMt	50	295
w/Cheese	(1 slice)	½ HFMt, ½ Fat	75	240
Garlic Loaf	(1 slice)	½ HFMt, 1 Fat	90	295
Wisconsin Made Ring	(1 oz.)	½ HFMt, 1 Fat	85	235
Braunschweiger				
Oscar Mayer				
German Brand, tube	(1 oz.)	½ HFMt, 1 Fat	95	345
Liver Sausage	(1 slice)	½ HFMt, 1 Fat	95	325
Liver Sausage, tube	(1 oz.)	½ HFMt, 1 Fat	95	320
Chicken				
Spreadables Sandwich Spread, Carnation, Chicken salad	(1.9 oz.)	1 LMt, 1 Fat	100	200
Swanson, canned				
Chunk Premium White in water	(2½ oz.)	2 LMt	90	240
Chunk Style Mix-in' Chicken	(2½ oz.)	2 LMt, ½ Fat	130	240

Food	Portion	Exchanges	Calories	Sodium (mg)
Chunk White & Dark in water	(2½ oz.)	2 LMt	100	240
Chunky Chicken Spread	(1 oz.)	½ LMt, ½ Fat	60	160
Weaver, Chicken Bologna	(3.5 oz.)	2 HFMt, 1 Fat	256	920
Corned Beef				
Buddig	(1½ oz.)	1 LMt	60	570
Carnation				
Corned Beef	(2.3 oz. of 7-oz. can)	2 MFMt	160	720
Corned Beef	(2.4 oz. of 12-oz. can)	2 MFMt	160	750
Corned Beef Hash	(7½ oz. of 15-oz. can)	1 S, 2 MFMt, 1 V, 3½ Fat	400	1260
Corned Beef Hash	(8 oz. of 24-oz. can)	1 S, 2 MFMt, 1 V, 3½ Fat	420	1330
Oscar Mayer Lean Cold Cuts				
Corned Beef, 98% fat-free	(3 slices)	1 LMt	45	600
Corned Beef Loaf, Jellied, 93% fat-free	(1 slice)	1 LMt	40	275
Frankfurters & Sausage				
Carnation, Vienna Sausage				
in Barbeque Sauce	(2½ oz. of 5-oz. can)	1 HFMt, 1½ F, ½ V	180	(N/A)
in Beef Broth	(2 oz. of 5-oz. can)	1 HFMt, 1½ Fat	160	330
in Beef Broth	(1.8 oz. of 9-oz. can)	1 HFMt, 1½ Fat	160	300
Chicken	(2 oz.)	1 HFMt, ½ Fat	123	851
Louis Rich, Turkey Franks*	(45-g. link)	1 HFMt	103	384
Cheese		1 HFMt	108	509
Oscar Mayer Lean Cold Cuts, New England Brand, 92% fat-free	(1 slice)	½ MFMt	30	290
Oscar Mayer Pork Sausage, Little Friers, cooked	(1 link)	½ MFMt, 1 Fat	80	220
Oscar Mayer, Summer Sausage, Thuringer Cervelat	(1 slice)	½ HFMt, ½ Fat	75	330
Beef		½ HFMt, ½ Fat	70	325
Oscar Mayer Smokies (1 link)				
Beef		½ HFMt, 1½ Fat	125	430
Cheese		1 HFMt, ½ Fat	125	455
Links Sausage		½ HFMt, 1½ Fat	125	435
Little Sausage		½ Fat	30	90
Oscar Mayer Wieners & Franks (1 link)				
Cheese Hot Dogs		½ HFMt, 2 Fat	145	475
Cheese Hot Dogs, Bacon & Cheddar		1 HFMt, 1 Fat	145	510
Cheese Hot Dogs, Nacho Style		½ HFMt, 1½ Fat	135	550

*Contains concentrated sources of carbohydrates

Food	Portion	Exchanges	Calories	Sodium (mg)
Frankfurters & Sausage, cont.				
Franks, Beef		½ HFMt, 2 Fat	145	460
Franks, Beef Jumbo		1 HFMt, 2 Fat	185	585
Franks, Beef "The Big One"		2 HFMt, 3½ Fat	360	1155
Franks, Bun Length Beef		1 HFMt, 2 Fat	185	585
Franks, Cheese		1 HFMt, 1 Fat	130	534
Wieners		½ HFMt, 2 Fat	145	460
Wieners, Bun Length		1 HFMt, 2 Fat	185	580
Wieners, Jumbo		1 HFMt, 2 Fat	185	580
Wieners, Little		½ Fat	30	90
Weaver, Chicken Franks	(1 frank)	1 HFMt, ½ Fat	122	508
w/Cheese		1 HFMt, 1 Fat	150	625
Ham				
Buddig	(1 oz.)	1 LMt	50	400
Carnation Spreadables Ham salad	(1.9 oz.)	1 LMt, 1 Fat	100	350
Oscar Mayer Jubilee				
Boneless	(1 oz.)	½ MFMt	45	370
Canned, w/Natural Juices	(1 oz.)	½ LMt	30	285
Slice, 95% fat-free, water added	(1 oz.)	½ LMt	30	350
Steaks, 95% fat-free, water added	(1 steak)	1 LMt	60	710
Oscar Mayer Lean Cold Cuts w/Natural Juices, 95% fat-free (1 slice)				
Boiled		½ LMt	25	250
Cracked Black Pepper		½ LMt	25	270
Honey		½ LMt	25	270
Italian-Style Cooked		½ LMt	25	265
Smoked Cooked		½ LMt	25	265
Oscar Mayer Meat Spreads				
Ham & Cheese	(1 oz.)	½ MFMt, ½ Fat	65	325
*Ham Salad**	(2 oz.)	½ Fr, 1 HFMt	120	540
Oscar Mayer Sliced Meats (1 slice)				
Chopped, w/Natural Juices		½ HFMt	55	330
Chopped Peppered, w/Natural Juices		½ HFMt	55	325
Ham & Cheese Loaf		½ HFMt, ½ Fat	75	360
Luncheon Meat		½ HFMt, 1 Fat	100	340
Ham, Deviled				
Carnation	(1½ oz.)	1 HFMt, ½ Fat	130	(N/A)

*Contains concentrated sources of carbohydrates

Food	Portion	Exchanges	Calories	Sodium (mg)
Liver Cheese,				
Oscar Meyer	(1 slice)	1 HFMt, ½ Fat	115	435
Loaf, Oscar Mayer				
Luxury, 95% fat-free	(1 slice)	½ LMt	40	300
Old Fashioned*	(2 slices)	½ Fr, 1 HFMt	130	670
Olive*	(2 slices)	½ Fr, 1 HFMt	120	790
Peppered, 93% fat-free	(1 slice)	½ MFMt	45	360
Pickle & Pimento*	(2 slices)	½ Fr, 1 HFMt	130	790
Picnic	(1 slice)	½ HFMt	60	330
Pastrami				
Buddig	(1½ oz.)	1 LMt	60	480
Oscar Mayer Lean Cold Cuts, 97% fat-free	(3 slices)	1 LMt	45	645
Potted Meat, Carnation	(1.83 oz.)	1 HFMt	100	320
Salami, Oscar Mayer Sliced Meats				
Cotto	(1 slice)	½ HFMt	55	290
Cotto, Beef	(1 slice)	½ HFMt	45	295
for Beer	(1 slice)	½ HFMt	55	280
for Beer, Beef	(1 slice)	½ HFMt, ½ Fat	65	280
Genoa	(3 slices)	1 HFMt	105	465
Hard	(3 slices)	1 HFMt	105	495
Sandwich Spread, Oscar Mayer*	(2 oz.)	½ Fr, 2 Fat	130	540
Spam, Hormel	(2 oz.)	1 HFMt, 1½ Fat	170	862
Tuna, Spreadables Sandwich Spread, Carnation, Tuna salad	(1.9 oz.)	1 LMt, 1 Fat	90	370
Turkey Combinations				
Buddig				
Turkey Ham	(1½ oz.)	1 LMt	60	645
Turkey Pastrami	(1½ oz.)	1 LMt	60	660
Louis Rich				
*Chopped Turkey Ham**	(28-g. slice)	1LMt	42	256
*Turkey Bologna**	(28-g. slice)	½ HFMt	58	225
*Turkey Cotto Salami**	(28-g. slice)	1 LMt	52	257
Turkey Ham (Cured Turkey Thigh Meat)*	(28-g. slice)	½ LMt	34	278
*Turkey Ham, cured Turkey Thigh Meat, water added**	(28-g. slice)	½ LMt	34	275
*Turkey Luncheon Loaf**	(28-g. slice)	1 LMt	43	277
Turkey Pastrami	(28-g. slice)	½ LMt	33	277

*Contains concentrated sources of carbohydrates

Food	Portion	Exchanges	Calories	Sodium (mg)
Turkey Combinations, cont.				
Turkey Pastrami, Square	(23-g. slice)	½ LMt	24	240
*Turkey Salami**	(28-g. slice)	1 LMt	52	244
*Turkey Smoked Sausage**	(28-g. slice)	1 LMt	55	230
*Turkey Summer Sausage**	(28-g. slice)	1 LMt	52	312
Spreadables Sandwich Spread, Carnation				
Turkey salad	(1.9 oz.)	1 LMt, 1 Fat	100	190

■ Chicken & Turkey

Chicken

Food	Portion	Exchanges	Calories	Sodium (mg)
Buddig	(1 oz.)	1 LMt	60	340
Louis Rich Oven Roasted Breast	(28-g. slice)	½ LMt	39	166
Oscar Mayer Lean Cold Cuts (1 slice)				
Breast, Oven Roasted, 97% fat-free		½ LMt	30	340
Breast, Smoked, 98% fat-free		½ LMt	25	385
Purdue Done It! (1 oz.)				
Breaded Breast Cutlets		½ S, ½ HFMt	70	116
Breaded Breast Nuggets		½ S, ½ HFMt	80	146
Breaded Breast Tenders		½ S, ½ MFMt	60	100
Hot & Spicy Drumettes/Wings		1 LMt	58	104
Hot & Spicy Flats, Mid-Sections		1 MFMt	66	133
Roasted Boneless Breast		1 LMt	45	123
Roasted Breast		1 LMt	45	123
Roasted Drumsticks		1 LMt	45	138
Roasted Leg Quarters		1 LMt	50	113
Roasted Thighs		1 LMt	60	117
Roasted Wings		1 MFMt	70	98
Whole Roasted		1 LMt	60	120
Whole Roasted Cornish Hen		1 LMt	55	57
Swanson Plump & Juicy				
Cutlets	(3 oz.)	1 S, 1½ MFMt, ½ Fat	200	370
Drumlets	(3 oz.)	1 S, 1½ MFMt, 1 Fat	220	370
Extra Crispy Fried	(3 oz.)	1 S, 1½ MFMt, 1½ Fat	250	320
Fried, Assorted Pieces	(3¼ oz.)	1 S, 1½ MFMt, 2 Fat	270	580
Fried, Breast Portions	(4½ oz.)	1½ S, 2½ MFMt, 1½ Fat	360	790
Nibbles	(3¼ oz.)	1 S, 1½ MFMt, 2½ Fat	300	640
Take-Out Fried, Assorted Pieces	(3¼ oz.)	1 S, 1½ MFMt, 2 Fat	270	640

*Contains concentrated sources of carbohydrates

Food	Portion	Exchanges	Calories	Sodium (mg)
Thighs & Drumsticks	(3¼ oz.)	1 S, 1½ MFMt, 2 Fat	280	520
Weaver				
Batter Dipped Breasts	(3.5 oz.)	½ S, 2 MFMt, 1½ Fat	257	210
Batter Dipped Thighs/Drums	(3.5 oz.)	½ S, 2 MFMt, 1½ Fat	261	210
Batter Dipped Party Pack	(3.5 oz.)	1 S, 1½ MFMt, 2½ Fat	284	210
Breast Fillets	(3.5 oz.)	1 S, 2 LMt, ½ Fat	196	525
Breast Fillet Strips	(3.5 oz.)	1 S, 2 LMt, ½ Fat	216	675
Breast Tenders	(3.5 oz.)	1 S, 2 LMt, 1 Fat	207	588
Chicken-To-Go	(3.5 oz.)	1 S, 2 MFMt, 1 Fat	248	400
Crispy Light Fried	(2.9 oz.)	½ S, 2 MFMt	163	305
Crispy Sticks	(3.5 oz.)	1 S, 1½ LMt, 1½ Fat	219	525
Croquettes	(3.5 oz.)	1 S, 1½ LMt, 2½ Fat	274	680
Dutch Frye Breasts	(3.5 oz.)	1 S, 2 MFMt, ½ Fat	246	390
Dutch Frye Party Pack	(3.5 oz.)	1 S, 1½ MFMt, 2 Fat	277	440
Dutch Frye Thighs/Drums	(3.5 oz.)	1 S, 2 MFMt, 1 Fat	246	390
Dutch Frye Variety Pack	(3.5 oz.)	1 S, 2 MFMt, 1 Fat	249	400
Mini-Drums-Crispy	(3 oz.)	1 S, 1½ LMt, 1 Fat	205	483
Mini-Drums-Herbs 'n' Spice	(3 oz.)	1 S, 1½ LMt, 1 Fat	208	344
Nuggets	(3 oz.)	1 S, 1½ LMt, 2 Fat	226	371
Nuggets, Teriyaki	(3.5 oz.)	1 S, 1½ LMt, 2½ Fat	266	454
Rondelets, Cheese	(3 oz.)	1 S, 1½ MFMt, 1 Fat	222	696
Rondelets, Homestyle	(3 oz.)	½ S, 2 LMt, 1½ Fat	206	640
Rondelets, Italian	(3 oz.)	1 S, 1½ MFMt, 1 Fat	215	570
Rondelets, Original	(3 oz.)	1 S, 1½ LMt, 1 Fat	195	454
Thigh Fillet Strips	(3.5 oz.)	1 S, 1½ LMt, 2 Fat	262	650
White Meat Roll	(3.5 oz.)	2½ LMt	128	780
Turkey				
Buddig				
Turkey	(1 oz.)	1 LMt	50	400
Turkey Breast	(1½ oz.)	1 LMt	35	(N/A)
Land O'Lakes Convenience				
Breast Fillets w/Cheese	(5 oz.)	1 S, 3 MFMt	300	835
Diced, White/Dark Mixed	(3 oz.)	2 LMt	120	590
Landola Roast, White w/gravy	(3 oz.)	2 LMt	110	510

Food	Portion	Exchanges	Calories	Sodium (mg)
Turkey, cont.				
Landola Roast, White/Dark w/gravy	(3 oz.)	2 LMt	120	490
Patties	(2¼ oz.)	½ S, 1 MFMt, 1 Fat	170	330
Sticks	(2 oz.)	½ S, 1 MFMt, 1 Fat	150	295
Turkey Ham	(3 oz.)	2½ LMt	100	845
Land O'Lakes Oven-Cooked Breasts (3 oz.)				
Bronze Label		2 LMt	100	510
Gold Label Browned		2½ LMt	120	635
Gold Label Skinless		3 LMt	90	715
Gold Label Skin On		2½ LMt	120	640
Silver Label		2½ LMt	100	565
Land O'Lakes Turkey Rolls (3 oz.)				
Blue Label Mixed		2 LMt	120	550
Blue Label White		2 LMt	110	560
Red Label Mixed		2 LMt	110	510
Red Label White		2 LMt	110	530
Louis Rich (1 oz.)				
*Barbecued Breast**		½ LMt	38	315
Breakfast Sausage		1 LMt	59	200
Breast		1 LMt	51	21
Breast Slices		1 LMt	44	28
Breast Tenderloins		1 LMt	41	22
*Chunk Smoked Turkey Breast**		½ LMt	34	260
Drumstick		1 LMt	55	20
Ground		1 LMt	61	29
*Hickory Smoked Breast**		½ LMt	35	229
Oven Roasted Breast		½ LMt	36	300
Thighs		1 LMt	65	20
Whole		1 LMt	57	20
Wing Drumettes		1 LMt	53	20
Wing Portion		1 LMt	54	17
Wings		1 LMt	54	17
Oscar Mayer Lean Cold Cuts, Turkey Breast (1 slice)				
Oven Roasted, 97% fat-free		½ LMt	20	265
Smoked, 98% fat-free		½ LMt	20	295
Weaver (3.5 oz.)				
Oven Roasted Breast		3 LMt	105	600
Turkey Ham		3 LMt	134	1060

*Contains concentrated sources of carbohydrates

Food	Portion	Exchanges	Calories	Sodium (mg)
Fish & Seafood				
Catfish, Mrs. Paul's				
Fillet	(1 fillet)	1 S, 1½ MFMt, ½ Fat	220	300
*Breaded Strips**	(4 oz.)	1½ S, ½ MFMt, 2 Fat	240	290
Light Fillets	(1 fillet)	1½ S, 2 LMt, 1 Fat	250	389
Strips	(4 oz.)	1½ S, 1 MFMt, 1½ Fat	240	290
Clams				
Doxsee				
Chopped Liquids & Solids	(6½ oz.)	2 LMt	90	1020
Juice	(3 fl. oz.)	free	4	110
Gorton's				
Crunchy Fried Strips	(½ pkg.)	1 S, ½ MFMt, 2½ Fat	240	460
Minced Clams	(½ can)	1½ LMt	70	640
Mrs. Paul's Prepared Battered (2½ oz.)				
Fried		1½ S, ½ LMt, 2 Fat	240	380
Fried, in a Light Batter		1½ S, ½ MFMt, 2 Fat	240	389
Snow's, Minced Liquid & Solids	(6½ oz.)	2 LMt	90	1020
Van De Kamp's Breaded	(2¼ oz.)	½ S, 2 MFMt	210	320
Cod				
Gorton's Fishmarket Fresh	(4 oz.)	3 LMt	90	70
Mrs. Paul's				
Au Natural Fillets	(4 oz.)	2 LMt	90	160
Light Fillets	(1 fillet)	1½ S, 2 LMt	220	412
Van De Kamp's Microwave Lightly Breaded	(5 oz.)	½ S, 2 MFMt, 2 Fat	290	370
Van De Kamp's Today's Catch	(5 oz.)	3½ LMt	110	220
Crab, Deviled				
Mrs. Paul's	(3 oz.)	1 S, 1 LMt, 1 Fat	170	390
Miniatures	(3½ oz.)	2 S, ½ LMt, 2 Fat	250	480
Mrs. Paul's Prepared Breaded	(1 piece)	1½ S, ½ MFMt, 1 Fat	190	370
Miniatures	(3½ oz.)	2 S, ½ MFMt, 1½ Fat	250	480
Fish Sticks, Fillets, Cakes, & Nuggets				
Gorton's				
Breaded Sticks	(4 sticks)	1½ S, ½ MFMt, 1 Fat	210	480
Crispy Batter Dipped Fillets	(1 fillet)	1 S, 1 MFMt, 2 Fat	250	440

*Contains concentrated sources of carbohydrates

Food	Portion	Exchanges	Calories	Sodium (mg)
Fish Sticks, Fillets, Cakes, & Nuggets, cont.				
Crispy Batter Dipped Sticks	(4 sticks)	1 S, 1 MFMt, 2 Fat	230	560
Crunchy Fillets	(2 fillets)	1 S, 1 MFMt, 4 Fat	350	440
Crunchy Sticks	(4 sticks)	1 S, ½ MFMt, 2½ Fat	220	370
Potato Crisp Fillets	(2 fillets)	1 S, 1 MFMt, 4 Fat	340	460
Potato Crisp Sticks	(4 sticks)	1 S, 1 MFMt, 3 Fat	280	400
Value Pack Sticks	(4 sticks)	1 S, 1 MFMt, 1 Fat	210	420
Gorton's Light Recipe				
Lightly Breaded Fillets	(1 fillet)	1 S, 1 MFMt, ½ Fat	170	380
Tempura Batter Fillets	(1 fillet)	1 S, 1 MFMt,1 Fat	190	400
Mrs. Paul's				
Buttered Fillets	(2 fillets)	3 LMt	170	390
Cakes	(2 cakes)	2 S, 1 LMt, 1½ Fat	250	840
Cake Thins	(2 cakes)	2 S, 1½ LMt, 1½ Fat	290	1210
Crispy Crunchy Fillets	(2 fillets)	1½ S, 1 LMt, 2½ Fat	280	550
Crispy Crunchy Sticks	(4 sticks)	1 S, 1 LMt, 1½ Fat	200	350
40 Crunchy Sticks, Minced	(4 sticks)	1 S, 1 LMt, 1½ Fat	200	340
Mrs. Paul's Prepared Battered				
Batter Dipped Fillets	(2 fillets)	2 S, 2 LMt, 1½ Fat	320	581
Crunchy Batter Fillets	(2 fillets)	2 S, 1 LMt, 2½ Fat	310	810
Crunchy Batter Sticks	(4 sticks)	1½ S, ½ LMt, 2 Fat	240	590
Crunchy Light Batter Fillets	(2 fillets)	2 S, 1 MFMt, 2 Fat	310	810
Crunchy Light Batter Sticks	(4 sticks)	1½ S, ½ MFMt, 2 Fat	240	590
Supreme Light Batter Fillets	(1 fillet)	1½ S, ½ MFMt, 1½ Fat	210	540
Mrs. Paul's Prepared Breaded				
Cakes	(2 cakes)	2 S, ½ MFMt, 1½ Fat	250	840
Cake Thins	(2 cakes)	2 S, 1 MFMt, 1½ Fat	290	1210
Crispy Crunchy Fillets	(2 fillets)	1½ S, 1 MFMt, 2 Fat	280	550
Crispy Crunchy Sticks	(4 sticks)	1 S, 1 MFMt, 1 Fat	200	350

Food	Portion	Exchanges	Calories	Sodium (mg)
Lightly Breaded Fillets	(1 fillet)	1½ S, 2½ MFMt	290	770
Van De Kamp's Batter Dipped				
& Chips	(1 pkg.)	4 S, 1 MFMt, 2½ Fat	470	610
Fillets	(1 fillet)	1 S, 1 MFMt, 1 Fat	180	230
Kabobs	(4 oz.)	1 S, 1½ MFMt, 1 Fat	240	430
Sticks	(4 sticks)	1 S, 1 MFMt, 1½ Fat	220	330
Van De Kamp's Breaded				
Country Seasoned	(1 piece)	1 S, ½ MFMt, 2 Fat	195	335
Fillets	(1 fillet)	½ S, ½ MFMt, 2½ Fat	180	175
Nuggets	(4 oz.)	1 S, 1½ MFMt, 1½ Fat	260	320
Sticks	(4 sticks)	1 S, 1 MFMt, 2½ Fat	270	300
Van De Kamp's Today's Catch, Fillets	(5 oz.)	3 LMt	100	110
Flounder				
Gorton's				
Fishmarket Fresh	(4 oz.)	3 LMt	90	140
Light Recipe, Entree Size Fillet	(1 fillet)	1½ S, 2 MFMt	260	710
Mrs. Paul's				
Au Natural Flounder Fillets	(4 oz.)	2 LMt	90	140
Crispy Crunchy Fillets	(2 fillets)	1 S, 3 LMt, 1 Fat	270	500
Light Fillets	(1 fillet)	2 S, 1 LMt, 1½ Fat	260	536
Mrs. Paul's Prepared Battered (2 fillets)				
Crunchy Batter Fillets		2 S, ½ LMt, 2½ Fat	310	790
Crunchy Light Batter Fillets		2 S, 1 MFMt, 2 Fat	310	790
Mrs. Paul's Prepared Breaded				
Crispy Crunchy Fillets	(2 fillets)	1½ S, 1 MFMt, 2 Fat	270	500
Lightly Breaded Fillets	(1 fillet)	1 S, 2½ MFMt	280	700
Van De Kamp's				
Microwave Lightly Breaded	(5 oz.)	1 S, 2 MFMt, 1½ Fat	290	410
Today's Catch	(5 oz.)	3 LMt	100	170
Haddock				
Gorton's				
Fishmarket Fresh	(4 oz.)	3 LMt	90	100
Light Recipe, Entree Size Fillet	(1 fillet)	1½ S, 2 MFMt	260	570
Mrs. Paul's Light Fillets	(1 fillet)	1½ S, 2 LMt	220	456

Food	Portion	Exchanges	Calories	Sodium (mg)
Haddock, cont.				
Mrs. Paul's Prepared Battered				
Crunchy Batter Fillets	(2 fillets)	2 S, ½ LMt, 3 Fat	330	670
Crunchy Light Batter Fillets	(2 fillets)	2 S, ½ MFMt, 3 Fat	330	670
Mrs. Paul's Prepared Breaded				
Crispy Crunchy Fillets	(2 fillets)	1½ S, 1½ MFMt, ½ Fat	250	485
Lightly Breaded Fillets	(1 fillet)	1½ S, 2½ MFMt	290	960
Van De Kamp's				
Batter Dipped	(2 pieces)	1 S, 1½ MFMt, 1 Fat	240	430
Breaded Fillets	(1 piece)	½ S, ½ MFMt, 2 Fat	180	160
Microwave Lightly Breaded	(5 oz.)	1 S, 2 MFMt, 2 Fat	300	310
Today's Catch	(5 oz.)	3½ MFMt	110	180
Halibut				
Van De Kamp's				
Batter Dipped	(3 pieces)	1 S, 1½ MFMt, 1½ Fat	260	440
Microwave Lightly Breaded	(4 oz.)	1 S, 2 MFMt	220	520
Ocean Perch				
Gorton's Fishmarket Fresh	(4 oz.)	3 LMt	100	100
Mrs. Paul's Crispy Crunchy Fillets	(1 fillet)	1½ S, 1 LMt, 3 Fat	320	460
Van De Kamp's				
Batter Dipped	(2 pieces)	1½ S, 1 MFMt, 2 Fat	270	510
Breaded Fillets	(1 fillet)	½ S, ½ MFMt, 2 Fat	170	115
Microwave Lightly Breaded	(5 oz.)	1 S, 2½ MFMt, 1½ Fat	300	330
Perch				
Mrs. Paul's				
Au Natural Fillets	(4 oz.)	2 LMt	80	160
Light Fillets	(1 fillet)	1½ S, 2 LMt, 1½ Fat	270	391
Prepared Breaded, Crispy Crunchy Fillets	(2 fillets)	1½ S, 1 MFMt, 3 Fat	320	460
Van De Kamp's Today's Catch	(5 oz.)	3½ LMt	160	150
Pollock, Mrs. Paul's Light Fillets	(1 fillet)	1 S, 2 LMt, 1 Fat	240	530

Food	Portion	Exchanges	Calories	Sodium (mg)
Salmon, Carnation (7¾ oz.)				
Pink		6 LMt	310	(N/A)
Sockeye Red		6½ LMt	380	(N/A)
Sardines, Underwood				
in Mustard Sauce, undrained	(3.75 oz.)	2½ MFMt, ½ Fat	220	650
in Soya Bean Oil, drained	(3 oz.)	2½ MFMt, 1 Fat	230	400
in Tabasco Brand Pepper Sauce, drained	(3 oz.)	2½ MFMt, ½ Fat	220	400
in Tomato Sauce, undrained	(3.75 oz.)	2½ MFMt, ½ Fat	220	500
Scallops, Mrs. Paul's				
Fried	(3½ oz.)	1½ S, 1 LMt, 1 Fat	230	480
Prepared Breaded, French Fried	(3½ oz.)	1½ S, 1 MFMt, 1 Fat	230	480
Shrimp, Mrs. Paul's				
Fried	(3 oz.)	1 S, 1 LMt, 1½ Fat	200	430
Prepared Breaded, Fried	(3 oz.)	1 S, 1 MFMt, 1 Fat	200	430
Sole				
Gorton's Fishmarket				
Fresh	(4 oz.)	3 LMt	90	110
Mrs. Paul's				
Au Natural Fillets	(4 oz.)	2 LMt	90	160
Light Fillets	(1 fillet)	2 S, 1 LMt, 1½ Fat	260	535
Prepared Breaded, Lightly Breaded Fillets	(1 fillet)	1 S, 2½ MFMt	280	700
Van De Kamp's				
Microwave Lightly Breaded	(5 oz.)	1 S, 2 MFMt, 1½ Fat	290	410
Today's Catch, Baby Sole	(5 oz.)	3 LMt	100	150

4

VEGETABLES, MIXED VEGETABLES, & VEGETABLE JUICES

Vegetables can add great variety and appeal to your diet.

In terms of general nutrition, it's a good idea to eat one dark green or deep yellow vegetable at least four times each week.

Whole vegetables add fiber to your diet, and vegetable juices are rich in vitamins and minerals. Vegetables have more free food exchanges than most foods, but for preserved vegetables, watch the sodium values.

Food	Portion	Exchanges	Calories	Sodium (mg)
■ Vegetables				
Asparagus				
Green Giant, canned (½ cup)				
Cuts		1 V	20	450
Le Sueur Spears		1 V	30	390
Joan of Arc, cuts, canned	(½ cup)	1 V	30	340
Beans, Baked				
Campbell's, canned				
Barbecue Beans	(7⅞ oz.)	2½ S, 1 V, ½ MFMt	250	900
Home Style Beans	(8 oz.)	3 S, ½ V, ½ Fat	270	900
*Old Fashioned Beans in Molasses & Brown Sugar**	(8 oz.)	3 S, ½ V, ½ Fat	270	730
Pork & Beans in Tomato Sauce	(8 oz.)	2½ S, 1 V, ½ Fat	240	740
Ranchero Beans	(7⅞ oz.)	2 S, 1 V, 1 Fat	220	830
Hanover, canned (½ cup)				
Barbeque Baked Beans		1½ S, ½ Fat	140	440
Brown Sugar & Bacon Baked Beans		1½ S	120	530
Pork & Beans		1½ S	120	420
Vegetarian Baked Beans		1 S, 1 V	100	410
Hunt's, canned				
Big John's Beans 'n' Fixin's				
Beans	(3 oz.)	1 S, 1 V	100	370
Fixin's	(1 oz.)	1 V, ½ Fat	50	125
Pork & Beans	(4 oz.)	1½ S, 1 V	140	400
Joan of Arc, Pork & Beans, canned	(½ cup)	1 S, 2 V	130	660
Van Camp's, canned (1 cup)				
*Brown Sugar Beans**		2½ S, ½ Fr, ½ HFMt	280	690
Pork & Beans		2½ S, ½ MFMt	220	1010
Vegetarian Style Beans		2½ S	210	990
Western Style Beans		2 S, ½ HFMt	210	1010
Beans, Butter				
Joan of Arc, canned	(½ cup)	1½ S	100	420
Van Camp's, canned	(1 cup)	2 S, ½ LMt	160	750
Beans, Chili				
Joan of Arc, canned	(½ cup)	1½ S	100	660
Van Camp's, Mexican Style, canned	(1 cup)	2½ S, ½ Fat	210	720

*Contains concentrated sources of carbohydrates

Food	Portion	Exchanges	Calories	Sodium (mg)
Beans, Garbanzo, Joan of Arc, canned	(½ cup)	1 S	90	420
Beans, Great Northern, Joan of Arc, canned	(½ cup)	1 S	90	420
Beans, Green				
Green Giant, in butter sauce	(½ cup)			
Cut		1 V, ½ Fat	35	300
French-Style		1 V, ½ Fat	40	360
Green Giant, canned	(½ cup)			
French-Style Cut		1 V	18	270
Kitchen Cut		1 V	20	260
1½" cut		1 V	20	310
Green Giant Harvest, Cut	(½ cup)	1 V	20	150
Green Giant Polybag	(½ cup)	1 V	20	10
Hanover, cut, canned	(½ cup)	1 V	20	280
Hanover, frozen	(3.2 oz.)			
Cut Blue Lake		1 V	30	4
French		1 V	25	4
Whole Blue Lake		1 V	30	5
Joan of Arc, canned	(½ cup)	1 V	25	380
Stouffer's, Green Bean Mushroom Casserole	(4¾ oz.)	½ S, 1 V, 2½ Fat	170	640
Beans, Kidney				
Hanover, Redskin, canned	(½ cup)	1½ S	120	440
Joan of Arc, canned	(½ cup)			
Dark Red		1½ S	110	340
Light Red		1 S	90	390
Van Camp's, canned	(1 cup)			
Dark Red		2 S, 1 LMt	180	730
Light Red		2 S, 1 LMt	180	690
New Orleans Style		2 S, 1 LMt	180	790
Beans, Lima				
Green Giant, in butter sauce, Baby	(½ cup)	1S, ½ V, ½ Fat	110	460
Green Giant Harvest Fresh	(½ cup)	1 S	70	210
Green Giant Polybag	(½ cup)	1 S, 1 V	100	30
Hanover, frozen	(3.2 oz.)			
Baby		1½ S	110	79
Fordhook		1 S, 1 V	100	140

Food	Portion	Exchanges	Calories	Sodium (mg)
Hanover, canned, Limagrands, Superfine	(½ cup)	1 S	90	410
Beans, Navy, Green Giant, canned	(½ cup)	1½ S	100	550
Beans, Pinto, Joan of Arc, canned	(½ cup)	1½ S	100	400
Beans, Red				
Joan of Arc, canned	(½ cup)	1½ S	100	450
Van Camp's, canned	(1 cup)	2½ S, ½ LMt	190	930
Beans, Refried, Little Pancho Refried Beans & Green Chili	(½ cup)	1 S	80	330
Beans, Romano, Hanover, Cut, frozen	(3.2 oz.)	1½ V	35	4
Beans, Wax, Joan of Arc, canned	(½ cup)	1 V	25	330
Broccoli				
Green Giant, in butter sauce (½ cup)				
Broccoli, Cauliflower, Carrots		½ V, ½ Fat	30	340
Broccoli Spears		1 V, ½ Fat	45	340
Green Giant, in cheese-flavored sauce (½ cup)				
Broccoli		2 V, ½ Fat	70	530
Broccoli, Cauliflower, Carrots		2 V, ½ Fat	70	490
Broccoli in White Cheddar		1½ V, ½ Fat	60	450
Green Giant Harvest Fresh (½ cup)				
Broccoli Spears		1 V	30	200
Cut Broccoli		1 V	25	200
Green Giant Harvest Get Togethers (½ cup)				
Broccoli Cauliflower Medley		2 V	60	470
Broccoli Fanfare		1 S	70	470
Green Giant Polybag (½ cup)				
Broccoli Cuts		1 V	16	10
Broccoli Minispears		1 V	16	10
Green Giant Valley Combination Polybag (½ cup)				
Broccoli Carrot Fanfare		1 V	20	30
Broccoli Cauliflower Supreme		1 V	18	30
Hanover, Broccoli Cuts, frozen	(3.2 oz.)	1 V	25	10
Pepperidge Farm Vegetables in Pastry, Broccoli w/Cheese	(1 pastry)	½ S, 2 V, 3 Fat	250	450
Stouffer's, Broccoli in Cheddar Cheese Sauce	(½ pkg.)	1 V, 1 HFMt, ½ Fat	150	480
Valley Combination Dual Pouch (½ cup)				
Broccoli Cauliflower Medley		1½ V, ½ Fat	60	430

Food	Portion	Exchanges	Calories	Sodium (mg)
Broccoli, cont.				
Broccoli Fanfare		½ S, ½ V, ½ Fat	80	430
Brussels Sprouts				
Green Giant, in butter sauce	(½ cup)	½ S, ½ Fat	60	320
Green Giant, in cheese-flavored sauce, Baby	(½ cup)	½ S, 1 V, ½ Fat	80	470
Green Giant Polybag	(½ cup)	1 V	30	10
Hanover, frozen	(3.2 oz.)	1½ V	40	10
Carrots, Hanover, Sliced, frozen	(3.2 oz.)	1½ V	35	24
Cauliflower				
Green Giant, in butter sauce	(½ cup)	½ V, ½ Fat	30	310
Green Giant, in cheese-flavored sauce	(½ cup)	2 V, ½ Fat	60	450
in White Cheddar	(½ cup)	1½ V, ½ Fat	70	420
Green Giant Harvest Get Togethers, Cauliflower Carrot Bonanza	(½ cup)	1 V, ½ Fat	60	290
Green Giant Polybag Cauliflower Cuts	(½ cup)	½ V	12	15
Green Giant Valley Combination Polybag, Cauliflower Green Bean Festival	(½ cup)	1 V	16	30
Hanover, frozen (3.2 oz.)				
Cauliflower Cuts		1 V	20	7
Cauliflower Florets		1 V	20	6
Pepperidge Farm Vegetables in Pastry, Cauliflower & Cheese Sauce	(1 pastry)	½ S, 2 V, 2½ Fat	210	460
Chinese				
Chun King, drained				
Bamboo Shoots	(4 oz.)	1 V	32	0
Bean Sprouts	(4 oz.)	1½ V	40	5
Chow Mein Vegetables	(4 oz.)	1 V	35	20
Water Chestnuts, Whole, Sliced	(2 oz.)	½ S	45	15
Hanover, Oriental Blend, frozen	(3.2 oz.)	1 V	25	10
La Choy, canned				
Bamboo Shoots	(¼ cup)	free	6	0
Bean Sprouts	(⅔ cup)	free	8	20
Chop Suey Vegetables, drained	(½ cup)	½ V	10	320

Food	Portion	Exchanges	Calories	Sodium (mg)
Fancy Mixed Chinese Vegetables, drained	(½ cup)	½ V	12	30
Fried Rice	(¾ cup)	2½ S	190	820
Water Chestnuts, drained	(¼ cup)	½ V	16	0
La Choy, Chinese Pea Pods, frozen	(½ pkg.)	1 V	35	< 10
Corn				
Green Giant, in butter sauce (½ cup)				
Niblets Corn		1 S, ½ Fat	100	280
White Shoepeg Corn		1 S, ½ Fat	110	340
Green Giant, canned (½ cup)				
Cream-Style Corn		1½ S	100	320
Golden Shoepeg Corn		1 S	90	270
Le Sueur Whole Kernel Corn		1 S	80	290
Mexicorn w/Peppers		1 S	80	330
White Shoepeg Corn Vacuum Pak		1 S	90	270
Whole Kernel Corn Vacuum Pak		1 S	90	230
Green Giant, in cream sauce, Cream-Style Corn	(½ cup)	1½ S	120	370
Green Giant Harvest Fresh (½ cup)				
Niblets Corn		1 S	90	150
White Shoepeg Corn		1 S, 1 V	100	270
Green Giant Polybag				
Niblets Corn	(½ cup)	1 S	80	5
Niblets Corn-on-the-Cob, 4 Ear	(1 ear)	2 S	150	20
Niblets Corn-on-the-Cob, 6 Ear	(2 ears)	2 S	150	20
White Shoepeg Corn	(½ cup)	1 S	80	0
Green Giant Valley Combination Polybag, Corn Broccoli Bounty	(½ cup)	½ S	45	15
Hanover, Yellow Corn, frozen	(3.2 oz.)	1 S	80	5
Joan of Arc, canned (½ cup)				
Cream-Style Corn		1½ S	120	360
Golden Whole Kernel Corn		1 S	90	190
Mrs. Paul's, Prepared Corn Fritters*	(2 fritters)	1 S, 1 Fr, 2½ Fat	250	630
Stouffer's Corn Souffle	(4 oz.)	½ S, ½ SMk, 1½ Fat	150	540

*Contains concentrated sources of carbohydrates

Food	Portion	Exchanges	Calories	Sodium (mg)
Eggplant				
Mrs. Paul's, Prepared				
Eggplant Parmigiana	(5 oz.)	1 S, 1 V, 3½ Fat	260	600
*Fried Eggplant Sticks**	(3½ oz.)	1 S, 1 Fr, 2 Fat	240	610
Mushrooms				
Green Giant, canned (2 oz.)				
B in B Mushrooms		1 V	25	530
Mushrooms in Butter Sauce		1 V	25	530
Mushrooms, Pieces & Stems Buttons		½ V	14	260
Okra				
Hanover, frozen (3.2 oz.)				
Cut		1 V	25	8
Whole		1½ V	35	11
Onions				
Hanover, Superfine Whole, canned	(½ cup)	1½ V	35	140
Mrs. Paul's Crispy Onion Rings, prepared	(2½ oz.)	1½ S, 2 Fat	180	270
Peas				
Green Giant, in butter sauce (½ cup)				
LeSueur Early Peas		1 S, ½ Fat	90	590
LeSueur Mini Peas, Pea Pods & Water Chestnuts		½ S, 1 V, ½ Fat	80	410
LeSueur Peas, Onions & Carrots		½ S, 1 V, ½ Fat	80	470
Sweet Peas		1 S, ½ Fat	90	490
Green Giant, canned (½ cup)				
Blackeye Peas		1 S	90	350
Early June Peas		1 S	60	380
Mini Sweet Peas		1 S	60	420
Sweet Peas		1 S	60	370
Sweet Peas & Onions		1 S	60	550
Green Giant, in cream sauce	(½ cup)	2 V, 1 Fat	100	320
Green Giant Harvest Fresh (½ cup)				
Early June Peas		1 S	80	170
Sweet Peas		1 S	60	220
Green Giant Polybag (½ cup)				
Early June Peas		1 S	60	170
Sweet Peas		2 V	60	110
Green Giant Valley Combination Polybag, Sweet Pea Cauliflower Medley	(½ cup)	1 V	30	60

*Contains concentrated sources of carbohydrates

Food	Portion	Exchanges	Calories	Sodium (mg)
Hanover, Sweet Peas, frozen	(3.2 oz.)	1 S	70	81
Joan of Arc, Sweet Peas, canned	(½ cup)	1 S	70	240
Peppers, Green, Hanover, Diced, frozen	(3.2 oz.)	1 V	20	5
Potatoes, canned				
Joan of Arc (½ cup)				
Cut Sweet Potatoes		1½ S	110	45
Mashed Sweet Potatoes		1½ S	130	60
*Sweet Potatoes in Orange Pineapple Sauce**		1 S, 1½ Fr	180	60
*Whole Sweet Potatoes in Heavy Syrup**		1 S, 1 Fr	150	40
Potatoes, Frozen				
Green Giant Stuffed Baked (5 oz.)				
w/Cheese-Flavored Topping		2 S, 1 Fat	200	520
Cream & Chives		2 S, 1 Fat	200	520
Ore Ida Formed potatoes (3 oz.)				
Crispers		1½ S, 3 Fat	230	545
Crispy Crowns		1 S, 2 Fat	160	525
Tater Tots		1 S, 1½ Fat	140	550
Ore Ida French Fries (3 oz.)				
Country-Style Dinner Fries		1 S, ½ Fat	110	30
Golden Crinkles		1 S, 1 Fat	120	35
Golden Fries		1 S, 1 Fat	120	35
Pixie Crinkles		1½ S, 1 Fat	140	40
Ore Ida Lites				
Crinkle Cuts	(3 oz.)	1 S, ½ Fat	90	35
Hash Browns Golden Patties	(2.5 oz.)	1 S, 1½ Fat	140	295
Shredded Hash Browns	(3 oz.)	1 S	70	40
Ore Ida Microwave				
Crinkle Cuts	(3.5 oz.)	1½ S, 1½ Fat	180	35
Hash Browns	(2 oz.)	1 S, 1½ Fat	130	170
Tater Tots	(4 oz.)	2 S, 2 Fat	200	670
Stouffer's (⅓ of 11½ oz. pkg.)				
Potatoes au Gratin		1 S, 1 Fat	120	480
Scalloped Potatoes		1 S, 1 Fat	110	410
Potato Mixes				
Country Store, Mashed Potatoes	(⅓ cup flakes)	1 S	70	10

*Contains concentrated sources of carbohydrates

Food	Portion	Exchanges	Calories	Sodium (mg)
Potato Mixes, cont.				
French's (½ cup)				
Creamy Italian-Style Potatoes w/Parmesan Sauce		1½ S, ½ Fat	130	430
Creamy Stroganoff Potatoes		1½ S, ½ Fat	130	520
Crispy Top Scalloped Potatoes w/Savory Onion		1 S, ½ V, 1 Fat	140	420
Dinner Potato Pancakes		1 S	80	410
Idaho Mashed Potatoes		1 S, 1 Fat	130	340
Spuds Mashed Potatoes		1 S, 1½ Fat	140	370
Real Cheese Scalloped Potatoes		1 S, ½ V, 1 Fat	140	370
Real Sour Cream & Chives Potatoes		1 S, ½ V, 1 Fat	150	560
Tangy au Gratin		1 S, ½ V, 1 Fat	140	470
General Mills (½ cup)				
Au Gratin		1½ S, 1 Fat	150	630
Chicken 'n' Herb		1 S, 1 Fat	120	600
Family-Style, Twice Baked Potatoes, Bacon & Cheese		1½ S, ½ MFMt, 1½ Fat	210	600
Family-Style, Twice Baked Potatoes, Herbed Butter		1 S, ½ MFMt, 2 Fat	220	540
Hash Browns w/Onions		1½ S, 1 Fat	160	460
Julienne		1 S, 1 Fat	140	600
Parsley Creamed		1½ S, 1½ Fat	180	420
Potato Buds		1 S, 1 Fat	130	360
Scalloped		1 S, 1 Fat	140	570
Smoky Cheddar		1½ S, 1 Fat	150	700
Sour Cream 'n' Chives		1½ S, 1 Fat	160	530
Twice Baked Potatoes, Mild Cheddar w/Onion		1 S, ½ MFMt, 1½ Fat	190	640
Twice Baked Potatoes, Sour Cream 'n' Chives		1 S, ½ MFMt, 1½ Fat	200	540
Hungry Jack, Mashed Potato Flakes	(½ cup)	1 S, 1½ Fat	140	380
Pumpkin, Joan of Arc, canned	(½ cup)	½ S, ½ Fat	50	25
Salad				
Fresh Chef (4 oz.)				
*Holiday Coleslaw**		1 Fr, 3 Fat	200	240
Old-Fashioned Potato		1 S, 3 Fat	210	330
General Mills Suddenly Salad, Creamy Potato	(1/6 pkg.)	1½ S, 3 Fat	250	420
Green Giant, Three-Bean, canned	(½ cup)	1 S	80	540
Hanover, frozen (3.2 oz.)				
Italian Pasta		1 S	70	7

*Contains concentrated sources of carbohydrates

Food	Portion	Exchanges	Calories	Sodium (mg)
Milano Pasta		½ S	50	5
Pasta Primavera		1 S	60	7
Sicilian Pasta		1 S	60	40
Hanover Salads (½ cup)				
Four-Bean		1 S	80	35
*Three-Bean**		1 S, ½ Fr, ½ Fat	130	10
Vegetable		1 S	90	15
Joan of Arc, canned (½ cup)				
Four-Bean		1½ S	120	850
Garden		1 S	80	600
German-Style Green Bean		½ S, 1½ V, ½ Fat	90	730
*German-Style Potato**		1 S, ½ Fr, ½ Fat	120	830
Home-Style Potato		1 S, 2 Fat	160	750
Three-Bean		1 S	90	920
Sauerkraut, Old-Fashioned	(1 oz.)	free	4	280
Spinach				
Green Giant, in butter sauce, Cut Leaf	(½ cup)	1½ V, ½ Fat	60	520
Green Giant, in cream sauce	(½ cup)	2 V, ½ Fat	80	480
Green Giant Harvest Fresh	(½ cup)	1 V	40	360
Green Giant Polybag	(½ cup)	1 V	25	60
Stouffer's				
Creamed Spinach	(4½ oz.)	1 V, ½ SMk, 3 Fat	190	440
Spinach Souffle	(4 oz.)	½ S, ½ V, ½ MFMt, 1 Fat	140	560
Succotash, Hanover, frozen	(3.2 oz.)	1 S	80	49
Tomatoes, Stewed				
Contadina	(½ cup)	1½ V	35	330
Hunt's	(3 oz.)	1 V	26	345
No Salt Added		1 V	26	15
Tomatoes, Whole				
Hunt's	(4 oz.)	1 V	20	420
No Salt Added		1 V	20	15
Yams				
Mrs. Paul's (4 oz.)				
*Candied Yams**		3½ Fr	200	125
*Candied Yams 'n' Apples**		2½ Fr	160	70
Stouffer's Yams & Apples	(5 oz.)	½ S, 2 Fr, ½ Fat	160	200

*Contains concentrated sources of carbohydrates

Food	Portion	Exchanges	Calories	Sodium (mg)
Zucchini, Mrs. Paul's Prepared Light				
Batter Sticks	(3 oz.)	1½ S, 2½ Fat	200	440

■ Mixed Vegetables

Food	Portion	Exchanges	Calories	Sodium (mg)
Green Giant, in butter sauce	(½ cup)	½ S, 1 V, ½ Fat	80	370
Green Giant Harvest Fresh	(½ cup)	½ S	45	170
Green Giant Polybag	(½ cup)	½ S	50	30
Hanover Frozen Blend from 16-oz. Polybags				
Autumn	(3.2 oz.)	1 V	20	9
Caribbean	(3.2 oz.)	1 V	25	28
Romano Medley	(3.2 oz.)	1 V	25	10
Soup Vegetables	(3.2 oz.)	½ S, ½ V	60	5
Summer Vegetables	(3.2 oz.)	1½ V	35	17
Valley Combination Dual-Pouch (½ cup)				
American-Style		1 S, ½ Fat	90	340
Italian-Style		1 V, ½ Fat	50	310
Japanese-Style		1½ V	45	420
LeSueur-Style		½ S, 1 V, ½ Fat	90	340
Mexican-Style		1 S, 1 V, 1 Fat	150	540

■ Vegetable Juices

Food	Portion	Exchanges	Calories	Sodium (mg)
Tomato				
Campbell's canned	(6 oz.)	½ Fr	35	570
Hunt's No Salt Added	(4 oz.)	1 V	20	20
Ortega Snap-E Tomato Cocktail	(6 oz.)	1½ V	40	750
Welch's	(6 oz.)	1 V	35	550
V8, canned	(6 oz.)	½ Fr	35	62
No Salt Added		½ Fr	40	45
Spicy Hot		½ Fr	35	620

5

FRUIT, FRUIT JUICES & DRINKS, FROZEN FRUIT SNACKS

Fruits and fruit juices add vitamins, minerals, and fiber to your diet without adding any fat or protein. Fresh whole fruits provide more fiber than processed juices or frozen fruit snacks. It's wise to consume one fruit high in vitamin C daily, such as citrus fruit, strawberries, or kiwi.

Fruits must be carefully measured and calculated, since the amounts of carbohydrates they contain differ widely. The riper the fruit, the higher the sugar content and the lower the amount of complex carbohydrates. Dried fruits such as figs and raisins have more sugar than their fresh counterparts. Some soft-serve frozen fruit treats can be a pleasant fruit exchange on a hot day.

Before you select a fruit drink or frozen fruit snack, check the label to see how much sugar is added.

Food	Portion	Exchanges	Calories	Sodium (mg)
■ Fruit & Fruit Mixtures				
Apples				
Mrs. Paul's Apple Fritters, frozen	(2 fritters)	1 S, 1½ Fr, 2½ Fat	270	610
Stouffer's, Escalloped Apples, frozen	(⅓ pkg.)	2 Fr, ½ Fat	140	20
Weight Watchers, Apple Snacks: Cinnamon, Peach, Strawberry, dried	(½ oz.)	1 Fr	50	75
Apricots, Sun-Maid, dried	(2 oz.)	2½ Fr	140	(N/A)
Currants, Sun-Maid, dried	(½ cup)	3½ Fr	210	(N/A)
Combination. ***See*** **Mixed Fruit**				
Figs, dried				
Blue Ribbon Calimyrna	(½ cup)	4 Fr, ½ Fat	250	(N/A)
Sun-Maid Mission	(½ cup)	3½ Fr	210	(N/A)
Mixed Fruit				
Del Monte Sierra Trail Mix, dried	(.9 oz.)	1 Fr, ½ MFMt, 1 Fat	130	35
Del Monte Tropical Fruit Mix, dried	(.9 oz.)	½ S, 1 Fr	90	15
Hunt's Snack Pack Fruit Cup, canned	(5 oz.)	2 Fr	120	5
Sun-Maid Fruit Bits, dried	(2 oz.)	3 Fr	160	(N/A)
Sun-Maid Mixed Fruit, dried	(2 oz.)	2½ Fr	150	(N/A)
Oranges, Mandarin, Dole, in light syrup	(½ cup)	1½ Fr	76	8
Peaches, diced, Hunt's Snack Pack	(5 oz.)	2 Fr	110	5
Pineapple				
Del Monte Nuggets	(.9 oz.)	1½ Fr	90	25
Dole, canned (½ cup)				
All Cuts in Juice		1 Fr	70	1.1
All Cuts in Syrup		1½ Fr	95	1.5
Prunes, Sunsweet, Pitted	(2 oz.)	2½ Fr	140	(N/A)
Raisins				
Del Monte (.9 oz.)				
*Yogurt Raisins**		½ S, ½ Fr, 1 Fat	120	25
*Yogurt Raisins, Strawberry**		½ S, ½ Fr, 1 Fat	120	200

*Contains concentrated sources of carbohydrates

Food	Portion	Exchanges	Calories	Sodium (mg)
Sun-Maid, Seedless Raisins	(½ cup)	4½ Fr	250	(N/A)
Salad, Fresh Chef, Tropical Delight	(7 oz.)	1 S, 1 Fr, 2 Fat	240	270
Spreads: Grape, Raspberry, Strawberry, Weight Watchers*	(4 tsp.)	½ Fr	32	0

■ Fruit Juices & Drinks

Food	Portion	Exchanges	Calories	Sodium (mg)
Apple				
Campbell's, canned (6 oz.)				
Juice Works, Apple		1½ Fr	100	30
Juice Works, Appleberry		1½ Fr	100	30
HI-C 100	(6 oz.)	1½ Fr	89	23
Minute Maid, chilled	(6 oz.)	1½ Fr	90	16
Minute Maid, frozen concentrate	(6 oz.)	1½ Fr	90	2
Mott's U.S.A. (6 oz.)				
Apple		1½ Fr	88	13
Apple Cranberry		1½ Fr	83	17
Apple Grape		1½ Fr	86	17
Apple Raspberry		1½ Fr	83	49
Natural Apple		1½ Fr	76	28
Sippin' Pak, concentrate	(8.45 oz.)	2 Fr	110	25
Welch, Orchard Frozen Apple-Grape	(6 oz.)	2 Fr	110	10
Cherry				
Campbell's, Juice Works, canned	(6 oz.)	1½ Fr	100	15
Welch's Orchard	(6 oz.)	1½ Fr	90	10
Citrus				
Five Alive, chilled	(6 oz.)	1½ Fr	87	16
Berry		1½ Fr	88	15
Tropical		1½ Fr	88	15
Five Alive, frozen concentrate	(6 oz.)	1½ Fr	87	2
Berry		1½ Fr	88	1
Tropical		1½ Fr	85	1
Clamato, Mott's U.S.A.	(6 oz.)	1 Fr, 1 V	96	815
Cranberry				
Ocean Spray (6 oz.)				
Cranapple		2 Fr	130	< 10
Cranberry		2 Fr	110	< 10

*Contains concentrated sources of carbohydrates

Food	Portion	Exchanges	Calories	Sodium (mg)
Cranberry, cont.				
Cranraspberry		2 Fr	110	< 10
Low-Calorie Cranapple		½ Fr	40	< 10
Low-Calorie Cranberry		½ Fr	40	< 10
Low-Calorie Cranraspberry		½ Fr	40	10
Grape				
Bama, 10% Grape Juice*	(8.45 fl. oz.)	2 Fr	120	25
Campbell's Juice Works, canned	(6 oz.)	1½ Fr	100	15
Hawaiian Punch*	(6 oz.)	1½ Fr	90	30
Hi-C 100	(6 oz.)	1½ Fr	94	22
Light 'n' Juicy, chilled	(15 oz.)	½ Fr	30	43
Light 'n' Juicy, frozen	(15 oz.)	½ Fr	30	3
Minute Maid Grapeade, chilled	(6 oz.)	1½ Fr	94	15
Minute Maid, frozen (6 oz.)				
Grape Juice, sweetened		1½ Fr	98	3
Grapeade		1½ Fr	94	(trace)
Sippin' Pak, concentrate	(8.45 fl. oz.)	2 Fr	130	25
Welch's (6 oz.)				
Purple Grape		2 Fr	120	5
Red Grape		2 Fr	120	15
Sparkling Red Grape		2 Fr	128	30
Sparkling White Grape		2 Fr	120	30
White Grape		2 Fr	120	15
Welch's, frozen (6 oz.)				
Orchard, unsweetened		2 Fr	120	10
Sweetened		1½ Fr	100	0
Grapefruit				
Minute Maid, chilled	(6 oz.)	1 Fr	65	16
Minute Maid, frozen concentrate	(6 oz.)	1 Fr	71	2
Pink		1 Fr	71	2
Ocean Spray	(6 oz.)	1 Fr	70	< 10
Pink		1½ Fr	80	15
Lemon/Lime				
Gatorade, Lemon-Lime or Orange, instant	(8 fl. oz.)	1 Fr	60	110
Light 'n' Juicy, Lemonade, chilled	(30 oz.)	½ Fr	26	85

*Contains concentrated sources of carbohydrates

Food	Portion	Exchanges	Calories	Sodium (mg)
Light 'n' Juicy, Lemonade, frozen	(30 oz.)	½ Fr	26	10
Minute Maid, Lemonade, chilled	(6 oz.)	1½ Fr	81	15
Minute Maid, frozen concentrate (6 oz.)				
Lemon		½ Fr	22	17
Lemonade		1½ Fr	77	(trace)
Lemon/Limeade		1½ Fr	77	(trace)
Limeade		1½ Fr	77	(trace)
Pink Lemonade		1½ Fr	77	(trace)
Realemon, concentrate (3.5 fl. oz.)				
Natural Strength Lemon		½ Fr	21	35
100% Pure Lemon		½ Fr	21	17.5
Realime, Natural Strength Lime, concentrate	(3.5 fl. oz.)	½ Fr	21	35
Mixed Fruit Juices				
Bama*	(8.45 fl. oz.)	2 Fr	130	15
Hi-C, Double Fruit Cooler	(6 oz.)	1½ Fr	86	19
Land O'Lakes, Flavored*	(8 fl. oz.)	2 Fr	120	10
Max Sports Drink	(6 oz.)	½ Fr	35	4
Orchard Frozen Harvest	(6 oz.)	2 Fr	110	10
Orange				
Bama, 10% Orange Juice*	(8.45 fl. oz.)	2 Fr	120	60
Bright & Early Imitation Orange Beverage, chilled	(6 oz.)	1½ Fr	90	14
Bright & Early Imitation Orange Beverage, frozen concentrate	(6 oz.)	1½ Fr	90	0
Campbell's Juice Works, Orange, canned	(6 oz.)	1½ Fr	90	65
Hi-C 100, Orange	(6 oz.)	1½ Fr	94	20
Light 'n' Juicy, chilled	(12 oz.)	½ Fr	28	34
Light 'n' Juicy, frozen	(12 oz.)	½ Fr	28	4
Minute Maid, Calcium Fortified Orange Juice	(6 oz.)	1½ Fr	84	19
Minute Maid, chilled (6 oz.)				
Orange Juice		1½ Fr	82	16
Country-Style Orange Juice		1½ Fr	82	16

*Contains concentrated sources of carbohydrates

Food	Portion	Exchanges	Calories	Sodium (mg)
Orange, cont.				
Minute Maid, frozen concentrate	(6 oz.)			
Country-Style Orange Juice		1½ Fr	82	2
Orange Juice		1½ Fr	82	1
Orange, reduced acid		1½ Fr	82	2
Orangeade		1½ Fr	85	3
Sippin' Pak, Orange, concentrate	(8.45 oz.)	2 Fr	110	25
Pineapple				
Dole	(6 oz.)			
Pineapple		1½ Fr	103	2
Pineapple Pink Grapefruit		1½ Fr	101	(trace)
Dole New Pineapple, reconstituted	(6 oz.)			
Pineapple		1½ Fr	100	7
Pineapple-Grapefruit		1½ Fr	90	8.4
Pineapple-Orange		1½ Fr	100	8.4
Minute Maid, frozen concentrate	(6 oz.)			
Pineapple		1½ Fr	93	2
Pineapple/Orange		1½ Fr	93	2
Ocean Spray, Pineapple Grapefruit	(6 oz.)	2 Fr	110	< 10
Prune, Mott's U.S.A.	(6 oz.)	2 Fr	130	8
Punch				
Hawaiian Punch, canned	(6 oz.)			
*Fruit Juicy Red**		1½ Fr	90	20
*Island Fruit Cocktail**		1½ Fr	90	30
*Lite Fruit Juicy Red**		1 Fr	60	30
*Orange**		1½ Fr	100	20
*Tropical Fruit**		1½ Fr	90	30
*Very Berry**		1½ Fr	90	30
*Wild Fruit**		1½ Fr	90	35
Hi-C 100 Fruit Punch	(6 oz.)	1½ Fr	92	23
Light 'n' Juicy, chilled	(15 oz.)	1½ Fr	30	43
Light 'n' Juicy, frozen	(15 oz.)	½ Fr	30	8
Minute Maid Fruit Punch, chilled	(6 oz.)	1½ Fr	91	15
Minute Maid Fruit Punch, frozen concentrate	(6 oz.)	1½ Fr	91	(trace)
Raspberry, Welch, Orchard North Country Raspberry	(6 oz.)	1½ Fr	90	10
Strawberry, Campbell's, Juice Works, canned	(6 oz.)	1½ Fr	100	40

*Contains concentrated sources of carbohydrates

Food	Portion	Exchanges	Calories	Sodium (mg)
Tangerine, Minute Maid, sweetened, frozen concentrate	(6 oz.)	1½ Fr	82	1
■ Frozen Fruit Snacks				
Banana, Dole Fruit 'n' Juice Bars	(1 bar)	1½ Fr	80	12.7
Blueberry, Dole Fruit & Cream Bars	(1 bar)	1½ Fr	90	20
Cherry				
Dole Fruit 'n' Juice Bars	(1 bar)	1 Fr	70	13
Minute Maid	(2.25 oz.)	1 Fr	60	10
Welch	(1 bar,1.75 fl. oz.)	1 Fr	45	0
	(1 bar, 3 fl. oz.)	1½ Fr	80	0
Grape				
Minute Maid	(2.25 oz.)	1 Fr	60	(N/A)
Weight Watchers	(1.7 fl. oz.)	½ Fr	35	10
Mixed				
Minute Maid				
Snack Pack	(1 oz.)	½ Fr	25	5
Variety Pack	(2.25 oz.)	1 Fr	60	10
Welch	(1 bar, 1.75 fl. oz.)	1 Fr	45	0
Orange				
Dole Fruit 'n' Juice Bars, w/Mandarin	(1 bar)	1 Fr	70	14.4
Minute Maid	(2.25 oz.)	1 Fr	60	(N/A)
Vitari Soft Serve	(3 oz.)	1 Fr	60	15
Passion Fruit, Vitari Soft Serve	(3 oz.)	1 Fr	60	15
Peach				
Dole Fruit & Cream Bars	(1 bar)	1½ Fr	90	19
Vitari Soft Serve	(3 oz.)	1 Fr	60	15
Piña Colada, Dole Fruit 'n' Juice Bars	(1 bar)	1 Fr, ½ Fat	90	2
Pineapple, Dole Fruit 'n' Juice Bars	(1 bar)	1 Fr	70	4.4
Punch, Fruit, Minute Maid	(2.25 oz.)	1 Fr	60	(N/A)
Raspberry				
Dole Fruit 'n' Juice Bars	(1 bar)	1 Fr	70	13.6
Weight Watchers	(1.7 fl. oz.)	½ Fr	35	10
Welch	(1 bar, 1.75 fl. oz.)	1 Fr	45	0
	(1 bar, 3 fl. oz.)	1½ Fr	80	0
Strawberry				
Dole Fruit & Cream Bars	(1 bar)	1½ Fr	90	22

Food	Portion	Exchanges	Calories	Sodium (mg)
Strawberry, cont.				
Dole Fruit 'n' Juice Bars	(1 bar)	1 Fr	70	6
Minute Maid	(2.25 oz.)	1 Fr	60	5
Vitari Soft Serve	(3 oz.)	1 Fr	60	15
Weight Watchers	(1.7 fl. oz.)	½ Fr	35	10
Welch	(1 bar, 1.75 fl. oz.)	1 Fr	45	0
	(1 bar, 3 fl. oz.)	1½ Fr	80	0
Wildberry, Vitari Soft Serve	(3 oz.)	1 Fr	60	15

6

PASTA & PIZZA

You can find pasta in more than 150 different shapes and sizes. Most pasta is made from hard durum wheat, which makes pasta high in complex carbohydrates, rich in iron, and a good source of essential B vitamins—niacin, thiamin, and riboflavin. However, the sauce and/or cheese traditionally served with pasta may contain high concentrations of salt and fat, and may be high in calories.

Pizza is another versatile food—there's no limit to the combinations you can put together for toppings. Vegetable toppings are the most nutritious and the lowest in fat. Watch the fat and salt content of pepperoni and combination pizzas.

Food	Portion	Exchanges	Calories	Sodium (mg)
■ Pasta				
Cannelloni, Stouffer's Lean Cuisine, Cheese Cannelloni w/Tomato Sauce	(9⅛ oz.)	1½ S, ½ V, 2½ LMt, ½ Fat	270	900
Elbows, Ragu Pasta Meals, Elbows in Sauce w/Ground Beef, Mushrooms & Green Peppers	(7.5 oz.)	2 S, 1 V, ½ Fat	200	540
Fettucini				
Stouffer's				
Fettucini Alfredo	(5 oz.)	1 S, 1 MFMt, 3 Fat	280	570
Fettucini Primavera	(5⅜ oz.)	½ S, ½ V, ½ MFMt, 3½ Fat	270	520
Lasagna				
Green Giant Frozen Entrees				
Lasagna	(12 oz.)	2½ S, 1 V, 3½ MFMt, ½ Fat	490	1660
Lasagna	(18 oz.)	3½ S, 2½ V, 5 MFMt, 1 Fat	735	2490
Hamburger Helper, Lasagna	(⅕ pkg.)	1½ S, 2 V, 1½ MFMt, 1½ Fat	340	1070
Hormel, Lasagna	(7½ oz.)	1½ S, ½ HFMt, 2 Fat	260	1083
Hungry-Man Dinners, Lasagna	(1 complete dinner)	5 S, 1 Fr, 1 V, 1 MFMt, 4 Fat	740	1520
Hungry-Man Entrees, Lasagna w/Meat	(1 complete entree)	4 S, 1 V, 1 MFMt, 2 Fat	480	1250
Le Menu Dinners, Vegetable Lasagna	(1 complete dinner)	1½ S, 2 V, ½ MFMt, 3½ Fat	360	1050
Ragu Pasta Meals, Mini Lasagna in Sauce	(7.5 oz.)	2 S, ½ V	160	580
Stouffer's Entrees (10½ oz.)				
Lasagna		2 S, 1 V, 3 LMt, 1 Fat	370	1030
Vegetable Lasagna		1½ S, 1 V, 3 MFMt, 2 Fat	450	910
Stouffer's Lean Cuisine				
Tuna Lasagna w/Spinach Noodles & Vegetables	(9¾ oz.)	1½ S, 1 V, 2½ LMt, ½ Fat	280	990
Veal Lasagna	(10¼ oz.)	1½ S, ½ V, 3 LMt	280	1000
Zucchini Lasagna	(11 oz.)	1½ S, 1 V, 2 LMt	260	975
Swanson Frozen Entrees, Lasagna w/Meat	(1 complete entree)	3 S, 1 V, 2 MFMt, 1½ Fat	470	1120
Weight Watchers				
Italian Cheese Lasagna w/Ricotta, Mozzarella & Romano Cheeses	(12 oz.)	2 S, 1 V, 1½ MFMt, 1½ Fat	360	1040
*Lasagna w/Meat Sauce**	(11 oz.)	2 S, ½ V, 2 MFMt, ½ Fat	330	1080

*Contains concentrated sources of carbohydrates

Food	*Portion*	*Exchanges*	*Calories*	*Sodium (mg)*
Linguini				
Stouffer's, Linguini w/Pesto Sauce	(4⅛ oz.)	1 S, 1 V, ½ MFMt, 1½ Fat	210	250
Stouffer's Lean Cuisine, Linguini w/Clam Sauce	(9⅝ oz.)	1½ S, ½ V, ½ SMk, 1 LMt, 1 Fat	260	800
Weight Watchers, Seafood Linguini	(9 oz.)	1½ S, 1 V, ½ LMt, 1 Fat	220	770
Macaroni				
Creamette, uncooked (2 oz.)				
Enriched Elbow Macaroni		2½ S	210	5
Enriched Spinach Macaroni Ribbons		2½ S	210	70
Franco-American Macaroni & Cheese	(7⅜ oz.)	1½ S, ½ MFMt, ½ Fat	170	960
Green Giant Frozen Entrees, Macaroni & Cheese	(1 pkg.)	2½ S, 1 MFMt, 1 Fat	290	1120
Mueller's, uncooked	(2 oz.)	3 S	210	0
Twist Trio		3 S	210	0
Stouffer's Entrees				
Macaroni & Beef w/Tomatoes	(11½ oz.)	2 S, ½ V, 2 MFMt, 1 Fat	360	1600
Macaroni & Cheese	(6 oz.)	1 S, ½ HFMt, ½ LFMk, 1 Fat	250	750
Swanson Frozen Entrees, Macaroni & Cheese	(1 complete entree)	3 S, 1 MFMt, 2 Fat	390	1870
Swanson Pot Pies, Macaroni & Cheese	(1 pie)	1½ S, ½ MFMt, 1 Fat	220	880
Swanson 3 Compartment Dinners (1 complete dinner)				
*Macaroni & Beef**		2 S, 1 Fr, ½ MFMt, 1 V, 2½ Fat	380	850
Macaroni & Cheese		2 S, 1 Fr, 1 MFMt, 2 Fat	380	990
Manicotti				
Le Menu Entrees, Manicotti	(1 complete entree)	1½ S, 1 V, 2 MFMt	300	910
Weight Watchers, Cheese Manicotti	(9¼ oz.)	1½ S, 1½ V, 1½ MFMt, 1½ Fat	320	740
Noodles				
Creamette Enriched Egg Noodles, uncooked	(2 oz.)	2½ S, ½ Fat	220	20
Dinty Moore, Noodles & Chicken	(7½ oz.)	1 S, 1 HFMt, 1 Fat	210	1144
La Choy				
Chow Mein Noodles	(½ cup)	1 S, 1½ Fat	150	230

*Contains concentrated sources of carbohydrates

Food	Portion	Exchanges	Calories	Sodium (mg)
Noodles, cont.				
Ramen Noodles w/Chicken Flavoring	(½ pkg.)	1½ S, 1½ Fat	190	1155
Ramen Noodles w/Oriental Flavoring	(½ pkg.)	1½ S, 1½ Fat	190	740
Rice Noodles	(½ cup)	1 S, 1 Fat	130	420
Lipton Noodles & Sauce (½ cup)				
Alfredo		1½ S, ½ HFMt, 1½ Fat	220	590
Chicken Flavor		1½ S, 1½ Fat	180	470
Pasta & Sauce Cheese Supreme		1½ S, ½ HFMt, 1 Fat	210	490
Mueller's Egg Noodles, uncooked	(2 oz.)	2½ S, ½ Fat	220	10
Noodle Roni				
Chicken & Mushroom Flavor	(½ cup)	1½ S, ½ Fat	150	550
Fettucini	(½ cup)	2 S, 3½ Fat	300	530
Garlic & Butter	(½ cup)	2 S, 3 Fat	290	590
Herbs & Butter	(½ cup)	1 S, 1 V, 1½ Fat	160	270
Parmesano	(½ cup)	1½ S, 2½ Fat	230	440
Pesto Italiano	(½ cup)	1½ S, 2 Fat	210	320
Romanoff	(½ cup)	2 S, 2 Fat	240	710
Stroganoff	(¾ cup)	2 S, ½ WMk, 3 Fat	360	1170
Rice a Roni Stroganoff w/Sour Cream	(½ cup)	2 S, 1½ Fat	200	810
Stouffer's Noodles Romanoff	(⅓ pkg.)	1 S, ½ MFMt, 1 Fat	170	700
Swanson 3-Compartment Dinners, Noodles & Chicken	(1 complete dinner)	1½ S, 1 Fr, 1 LMt, 1 Fat	260	860
Weight Watchers, Pasta Rigati-Meat Sauce w/Pasta & Cheese	(11 oz.)	2 S, 1 V, 1½ MFMt	290	790
PizzO's, Franco-American	(7½ oz.)	2 S, ½ Fat	170	1060
Ravioli				
Franco-American (7½ oz.)				
Beef Ravioli in Meat Sauce		2 S, 1 V, 1 Fat	230	1090
Beef RavioliO's in Meat Sauce		2 S, 1 V, 1½ Fat	250	900
Salad				
Fresh Chef Italian Pasta	(3¼ oz.)	1 S, 1 Fat	110	340
Hanover Italian Pasta Salad, in glass	(½ cup)	1 V, 1 Fat	80	819
Joan of Arc Macaroni Salad, canned	(½ cup)	1 S, 2½ Fat	200	850
Suddenly Salad (⅙ pkg.)				
Classic Pasta		1 S, 1 V, 1 Fat	150	330

Food	Portion	Exchanges	Calories	Sodium (mg)
Creamy Macaroni		1 S, 1 V, 2 Fat	200	260
Italian Pasta		1 S, 1 V, 1 Fat	160	350
Shells				
Le Menu Light Style Dinners, 3-Cheese Stuffed Shells	(1 complete dinner)	2 S, 1 V, 1 MFMt, ½ Fat	280	720
Ragu Pasta Meals Shells in Sauce w/Ground Beef	(7.5 oz.)	1½ S, 1½ V, 1 Fat	190	610
Stouffer's Entrees (9 oz.)				
Beef & Spinach Stuffed Pasta Shells w/Tomato Sauce		1½ S, 1 V, 2 MFMt, ½ Fat	300	1100
Cheese-Stuffed Pasta Shells w/Meat Sauce		1½ S, ½ V, 2½ MFMt, ½ Fat	340	1200
Spaghetti				
Creamette Enriched Spaghetti, uncooked	(2 oz.)	2½ S	210	5
Franco-American (7⅜ oz.)				
Spaghetti in Tomato Sauce w/Cheese		2 S, ½ V, ½ Fat	190	810
Spaghetti w/Meatballs in Tomato Sauce		1½ S, 1 V, ½ MFMt, 1 Fat	220	830
"SpaghettiO's" in Tomato & Cheese Sauce		2 S, ½ Fat	170	910
"SpaghettiO's" w/Meatballs in Tomato Sauce		1½ S, ½ MFMt, ½ V, 1 Fat	220	910
"SpaghettiO's" w/Sliced Beef Franks in Tomato Sauce		1½ S, ½ MFMt, ½ V, 1 Fat	220	970
Hamburger Helper, Spaghetti	(⅕ pkg.)	1½ S, 2 V, 1½ MFMt, 1½ Fat	340	1110
Hormel (7½ oz.)				
Spaghetti 'n' Beef		1½ S, ½ HFMt, 2 Fat	260	1091
Spaghetti & Meatballs		1½ S, 1 HFMt	210	(N/A)
Mueller's uncooked	(2 oz.)	3 S	210	0
Ragu Pasta Meals (7.5 oz.)				
Spaghetti in Sauce		2 S, ½ V	170	580
Spaghetti in Sauce w/Ground Beef		2 S, 1 V, ½ Fat	210	630
Stouffer's Entrees				
Spaghetti w/Meatballs	(12⅝ oz.)	2 S, 2½ V, 1½ MFMT, 1 Fat	370	1560
Spaghetti w/Meat Sauce	(14 oz.)	2½ S, 3 V, 1 MFMt, 2 Fat	440	1730
Stouffer's Lean Cuisine, Spaghetti w/Beef & Mushroom Sauce	(11½ oz.)	2 S, 1½ V, 1 LMt, 1 Fat	280	1350
Swanson 3-Compartment Dinners, Spaghetti & Meatballs*	(1 complete dinner)	2 S, 1 Fr, 1 MFMt, 2 Fat	370	1010

*Contains concentrated sources of carbohydrates

Food	Portion	Exchanges	Calories	Sodium (mg)
Spaghetti, cont.				
Weight Watchers (10½ oz.)				
Chicken Cacciatore w/Spaghetti		2 S, 1½ V, 1 LMt	300	670
*Spaghetti w/Meat Sauce**		2 S, 1 V, 1½ MFMt	290	900
Twists, Ragu Pasta Meals, Twists in Sauce	(7.5 oz.)	2 S, ½ V	160	580

■ Pizza

Food	Portion	Exchanges	Calories	Sodium (mg)
Bacon, Totino's Party	(⅓ pizza)	1½ S, 1 V, ½ MFMt, 2 Fat	270	710
Canadian-Style				
Celeste	(¼ of a 19-oz. pizza)	1½ S, 1 V, 1½ HFMt, 1 Fat	340	1030
Bacon, Celeste	(7¾-oz. pizza)	3 S, 1½ V, 2 HFMt, 2 Fat	550	1750
Totino's My Classic	(¼ pizza)	2 S, 1½ V, 1 MFMt, 1 Fat	320	830
Totino's Party	(⅓ pizza)	1½ S, 1 V, 1 MFMt, ½ Fat	230	670
Cheese				
Celeste	(6½-oz. pizza)	3 S, ½ V, 1½ MFMt, 3 Fat	500	920
	(¼ of 17¾-oz. pizza)	1½ S, 1 V, 1 MFMt, 2 Fat	330	740
Fox Deluxe	(⅓ pizza)	1½ S, ½ MFMt, ½ Fat	170	520
Pepperidge Farm Croissant Pastry	(1 pizza)	3 S, ½ V, 1 MFMt, 4 Fat	490	730
Pillsbury Heat 'n' Eat Microwave	(1 pizza)	1½ S, 1½ V, 1 MFMt, 1 Fat	270	670
Pillsbury Microwave	(1 pizza)	3½ S, 1 V, 1 MFMt, 2½ Fat	480	1190
Pillsbury Microwave French Bread	(1 piece)	2 S, 2 V, ½ MFMt, 2 Fat	340	570
Stouffer's French Bread	(½ of 10⅜-oz. pkg.)	2½ S, ½ V, 1 MFMt, 1½ Fat	340	840
Totino's Extra!	(¼ pizza)	1½ S, ½ V, ½ MFMt, 2 Fat	250	450
Totino's Microwave	(1 pizza)	1½ S, 1 V, ½ MFMt, 1 Fat	250	630
Totino's Party	(⅓ pizza)	1½ S, 1 V, ½ MFMt, 1½ Fat	250	650
Totino's Slices	(1 piece)	1 S, 1 V, ½ MFMt, ½ Fat	170	350
Weight Watchers	(5¾ oz.)	2 S, 1 V, 2 LMt	300	1010
French Bread	(5⅛ oz.)	2 S, 1 V, 1 MFMt, 1½ Fat	320	640
Combination				
Pillsbury Heat 'n' Eat Microwave	(1 pizza)	1½ S, 2 V, 1 MFMt, 3 Fat	380	1190
Pillsbury Microwave	(1 pizza)	3½ S, 1½ V, 2 MFMt, 5 Fat	670	1550
Totino's Slices	(1 piece)	1 S, 1 V, ½ MFMt, 1½ Fat	200	630
Deluxe				
Celeste	(8¼-oz. pizza)	3 S, 2 V, 1½ HFMt, 4 Fat	600	1500
	(¼ of 22¼-oz. pizza)	1½ S, 2 V, 1 HFMt, 3 Fat	390	1050

*Contains concentrated sources of carbohydrates

Food	Portion	Exchanges	Calories	Sodium (mg)
Pepperidge Farm Croissant Pastry	(1 pizza)	3 S, 1 V, 1 MFMt, 4 Fat	520	940
Stouffer's French Bread	(½ of 12⅜-oz. pkg.)	2½ S, 1 V, 1 MFMt, 3 Fat	430	1130
Totino's My Classic (¼ pizza)				
Cheese		2 S, 1½ V, 1 MFMT, 2 Fat	350	810
Combination		2 S, 2 V, 1 MFMt, 4 Fat	460	1040
Pepperoni		2 S, 2 V, 1 MFMt, 3 Fat	410	1090
Sausage		2 S, 2 V, 1 MFMt, 3½ Fat	440	980
Weight Watchers				
Combination	(6¾ oz.)	2 S, 1 V, 2 LMt	280	780
French Bread	(6⅛ oz.)	2 S, 1 V, 2 MFMt, ½ Fat	340	830
Hamburger				
Fox Deluxe	(⅓ pizza)	1½ S, ½ MFMT, ½ Fat	180	470
Hamburger Helper Hamburger Pizza Dish	(⅕ pkg.)	2 S, 1½ V, 1½ MFMt, 1½ Fat	360	1010
Pepperidge Farm Croissant Pastry	(1 pizza)	3 S, 2 MFMt, 3 Fat	510	1040
Stouffer's French Bread	(½ of a 12¼-oz. pkg.)	2½ S, ½ V, 2 MFMt, 1½ Fat	410	1040
Totino's Party	(⅓ pizza)	1½ S, 1 V, ½ MFMt, 2 Fat	280	650
Mexican-Style, Totino's Party	(⅓ pizza)	1½ S, ½ MFMt, 2 Fat	240	600
Nacho, Totino's Party	(⅓ pizza)	1 S, 1 V, 1 MFMt, 1 Fat	230	480
Pepperoni				
Celeste	(6¾-oz. pizza)	3 S, 1 V, 1 HFMt, 4 Fat	540	1560
	(¼ of 19-oz. pizza)	1½ S, 1½ V, 1 HFMt, 2½ Fat	370	1170
Fox Deluxe	(⅓ pizza)	1½ S, ½ MFMt, ½ Fat	170	520
Pepperidge Farm Croissant Pastry	(1 pizza)	3 S, 1 V, 1 MFMt, 4 Fat	490	810
Pillsbury Heat 'n' Eat Microwave	(1 pizza)	1½ S, 1½ V, 1 MFMt, 2½ Fat	350	1070
Pillsbury Microwave	(1 pizza)	3½ S, 1 V, 2 MFMt, 3½ Fat	590	1560
Pillsbury Microwave French Bread	(1 piece)	2 S, 2 V, 1 MFMt, 3 Fat	410	1160
Stouffer's French Bread	(½ of 11¼-oz. pkg.)	2½ S, 1 V, 1 HFMt, 2 Fat	390	1040
Totino's Extra!	(¼ pizza)	1½ S, ½ V, ½ MFMt, 2 Fat	260	700
Totino's Microwave	(1 pizza)	1½ S, 1½ V, ½ MFMt, 2 Fat	290	1270
Totino's Party	(⅓ pizza)	1½ S, 1 V, ½ MFMt, 1½ Fat	260	720

Food	Portion	Exchanges	Calories	Sodium (mg)
Pepperoni Pizza, cont.				
Totino's Slices	(1 piece)	1 S, 1 V, ½ MFMt, 1 Fat	190	530
Weight Watchers	(5⅞ oz.)	2 S, 1 V, 2 MFMt	320	880
French Bread	(5¼ oz.)	2 S, 1 V, 1½ MFMt, 1½ Fat	330	850
Pizzabake, Hamburger Helper	(⅙ pkg.)	1½ S, 1½ V, 1½ MFMt, 1 Fat	320	840
Sausage				
Celeste	(7½-oz. pizza)	3 S, 1 V, 1½ HFMt, 4 Fat	580	1510
	(¼ of 20-oz. pizza)	1½ S, 1½ V, 1 HFMt, 3 Fat	390	1080
Fox Deluxe	(⅓ pizza)	1½ S, ½ MFMt, ½ Fat	180	530
Pepperidge Farm Croissant Pastry	(1 pizza)	3 S, 1 V, 1 MFMt, 4½ Fat	540	910
Pillsbury Heat 'n' Eat Microwave	(1 pizza)	1½ S, 1½ V, 1 MFMt, 3 Fat	360	1130
Pillsbury Microwave	(1 pizza)	3½ S, 1½ V, 1½ MFMt, 5 Fat	650	1420
Pillsbury Microwave French Bread	(1 piece)	2 S, 2 V, 1 MFMt, 3 Fat	410	1020
Stouffer's French Bread	(½ of 12-oz. pkg.)	2½ S, 1 V, 1½ HFMt, 1½ Fat	420	1080
Totino's Extra!	(¼ pizza)	1½ S, ½ V, ½ MFMt, 2½ Fat	280	770
Totino's Microwave	(1 pizza)	1½ S, 1½ V, ½ MFMt, 2½ Fat	300	920
Totino's Party	(⅓ pizza)	1½ S, 1 V, ½ MFMt, 2 Fat	270	780
Totino's Slices	(1 piece)	1 S, 1 V, ½ MFMt, 1½ Fat	200	540
Weight Watchers	(6¼ oz.)	2 S, 1 V, 2 LMt	290	800
Sausage & Mushroom				
Celeste	(8½-oz. pizza)	3 S, 2 V, 1½ HFMt, 4 Fat	600	1490
	(¼ of 22¼-oz. pizza)	1½ S, 2 V, 1 HFMt, 3 Fat	410	1140
Stouffer's French Bread	(½ of 12½-oz. pkg.)	2½ S, 1 V, 1½ MFMt, 2 Fat	400	1160
Sausage & Pepperoni				
Fox Deluxe	(⅓ pizza)	1½ S, ½ MFMt, ½ Fat	170	530
Pillsbury Microwave French Bread	(1 piece)	2 S, 2 V, 1 MFMt, 3 Fat	430	1140
Totino's Extra!	(¼ pizza)	1½ S, ½ V, 1 MFMt, 2 Fat	290	800
Totino's Microwave	(1 pizza)	1½ S, 1½ V, ½ MFMt, 2½ Fat	310	1090
Totino's Party	(⅓ pizza)	1½ S, 1 V, ½ MFMt, 2 Fat	270	770

Food	Portion	Exchanges	Calories	Sodium (mg)
Suprema				
Celeste	(9-oz. pizza)	3 S, 2½ V, 1½ HFMt, 5½ Fat	690	1860
Celeste	(¼ of 23-oz. pizza)	1½ S, 1½ V, 1 HFMt, 3 Fat	410	1140
Vegetable, Totino's				
Party	(⅓ pizza)	1½ S, 1½ V, 1½ Fat	220	630

7

BREADS & OTHER GRAIN PRODUCTS

This chapter includes a wide variety of foods. From a nutritional standpoint, it's best to choose whole-grain products as often as possible. Whole-grain foods can add fiber to your diet, are excellent sources of B-complex vitamins, and they also help to prevent constipation.

Many of the baked goods listed in this chapter contain concentrated sources of carbohydrates. As a reminder, these items are marked with the symbol (*). Discuss these with your dietitian before you use them. In deciding if these products should be included in this book, the author found that many of them are used occasionally by her own clients, but that some clients were not counting these foods in their exchange plans. Remember to count everything you eat in your meal plan.

Snack foods also are included in this chapter. You might find yourself in a place where the only foods available are provided by vending machines. This chapter will make you more aware of which foods in these categories are better choices. Fruit exchanges are used to account for concentrated sources of carbohydrates. It's much healthier to use whole fruits for these exchanges, since fruit contains fiber, vitamins, and minerals that your body needs.

Some snacks are not high in concentrated carbohydrates, but are high in fat. Commercial popcorns vary widely in the amount of fat they contain. Some contain fat equal to 1½ fat exchanges, but others contain no fat. It's a good idea to discuss with your dietitian how many snacks your diet can include.

Food	*Portion*	*Exchanges*	*Calories*	*Sodium (mg)*
■ Biscuits, Mini Loaves, Muffins, Quick Breads, Rolls				
Biscuits				
Baking Powder, Pillsbury, Tenderflake	(2 biscuits)	1 S, 1 Fat	110	340
Butter, Pillsbury	(2 biscuits)	1½ S	100	360
Butter Tastin', Pillsbury	(2 biscuits)			
Big Country		1½ S, 1½ Fat	190	650
Hungry Jack Flaky		1½ S, 1½ Fat	180	310
Buttermilk, Hungry Jack	(2 biscuits)			
Extra Rich		1 S, ½ Fat	110	350
Flaky		1½ S, 1 Fat	170	590
Fluffy		1½ S, 1½ Fat	180	560
Buttermilk, Pillsbury	(2 biscuits)	1½ S	100	360
Big Country		1½ S, 1½ Fat	200	650
Extra Lights Flaky		1 S, ½ Fat	110	340
Heat 'n' Eat		1½ S, 1 Fat	170	530
Heat 'n' Eat, Deluxe		2 S, 3 Fat	280	610
Buttermilk, Weight Watchers, Country-Style	(2 biscuits)	1½ S	100	440
Country, Pillsbury	(2 biscuits)	1½ S	100	360
Mini Loaves, Earth Grain	(1 oz.)			
Country White		1 S	70	150
Cracked Wheat		1 S	70	170
Sourdough		1 S	80	210
Muffins				
Apple				
General Mills, Apple Cinnamon	(1 muffin)	½ S, ½ Fr, 1 Fat	120	140
*Pillsbury Toaster, Apple Spice Breakfast**	(1 muffin)	½ S, 1 Fr, 1 Fat	140	120
Banana				
General Mills, Banana Nut	(1 muffin)	½ S, 1 Fr, 1 Fat	150	200
*Pillsbury Toaster, Banana Nut Breakfast**	(1 muffin)	½ S, 1 Fr, 1 Fat	140	80
Blueberry				
General Mills, Wild Blueberry	(1 muffin)	½ S, ½ Fr, 1 Fat	120	150
Pepperidge Farm Old Fashioned, Blueberry	(1 muffin)	1 S, 1 Fr, 1 Fat	185	250
*Pillsbury Toaster, Wild Maine Blueberry Breakfast**	(1 muffin)	½ S, 1 Fr, ½ Fat	130	120

*Contains concentrated sources of carbohydrates

Food	Portion	Exchanges	Calories	Sodium (mg)
Muffins, cont.				
Bran				
Pepperidge Farm Old Fashioned, Bran w/Raisins	(1 muffin)	1 S, 1 Fr, 1 Fat	185	250
*Pillsbury Toaster, Raisin Bran Breakfast**	(1 muffin)	½ S, 1 Fr, ½ Fat	120	220
Carrot				
General Mills, Carrot Nut	(1 muffin)	½ S, 1 Fr, ½ V, 1 Fat	150	170
*Pepperidge Farm Old Fashioned, Carrot Walnut**	(1 muffin)	1 S, 1 Fr, 1 Fat	200	220
Cherry, General Mills, Tart Cherry	(1 muffin)	½ S, ½ Fr, 1 Fat	120	140
Chocolate Chip				
*General Mills**	(1 muffin)	½ S, 1 Fr, 1 Fat	150	180
*Pepperidge Farm Old Fashioned**	(1 muffin)	1 S, 1 Fr, 1½ Fat	210	180
Cinnamon Swirl, Pepperidge Farm Old-Fashioned*	(1 muffin)	1 S, 1 Fr, 1 Fat	190	170
Corn				
*Flako, Corn**	(1 muffin)	1 S, ½ Fr, 1 Fat	140	370
*Nabisco, Dromedary Corn**	(1 muffin)	1 S, ½ Fr, ½ Fat	120	270
*Pepperidge Farm Old Fashioned, Corn**	(1 muffin)	1 S, ½ Fr, 1½ Fat	180	260
*Pillsbury Toaster, Old Fashioned Corn Breakfast**	(1 muffin)	1 S, ½ Fr, 1 Fat	140	250
English				
Earth Grain (1 muffin)				
Plain		2 S	150	45
Raisin		2 S	150	390
Wheatberry		2 S	150	460
Whole Wheat		2 S	170	540
Pepperidge Farm (1 muffin)				
Cinnamon Raisin		2 S	150	180
Plain		2 S	140	180
Wonder (2 oz.)				
English		1½ S	130	280
Raisin Rounds		1½ S, ½ Fat	140	280
Sour Dough		1½ S	130	250
Oatmeal Raisin, General Mills	(1 muffin)	1 S, ½ Fr, ½ Fat	140	125

*Contains concentrated sources of carbohydrates

Food	Portion	Exchanges	Calories	Sodium (mg)
Quick Breads				
Applesauce Spice, Pillsbury*	(1/12 loaf)	1 S, 1 Fr, ½ Fat	150	150
Apricot Nut, Pillsbury*	(1/12 loaf)	1 S, 1 Fr, ½ Fat	160	150
Banana, Pillsbury*	(1/12 loaf)	1 S, ½ Fr, 1 Fat	160	210
Blueberry Nut, Pillsbury*	(1/12 loaf)	1 S, 1 Fr, ½ Fat	150	150
Carrot Nut, Pillsbury*	(1/12 loaf)	1 S, 1 Fr, ½ Fat	150	180
Cherry Nut, Pillsbury*	(1/12 loaf)	1 S, 1 Fr, 1 Fat	180	150
Corn				
Aunt Jemima	(1/6 loaf)	2 S, 1½ Fat	220	600
*Nabisco, Dromedary**	(2″ square)	1 S, ½ Fr, ½ Fat	130	480
Cranberry, Pillsbury*	(1/12 loaf)	1 S, 1 Fr, ½ Fat	160	150
Date, Pillsbury*	(1/12 loaf)	1 S, 1 Fr, ½ Fat	160	150
Honey Granola, Pillsbury*	(1/12 loaf)	1 S, 1 Fr, ½ Fat	170	180
Nut, Pillsbury*	(1/12 loaf)	1 S, 1 Fr, 1 Fat	170	150
Rolls				
Butter Crescent, Pepperidge Farm Rolls	(1 roll)	1 S, 1 Fat	110	150
Butterflake, Pillsbury Refrigerated Dinner Rolls	(1 roll)	1 S, Fat	110	410
Buttermilk, Wonder Brown 'n' Serve	(1 roll)	1 S	80	140
Club, Pepperidge Farm Brown 'n' Serve	(1 roll)	1½ S	100	200
Crescent, Pillsbury Refrigerated Dinner Rolls	(2 rolls)	1½ S, 2 Fat	200	460
French				
Earth Grain	(1.2 oz.)	1½ S	100	270
Sourdough		1½ S	100	0
Pepperidge Farm (1 roll)				
French-Style		1½ S	110	230
Sourdough-Style French		1½ S	100	230
Wonder Brown 'n' Serve Petite French	(3.5 oz.)	3 S	230	490
Gem Style, Wonder Brown 'n' Serve	(1 roll)	1 S	80	140
Golden Twist, Pepperidge Farm	(1 roll)	1 S, 1 Fat	110	150

*Contains concentrated sources of carbohydrates

Food	Portion	Exchanges	Calories	Sodium (mg)
Rolls, cont.				
Hamburger				
Pepperidge Farm	(1 roll)	1½ S	130	240
Rainbo/Colonial/ Kilpatrick's	(2 oz.)	2 S	150	320
Wonder	(1.5 oz.)	1½ S	120	230
Hoagie, Wonder	(5 oz.)	4½ S, 1 Fat	400	800
Hot Dog, Wonder	(1 oz.)	1 S	80	150
County Grain	(1.5 oz.)	1 S	100	230
Hot Roll Mix, Pillsbury	(2 rolls)	2½ S, 1 Fat	240	430
Italian, Wonder Brown 'n' Serve Rolls, Crusty, Italian du Jour	(1 roll)	1 S	80	200
Kaiser, Earth Grain	(2.3 oz.)	2 S, ½ Fat	190	520
Onion, Earth Grain	(2.3 oz.)	2 S, ½ Fat	190	530
Pan, Dinner, or Biscuits, Wonder	(1 oz.)	1 S	80	140
Parker House, Pepperidge Farm	(1 roll)	1 S	60	80
Sandwich, Pepperidge Farm (1 roll)				
Onion Sandwich w/Poppy Seeds		1½ S, ½ Fat	150	260
Sandwich w/Sesame Seeds		2 S, ½ Fat	160	220
Submarine, Earth Grain	(1 roll)	2 S, ½ Fat	180	0
Wheat				
Earth Grain	(1.4 oz.)	1½ S	110	260
Pillsbury Pipin' Hot Dinner Rolls, Wheat Loaf	(1″ slice)	1 S	80	170
Wonder Home Pride	(1 roll)	1 S	70	140
White				
Pillsbury Pipin' Hot Dinner Rolls, White Loaf	(1″ slice)	1 S	80	170
Wonder Home Pride	(1 roll)	1 S	80	170

■ Bread Loaves

Food	Portion	Exchanges	Calories	Sodium (mg)
Austrian, Wonder Brown 'n' Serve du Jour	(1 oz.)	1 S	70	140
Bran				
Earth Grain (1 oz.)				
Barley Bran		1 S	70	180
Gold 'n' Bran		1 S	70	150
Yogurt Bran		1 S	70	(N/A)
Pepperidge Farm, Honey Bran*	(2 slices)	2 S, ½ Fr	190	340

*Contains concentrated sources of carbohydrates

Food	Portion	Exchanges	Calories	Sodium (mg)
Buttermilk, Rainbo/Colonial/Kilpatrick's Grant's Farm	(1 oz. or 1 slice)	1 S	80	190
Cinnamon, Pepperidge Farm	(2 slices)	1½ S, 1 Fat	170	170
Country Meal, Rainbo/Colonial/ Kilpatrick's	(1 oz. or 1 slice)	1 S	80	135
Dark, Wonder, Hollywood	(1 slice)	1 S	70	160
Dijon, Pepperidge Farm, Party	(4 slices)	1 S	70	190
French				
Earth Grain (1 oz.)				
French		1 S	70	160–200
Sourdough French		1 S	70	120–140
Pillsbury Pipin' Hot Dinner Rolls & Sweet Rolls, Crusty French Loaf	(1″ slice)	1 S	60	120
Wonder				
Brown 'n' Serve, du Jour French	(1 oz.)	1 S	70	140
DiCarlo Parisian French	(1 slice)	1 S	70	180
French	(1 slice)	1 S	70	180
Honey				
Earth Grain (1 oz.)				
Honey & Buttermilk		1 S	80	190
Honey Oatberry		1 S	70	135
Rainbo/Colonial/Kilpatrick's (1 slice)				
Family Recipe, Honey Grain		1 S	70	180
Honey Grain		1 S	70	170
Italian, Wonder, Family	(1 slice)	1 S	70	160
Multigrain				
Earth Grain, Earth Bread	(1 oz.)	1 S	70	135–170
Earth Grain, Multi Grain	(1 oz.)	1 S	70	140
Pepperidge Farm, Multi-Grain, Very Thin	(2 slices)	1 S	80	180
Rainbo/Colonial/Kilpatrick's Grant's Farm, 7-Grain	(1 oz. or 1 slice)	1 S	70	140
Weight Watchers Multi-Grain				
Thick-Sliced	1 slice	½ S	40	95
Thin-Sliced	2 slices	1 S	80	190
Wonder Wheat (1 slice)				
Beefsteak Multigrain		1 S	70	130
Home Pride 7 Grain		1 S	70	140

Food	Portion	Exchanges	Calories	Sodium (mg)
Oatmeal, Pepperidge Farm	(2 slices)	1½ S, ½ Fat	140	370
Pumpernickel				
Pepperidge Farm				
Family	(2 slices)	2 S	160	450
Party	(4 slices)	1 S	70	180
Raisin				
Earth Grain Raisin	(1 oz.)	1 S	80	110
Pepperidge Farm, Raisin w/Cinnamon	(2 slices)	1½ S, ½ Fat	150	170
Weight Watchers, Light Cinnamon Raisin*	(1 slice)	1 S	60	85
Wonder, Cinnamon Raisin	(1 slice)	1 S	80	140
Rye				
Earth Grain (1 oz.)				
Light Rye		1 S	70	240
Party Rye		1 S	70	230
Pumpernickel Rye		1 S	70	220
Very Thin Light Rye		1 S	70	230
Pepperidge Farm				
Dijon Rye	(2 slices)	2 S	160	490
Party Rye	(5 slices)	1 S	75	350
Seeded Family Rye	(2 slices)	1 S	80	220
Seedless Rye	(2 slices)	2 S	160	420
Rainbo/Colonial/Kilpatrick's Grant's Farm, Honey Cracked Rye	(1 oz. or 1 slice)	1 S	70	190
Weight Watchers Rye				
Thick-Sliced	(1 slice)	½ S	40	95
Thin-Sliced	(2 slices)	1 S	80	190
Wonder (1 slice)				
Beefsteak Hearty Rye		1 S	70	180
Beefsteak Mild Rye		1 S	70	180
Beefsteak Onion Rye		1 S	70	170
Beefsteak Soft Rye		1 S	70	170
Beefsteak Wheatberry Rye		1 S	70	160
Braun's Old Allegheny		1 S	70	160
Rye		1 S	70	150
Salt-Free, Earth Grain, Sandwich	(1 oz.)	1 S	80	20
Sour Dough, Wonder, DiCarlo	(1 slice)	1 S	70	140

*Contains concentrated sources of carbohydrates

Food	Portion	Exchanges	Calories	Sodium (mg)
Wheat				
Earth Grain (1 oz.)				
Cracked Wheat		1 S	70	180
Honey Wheat Berry		1 S	70	160
Lite 35 Wheat		1 S	70	170
100% Whole Wheat		1 S	70	130
Stone Ground Wheat		1 S	70	160
Very Thin Wheat		1 S	70	150
Pepperidge Farm (2 slices)				
Cracked Wheat		1½ S, ½ Fat	140	280
Honey Wheat Berry		1½ S, ½ Fat	140	290
Wheat		2 S, ½ Fat	190	380
Wheat Germ		1½ S	130	280
Whole Wheat		1½ S	130	230
Whole Wheat, Very Thin		1 S	80	160
Rainbo/Colonial/Kilpatrick's (1 slice)				
Family Recipe, Honey-Buttered Split-Top Wheat		1 S	70	150
Family Recipe, Wheat		1 S	70	150
Grant's Farm, Stone Ground Wheat		1 S	70	150
Grant's Farm, Wheat Berry		1 S	70	170
Wheat		1 S	70	150
Whole Wheat		1 S	70	140
Weight Watchers Wheat				
Thick-Sliced	(1 slice)	½ S	40	95
Thin-Sliced	(2 slices)	1 S	80	190
Wonder (1 slice)				
Beefsteak Hearty Wheat		1 S	70	160
Beefsteak Soft Wheat		1 S	70	160
Country Grain		1 S	70	160
Cracked Wheat		1 S	70	180
Family Wheat		1 S	70	140
Fresh & Natural Wheat		1 S	70	140
High Fiber Wheat		½ S	40	80
Home Pride Butter Top Wheat		1 S	70	140
Home Pride Stoneground Wheat		1 S	70	140
100% Whole Wheat		1 S	70	160
Soft 100% Whole Wheat		1 S	70	140
Wheat Light		½ S	40	120
White				
Earth Grain, Very Thin				
White	(1 oz.)	1 S	80	160

Food	Portion	Exchanges	Calories	Sodium (mg)
White bread, cont.				
Pepperidge Farm (2 slices)				
Sandwich White		1½ S	130	270
Toasting White		2 S	170	430
White		1½ S, ½ Fat	145	270
White, Very Thin		1 S	80	160
Rainbo/Colonial/Kilpatrick's (1 slice)				
Family Recipe, Honey-Buttered Split-Top White		1 S	80	150
White Enriched		1 S	70	150
Weight Watchers White				
Thick-Sliced	(1 slice)	½ S	40	95
Thin-Sliced	(2 slices)	1 S	80	190
Wonder (1 slice)				
Beefsteak Robust White		1 S	70	140
w/Buttermilk		1 S	70	160
High Fiber		½ S	40	80
Hollywood Light		1 S	70	150
Home Pride Butter Top		1 S	70	140
Thin Sliced		½ S	50	120
White		1 S	70	140
White Light		½ S	40	110

■ Cereal (cold)

Food	Portion	Exchanges	Calories	Sodium (mg)
Bran & Fiber				
General Mills				
*Bran Muffin Crisp**	(⅔ cup)	1 S, ½ Fr, ½ Fat	130	250
Fiber One	(½ cup)	1½ S	60	230
Raisin Nut Bran	(½ cup)	1 S, ½ Fr	110	140
Kellogg's				
All-Bran	(⅓ cup)	1½ S	70	260
*All-Bran w/Extra Fiber**	(½ cup)	1 S, ½ Fr	60	270
All-Bran Fruit & Almonds	(⅔ cup)	1½ S, ½ Fr, ½ Fat	100	260
*Bran Buds**	(⅓ cup)	1 S, ½ Fr	70	170
*Bran Flakes**	(⅔ cup)	1 S, ½ Fr	90	220
*Fruitful Bran**	(⅔ cup)	1 S, 1 Fr	110	230
*Mueslix Bran**	(½ cup)	1 S, 1 Fr, ½ Fat	130	100
*Raisin Bran**	(¾ cup)	1 S, 1 Fr	120	220
Nabisco, 100% Bran	(1 oz.)	1½ S, ½ Fat	70	190
Quaker, Unprocessed Bran	(4 tbsp.)	½ S	40	0

*Contains concentrated sources of carbohydrates

Food	Portion	Exchanges	Calories	Sodium (mg)
Corn				
General Mills (1 cup)				
Country Corn Flakes		1½ S	110	310
Total Corn Flakes		1½ S	110	310
Kellogg's				
*Corn Flakes**	(1 cup)	1 S, ½ Fr	100	290
*Corn Pops**	(1 cup)	½ S, 1 Fr	110	90
*Frosted Flakes**	(¾ cup)	½ S, 1 Fr	110	200
*Frosted Krispies**	(¾ cup)	½ S, 1 Fr	110	220
*Nut & Honey Crunch**	(⅔ cup)	1 S, ½ Fr	110	200
*Nutri-Grain Corn**	(½ cup)	1 S, ½ Fr	100	170
Quaker, Corn Bran*	(⅔ cup)	1 S, ½ Fr	120	300
Fruit				
Kellogg's				
*Apple Cinnamon Squares**	(½ cup)	1 S, ½ Fr	90	5
*Apple Jacks**	(1 cup)	1 S, ½ Fr	110	125
*Apple Raisin Crisp**	(⅔ cup)	1 S, 1 Fr	130	230
*Just Right Fruit, Nut & Flake**	(¾ cup)	1 S, 1 Fr	140	190
*Strawberry Squares**	(½ cup)	1 S, ½ Fr	90	5
Nabisco Fruit Wheats (1 oz.)				
*Apple**		1 S, ½ Fr	100	15
*Raisin**		1 S, ½ Fr	100	5
*Strawberry**		1 S, ½ Fr	100	15
Granola				
Quaker 100% Natural Cereal	(¼ cup)	1 S, 1 Fat	140	15
Apple & Cinnamon		1 S, 1 Fat	130	20
Raisin & Date		1 S, 1 Fat	130	10
Graham, General Mills, Golden Grahams*	(¾ cup)	1 S, ½ Fr	110	280
Mixed-Grain				
General Mills, Clusters*	(½ cup)	½ S, ½ Fr, ½ MFMt	100	160
Kellogg's				
Crispix	(1 cup)	1 S, ½ Fr	110	220
*Just Right Nugget & Flake**	(⅔ cup)	1 S, ½ Fr	100	190
*Mueslix Five Grain**	(½ cup)	1½ S, ½ Fr, ½ Fat	150	60
*Nutrific**	(1 cup)	1½ S, ½ Fr, ½ Fat	120	240
*Product 19**	(1 cup)	1 S, ½ Fr	100	320
*Pro Grain**	(¾ cup)	1 S, ½ Fr	100	170

*Contains concentrated sources of carbohydrates

Food	Portion	Exchanges	Calories	Sodium (mg)
Mixed-Grain Cereal, cont.				
*Raisin Squares**	(½ cup)	1 S, ½ Fr	90	0
Special K	(1 cup)	1½ S	110	230
Nabisco, Team Flakes*	(1 oz.)	1 S, ½ Fr	110	90
Oat				
General Mills				
Cheerios	(1¼ cup)	1½ S	110	290
*Honey Nut Cheerios**	(¾ cup)	1 S, ½ Fr	110	250
*Oatmeal Raisin Crisp**	(½ cup)	1 S, ½ Fr	110	160
Kellogg's Cracklin' Oat Bran	(½ cup)	1 S, 1 Fat	110	140
Quaker				
*Cinnamon Life**	(⅔ cup)	1 S, ½ Fat	120	180
*Life**	(⅔ cup)	1 S, ½ Fat	120	180
*Quisp**	(1⅙ cup)	½ S, 1 Fr, ½ Fat	120	230
*Raisin Life**	(⅔ cup)	1 S, 1 Fr, ½ Fat	150	200
Rice				
Kellogg's Rice Krispies*	(1 cup)	1 S, ½ Fr	110	290
Quaker Puffed Rice	(1 cup)	½ S	50	0
Sweetened				
General Mills				
*Body Buddies, Brown Sugar & Honey**	(1 cup)	1 S, ½ Fr	110	290
*Body Buddies, Natural Fruit Flavor**	(1 cup)	1 S, ½ Fr	110	280
*Boo Berry**	(1 cup)	½ S, 1 Fr	110	210
*Cinnamon Toast Crunch**	(¾ cup)	½ S, 1 Fr, ½ Fat	120	220
*Circus Fun**	(1 cup)	½ S, 1 Fr	110	160
*Cocoa Puffs**	(1 cup)	1 S, ½ Fr	110	210
*Count Chocula**	(1 cup)	½ S, 1 Fr	110	210
*FrankenBerry**	(1 cup)	½ S, 1 Fr	110	210
Ice Cream Cones, Vanilla	(¾ cup)	½ S, 1 Fr	110	170
*Kaboom**	(1 cup)	1 S, ½ Fr	110	290
Kix	(1½ cup)	1½ S	110	290
*Lucky Charms**	(1 cup)	1 S, ½ Fr	110	180
*Pac-Man**	(1 cup)	1 S, ½ Fr	110	200
*Rocky Road**	(⅔ cup)	½ S, 1 Fr, ½ Fat	120	110
*S'mores Crunch**	(¾ cup)	½ S, 1 Fr, ½ Fat	120	250
*Trix**	(1 cup)	1 S, ½ Fr	110	170

*Contains concentrated sources of carbohydrates

Food	Portion	Exchanges	Calories	Sodium (mg)
Kellogg's				
*Cocoa Krispies**	(¾ cup)	½ S, 1 Fr	110	190
*Froot Loops**	(1 cup)	1 S, ½ Fr	110	125
*Fruity Marshmallow Krispies**	(1¼ cup)	1 S, 1 Fr	140	210
*Honey Smacks**	(¾ cup)	1 S, ½ Fr	110	70
Quaker				
*Cap'n Crunch**	(¾ cup)	½ S, 1 Fr, ½ Fat	120	220
*Cap'n Crunch Choco Crunch**	(¾ cup)	½ S, 1 Fr, ½ Fat	130	210
*Cap'n Crunch Crunchberries**	(¾ cup)	½ S, 1 Fr, ½ Fat	120	220
*Cap'n Crunch Peanut Butter**	(¾ cup)	½ S, 1 Fr, ½ Fat	130	250
*Hafsies**	(¾ cup)	½ S, 1 Fr	120	240
*King Vitaman**	(1¼ cup)	½ S, 1 Fr	110	280
*Mr. T**	(1 cup)	½ S, 1 Fr, ½ Fat	120	230
Wheat				
General Mills				
*Crispy Wheats 'n' Raisins**	(¾ cup)	1 S, ½ Fr	110	180
Honey Buc Wheat Crisp	(¾ cup)	1 S, ½ Fr	110	260
Total	(1 cup)	1½ S	110	310
Wheaties	(1 cup)	1½ S	110	270
Kellogg's				
*Frosted Mini-Wheats**	(4 biscuits)	1 S, ½ Fr	100	5
*Nutri-Grain Almond Raisin**	(⅔ cup)	1 S, 1 Fr, ½ Fat	140	220
*Nutri-Grain Nuggets**	(¼ cup)	1 S, ½ Fr	90	110
*Nutri-Grain Wheat**	(⅔ cup)	1 S, ½ Fr	100	170
*Nutri-Grain Wheat & Raisins**	(⅔ cup)	1 S, 1 Fr	130	170
Nabisco				
Shredded Wheat	(⅚ oz.)	1 S	90	0
Shredded Wheat 'n' Bran	(1 oz.)	1½ S	110	0
Spoon Size Shredded Wheat	(1 oz.)	1½ S	110	0
Toasted Wheat & Raisins	(1 oz.)	1 S, ½ Fr	100	0
Quaker				
Puffed Wheat	(1 cup)	½ S	50	0

*Contains concentrated sources of carbohydrates

Food	Portion	Exchanges	Calories	Sodium (mg)
Wheat Cereal, cont.				
Shredded Wheat	(2 biscuits)	2 S	160	0
Sunshine, Bite Size Shredded Wheat	(⅔ cup)	1½ S	110	0

■ Cereal (hot)

Food	Portion	Exchanges	Calories	Sodium (mg)
Cream of Rice, Nabisco	(1 oz.)	1 S, ½ Fr	100	0
Cream of Wheat, Nabisco				
Instant	(1 oz.)	1½ S	100	0
Mix 'n' Eat (1¼ oz.)				
*Apple & Cinnamon**		1 S, 1 Fr	130	240
*Brown Sugar Cinnamon**		1 S, 1 Fr	130	180
*Maple Brown Sugar**		1 S, 1 Fr	130	180
*Our Original**		1 S, ½ Fr	100	180
*Peach**		1 S, 1 Fr, ½ Fat	140	200
*Strawberry**		1 S, 1 Fr	130	300
Quick	(1 oz.)	1½ S	100	80
*Apples, Raisin, & Spice**		1 S, ½ Fr	110	0
*Maple Brown Sugar, Artificially Flavored**		1 S, Fr	110	0
*Regular**		1½ S	100	80
Farina				
Pillsbury, Farina, cooked	(⅔ cup)	1 S	80	270
Quaker, Quick Creamy Wheat Farina, uncooked	(2½ tbsp.)	1½ S	100	0
Grits, Quaker Instant (1 pkt.)				
w/Imitation Bacon Bits		1½ S	100	730
w/Imitation Ham Bits		1½ S	100	900
w/Real Cheddar Cheese Flavor		1½ S	100	700
White Hominy Product		1 S	80	520
Hominy				
Albers, Hominy Quick Grits, uncooked	(¼ cup)	2 S	150	5
Aunt Jemima Enriched White Hominy Grits Regular, Quick	(3 tbsp.)	1½ S	100	0
Quaker, Enriched Yellow Hominy Quick Grits	(3 tbsp.)	1½ S	100	0
Van Camp's (1 cup)				
Golden Hominy		2 S	130	700
Golden Hominy w/Red & Green Peppers		2 S	130	690
White Hominy		2 S	140	710
Oat Bran, Quaker Cereal, uncooked	(⅓ cup)	1 S, ½ Fat	110	0

*Contains concentrated sources of carbohydrates

Food	Portion	Exchanges	Calories	Sodium (mg)
Oatmeal				
General Mills, Total, uncooked				
*Instant, Cinnamon Raisin Almond**	(1.5 oz.)	1 S, 1 Fr, ½ Fat	150	120
*Instant, Mixed Nut**	(1.3 oz.)	1 S, ½ Fr, ½ Fat	140	125
Instant, Regular	(1 oz.)	1 S	90	220
Quick	(1 oz.)	1 S	90	5
Quaker Instant Regular Flavor	(1 pkt.)	1 S, ½ Fat	100	400
*w/Artificial Maple & Brown Sugar Flavors**		1½ S, ½ Fr, ½ Fat	160	330
*w/Artificial Peaches & Cream Flavor**		1 S, ½ Fr, ½ Fat	140	190
*w/Artificial Strawberries & Cream Flavor**		1 S, ½ Fr, ½ Fat	140	250
*w/Bran & Raisins**		1½ S, ½ Fr, ½ Fat	150	340
*w/Cinnamon & Spice**		1½ S, ½ Fr, ½ Fat	170	360
*w/Raisins, Dates & Walnuts**		1 S, ½ Fr, 1 Fat	160	220
*w/Raisins & Spice**		1½ S, ½ Fr, ½ Fat	160	310
*w/Real Apples & Cinnamon**		1 S, ½ Fr, ½ Fat	130	260
*w/Real Honey & Graham**		1 S, 1 Fr, ½ Fat	140	320
Oats, Quaker Quick & Old Fashioned, cooked	(⅔ cup)	1 S, ½ Fat	110	0
Wheat				
General Mills, Wheat Hearts, uncooked	(1 oz.)	1½ S	110	0
Quaker, Whole Wheat Hot Natural Cereal, cooked	(⅔ cup)	1 S, 1 Fat	100	0

■ Crackers

Portions are listed as the number of crackers unless noted otherwise.

Food	Portion	Exchanges	Calories	Sodium (mg)
Appetizer, Famous Foods of Virginia	(9)	1 S, 1 Fat	127	190
Assortment, Pepperidge Farm Distinctive	(4)	1 S, ½ Fat	100	180
Bacon, Nabisco				
Bacon-Flavored Thin	(7)	½ S, 1 Fat	70	210
Great Crisps, Real Bacon	(9)	½ S, 1 Fat	70	230
Biscuits				
Nabisco, Uneeda, Unsalted Tops	(3)	½ S, ½ Fat	60	100
Pepperidge Farm Distinctive English Water Biscuit*	(4)	½ S, ½ Fr	70	90
Butter-Flavored				
Nabisco, Escort	(3)	½ S, 1 Fat	80	110

*Contains concentrated sources of carbohydrates

Food	Portion	Exchanges	Calories	Sodium (mg)
Butter-Flavored Crackers, cont.				
Nabisco Great Crisps!				
Ritz	(4)	½ S, 1 Fat	70	120
Ritz Low-Salt	(4)	½ S, 1 Fat	70	60
Sociables	(6)	½ S, ½ Fat	70	130
Waverly	(4)	½ S, ½ Fat	70	160
Pepperidge Farm Snack Sticks, Original	(8)	1 S, 1 Fat	130	180
Pepperidge Farm Thin, Butter-Flavored	(4)	½ S, 1 Fat	80	100
Pepperidge Farm Tiny Goldfish, Original	(45)	1 S, 1½ Fat	140	180
Sunshine HiHo	(4)	½ S, 1 Fat	80	125
Cheese				
Austin				
Cheese Peanut Butter	(1.4 oz.)	1 S, ½ HFMt, 1 Fat	190	(N/A)
Snackers Cheese	(1⅜ oz.)	1½ S, 1½ Fat	180	(N/A)
Famous Foods of Virginia Cheddar Thins	(13)	1 S, 1 Fat	127	405
Lance				
Cheese on Wheat	(1 5/16 oz.)	1½ S, 1½ Fat	180	260
Cream Cheese & Chives on Captain's Wafer	(1 5/16 oz.)	1½ S, 1½ Fat	170	260
Gold-n-Chee	(1⅜ oz.)	1½ S, 1½ Fat	180	410
Lanchee	(1¼ oz.)	1 S, ½ HFMt, 1 Fat	180	110
Nip Chee	(1 5/16 oz.)	1½ S, 1½ Fat	180	320
Nabisco				
Better Blue Cheese Snack Thins	(10)	½ S, 1 Fat	70	260
Better Cheddars 'n' Bacon Snack Thins	(10)	½ S, 1 Fat	70	210
Better Cheddars Snack Thins	(11)	½ S, 1 Fat	70	130
Better Nacho Snack Thins	(9)	½ S, 1 Fat	70	220
Better Swiss Snack Thins	(10)	½ S, 1 Fat	70	230
Cheese Peanut Butter Sandwich	(2)	½ S, ½ Fat	70	150
Cheese Ritz	(5)	½ S, ½ Fat	70	120
Cheese Wheat Thins	(9)	½ S, ½ Fat	70	220
Cheese Tid-Bit	(16)	½ S, 1 Fat	70	200
Dip in a Chip Cheese 'n' Chive	(8)	½ S, 1 Fat	70	130

Food	Portion	Exchanges	Calories	Sodium (mg)
Nabisco Brand Great Crisps! Baked Crispy Snacks				
Cheese 'n' Chive	(9)	½ S, 1 Fat	70	170
Nacho	(8)	½ S, 1 Fat	70	250
Real Cheddar Cheese	(13)	½ S, ½ Fat	70	130
Pepperidge Farm Snack Sticks, Cheese	(8)	1 S, 1 Fat	130	180
Pepperidge Farm Tiny Goldfish (45)				
Cheddar Cheese		1 S, 1 Fat	140	180
Parmesan Cheese		1 S, 1 Fat	130	250
Planters, Square Cheese	(1 oz.)	1 S, 1½ Fat	140	270
Sunshine				
American Heritage, Cheddar	(4)	½ S, 1 Fat	80	150
American Heritage, Parmesan	(4)	½ S, 1 Fat	70	180
Cheez-it	(12)	½ S, 1 Fat	70	135
Cheeze-It, Low-Salt	(12 pieces)	½ S, 1 Fat	70	65
Chicken, Nabisco Chicken in a Biskit	(7)	½ S, 1 Fat	70	115
Cinnamon, Nabisco Cinnamon Treats*	(2)	½ S, ½ Fr	60	80
Garlic				
Fleetwood Snacks, Garlic, Butter 'n' Cheese	(1 oz.)	1 S, 1½ Fat	150	690
Nabisco Great Crisps! Savory Garlic	(8)	½ S, ½ Fat	70	190
Graham				
Lance Coated Grahams*	(1 5/16 oz.)	1 S, ½ Fr, 1½ Fat	180	60
Nabisco Grahams	(2)	1 S	60	115
Nabisco Great Crisps! Honey Maid Grahams	(2)	1 S	60	90
Sunshine				
*Cinnamon Graham**	(4)	½ S, ½ Fat	70	95
*Honey Graham**	(4)	½ S, ½ Fat	60	90
*Graham Cracker Crumbs**	(1 cup)	6 S, 3 Fat	550	990
*Grahamy Bears Honey Graham**	(9)	1 S, ½ Fr, 1 Fat	130	160
Ham 'n' Cheese, Famous Foods of Virginia	(10)	1 S, 1 Fat	135	320
Italian, Nabisco Great Crisps! (9)		½ S, 1 Fat	70	200
Malt Crackers, Lance	(1¼ oz.)	1 S, ½ HFMt, 1½ Fat	190	125

*Contains concentrated sources of carbohydrates

Food	Portion	Exchanges	Calories	Sodium (mg)
Milk, Nabisco Great Crisps! Royal Lunch Milk	(1)	½ S, ½ Fat	60	80
Onion				
Fleetwood Snacks, Onion 'n' Cheese	(1 oz.)	1 S, 1½ Fat	150	750
Nabisco French Onion	(7)	½ S, 1 Fat	70	90
Oyster				
Lance Oyster Crackers	(½ oz.)	½ S, ½ Fat	70	170
Nabisco Dandy Soup & Oyster Crackers	(20)	1 S	60	220
Nabisco Great Crisps! Oysterettes Soup & Oyster Crackers	(18)	1 S	60	130
Sunshine Oyster & Soup Crackers	(16)	½ S, ½ Fat	60	190
Peanut Butter				
Austin Toasty Peanut Butter	(1.4 oz.)	1 S, ½ HFMt, 1 Fat	190	(N/A)
Lance				
*Nekot**	(1½ oz.)	1 S, ½ Fr, ½ HFMt, 1 Fat	210	95
Peanut Butter on Wheat	(1$\frac{5}{16}$ oz.)	1 S, ½ HFMt, 1½ Fat	190	210
Toastchee	(1⅜ oz.)	1 S, ½ HFMt, 1½ Fat	190	310
Toasty	(1¼ oz.)	1 S, ½ HFMt, 1 Fat	180	160
Nabisco Great Crisps! (2)				
Malted Milk Peanut Butter Sandwich		½ S, ½ Fat	70	150
Toasted Peanut Butter Sandwich		½ S, 1 Fat	70	150
Pizza				
Famous Foods of Virginia	(11)	1 S, 1 Fat	127	280
Fleetwood Snacks	(1 oz.)	1 S, 1½ Fat	150	480
Nabisco Great Crisps!	(20)	½ S, ½ Fat	70	180
Pepperidge Farm Tiny Goldfish	(45)	1 S, 1½ Fat	140	180
Poppy Seed, Famous Foods of Virginia	(13)	1 S, 1 Fat	135	80
Pretzel, Pepperidge Farm Tiny Goldfish	(40)	1 S, 1 Fat	120	160
Pumpernickel, Pepperidge Farm Snack Sticks	(8)	1 S, 1 Fat	130	180
Rice, Famous Foods of Virginia	(8)	1 S, ½ Fat	105	520

*Contains concentrated sources of carbohydrates

Food	Portion	Exchanges	Calories	Sodium (mg)
Rye				
Lance				
Rye Chee	(1 7/16 oz.)	1½ S, 1½ Fat	190	320
Rye Twins	(6)	1 S, ½ Fat	90	195
Salt-Free, Fleetwood Snacks	(1 oz.)	1 S, 1½ Fat	150	40
Saltines				
Lance				
Saltines	(8)	1 S, ½ Fat	100	260
Saltines Slug Pack	(2 oz.)	1 S, ½ Fat	100	260
Nabisco Great Crisps! (5)				
Premium, Low-Salt		½ S, ½ Fat	60	115
Premium, Unsalted Tops		½ S, ½ Fat	60	135
Sunshine (5)				
Krispy		½ S	60	210
Krispy Unsalted Tops		½ S	60	120
Sesame				
Famous Foods of Virginia, Sesame Crisp	(8)	1 S, 1 Fat	120	175
Lance Sesame Twins	(2)	½ S	40	65
Nabisco Great Crisps!				
Meal Mates Sesame Bread Wafers	(3)	½ S, ½ Fat	70	140
Sesame	(9)	½ S, 1 Fat	70	190
Twigs, Sesame & Cheese Snack Sticks	(5)	½ S, 1 Fat	70	200
Pepperidge Farm Distinctive Sesame	(4)	½ S, 1 Fat	80	105
Pepperidge Farm Snack Sticks, Sesame	(8)	1 S, 1 Fat	130	160
Sunshine American Heritage, Sesame	(4)	½ S, 1 Fat	70	125
Soda				
Lance (6)				
Captain Wafers		1 S, ½ Fat	90	180
Very Low-Sodium Captain Wafers		1 S, ½ Fat	90	75
Nabisco Crown Pilot	(1)	1 S	60	70
Nabisco Great Crisps!				
Sea Rounds	(1)	½ S, ½ Fat	60	140
Sultana Soda	(4)	1 S	60	115
Sour Cream & Onion, Nabisco Great Crisps!	(8)	½ S, 1 Fat	70	200
Taco, Nabisco Great Crisps!	(14)	½ S, 1 Fat	70	200

Food	Portion	Exchanges	Calories	Sodium (mg)
Toast				
Nabisco Great Crisps!				
Holland Rusk Instant Toast	(1)	1 S	60	35
Zwieback Teething Toast	(2)	1 S	60	20
Planters Round Toast	(1 oz.)	1 S, 1½ Fat	140	270
Tomato & Celery, Nabisco Great Crisps!	(9)	½ S, 1 Fat	70	160
Vegetable Thins, Nabisco Great Crisps!	(7)	½ S, 1 Fat	70	100
Wheat				
Austin Snackers Wheat	(1⅜ oz.)	1½ S, 2 Fat	200	(N/A)
Famous Foods of Virginia (11)				
Stoned Wheat Appetizer		1 S, 1 Fat	115	85
Stoned Wheat Wafers		1 S, 1 Fat	115	230
Wheat Appetizer		1 S, 1 Fat	137	160
Lance (6)				
Wheatswafer		1 S, ½ Fat	90	150
Wheat Twins		1 S, ½ Fat	90	210
Nabisco Great Crisps!				
Nutty Wheat Thins	(7)	½ S, 1 Fat	80	250
Triscuit Wafers	(3)	½ S, ½ Fat	60	90
Triscuit Wafers, Low Salt	(3)	½ S, ½ Fat	60	35
Wheatsworth Stone Ground Wheat	(5)	½ S, ½ Fat	70	135
Wheat Thins	(8)	½ S, ½ Fat	70	120
Wheat Thins, Low Salt	(8)	½ S, ½ Fat	70	60
Pepperidge Farm Distinctive (4)				
Cracked Wheat		1 S, ½ Fat	110	200
Hearty Wheat		1 S, ½ Fat	100	180
Toasted Wheat w/Onion		½ S, ½ Fat	80	110
Sunshine				
American Heritage, Wheat snack crackers	(4)	½ S, ½ Fat	60	135
Wheat wafers	(8)	½ S, 1 Fat	80	190

Grain & Grain Products

Food	Portion	Exchanges	Calories	Sodium (mg)
Barley, Scotch (¼ cup)				
Medium Pearled		2½ S	170	5
Quick Pearled		2½ S	170	5

Food	Portion	Exchanges	Calories	Sodium (mg)
Bread Crumbs				
Contadina Seasoned Bread Crumbs	(2 tbsp.)	1 S	70	500
Kellogg's Corn Flake Crumbs*	(1 oz.)	1 S, ½ Fr	110	290
Nabisco, Graham Cracker Crumbs	(2 tbsp.)	1 S	60	90
Corn Meal				
Albers Corn Meal, uncooked (1 oz.)				
White		1½ S	100	.2
Yellow		1½ S	100	.2
Aunt Jemima				
Bolted White Corn Meal Mix	(⅙ cup)	1½ S	100	460
Bolted Yellow Corn Meal Mix	(⅙ cup)	1½ S	100	490
Buttermilk Self-Rising White Corn Meal Mix	(3 tbsp.)	1½ S	100	590
Enriched White Corn Meal	(3 tbsp.)	1½ S	100	0
Enriched Yellow Corn Meal	(3 tbsp.)	1½ S	100	0
Self-Rising White Corn Meal	(⅙ cup)	1½ S	100	510
Self-Rising White Enriched Bolted Corn Meal	(⅙ cup)	1½ S	100	520
Cracker Meal				
Lance	(1 oz.)	1½ S	100	1
Nabisco	(2 tbsp.)	1 S	50	0
Croutettes, Kellogg's dry mix	(.7 oz.)	1 S	70	260
Croutons				
Pepperidge Farm (½ oz.)				
Cheese & Garlic		½ S, ½ Fat	70	180
Onion & Garlic		½ S, ½ Fat	70	170
Seasoned		½ S, ½ Fat	70	200
Granola				
General Mills, Nature Valley (⅓ cup)				
*Cinnamon & Raisin**		½ S, 1 Fr, ½ Fat	120	90
*Coconut & Honey**		1 S, ½ Fr, 1 Fat	150	35
*Fruit & Nut**		½ S, 1 Fr, 1 Fat	130	80
*Toasted Oat Mixture**		½ S, 1 Fr, 1 Fat	130	90

*Contains concentrated sources of carbohydrates

Food	Portion	Exchanges	Calories	Sodium (mg)
Granola, cont.				
Quaker Oats, Sun Country (1 oz.)				
w/Almonds		1 S, 1 Fat	130	10
w/Raisins		1 S, ½ Fr, 1 Fat	130	10
w/Raisins & Dates		1 S, ½ Fr, 1 Fat	130	10
Granola Bars				
General Mills, Nature Valley (1 bar)				
*Almond**		½ S, ½ Fr, 1 Fat	120	85
*Chocolate Chip**		½ S, ½ Fr, 1 Fat	110	75
*Cinnamon**		½ S, ½ Fr, 1 Fat	120	70
*Coconut**		½ S, ½ Fr, 1½ Fat	130	65
*Oats 'n' Honey**		½ S, ½ Fr, 1 Fat	120	65
*Peanut**		½ S, ½ Fr, 1 Fat	120	80
*Peanut Butter**		½ S, ½ Fr, 1 Fat	120	70
Quaker Chewy (1 bar)				
*Chocolate Chip**		½ S, 1 Fr, 1 Fat	130	95
*Chocolate, Graham & Marshmallow**		½ S, 1 Fr, 1 Fat	130	110
*Chunky Nut & Raisin**		½ S, ½ Fr, 1 Fat	130	95
*Honey & Oats**		½ S, 1 Fr, 1 Fat	130	110
*Peanut Butter**		1 S, 1 Fat	140	130
*Peanut Butter & Chocolate Chip**		½ S, ½ Fr, 1 Fat	130	120
*Raisin & Cinnamon**		½ S, 1 Fr, 1 Fat	130	100
Quaker Dipps (1 bar)				
*Caramel Nut**		½ S, 1 Fr, 1 Fat	150	75
*Chocolate Chip**		½ S, 1 Fr, 1 Fat	140	80
*Honey & Oats**		½ S, 1 Fr, 1 Fat	140	80
*Mint Chocolate**		½ S, 1 Fr, 1 Fat	140	70
*Peanut Butter**		½ S, ½ Fr, 1½ Fat	150	105
*Raisin & Almond**		½ S, 1 Fr, 1 Fat	140	100
*Rocky Road**		½ S, 1 Fr, 1½ Fat	140	70
Flour				
Aunt Jemima, Enriched Self-Rising Flour	(¼ cup)	1½ S	100	500
Quaker (⅓ cup)				
Masa Harina De Maiz		2 S	140	0
Masa Trigo		1½ S, 1 Fat	150	300
Matos, Matzos, & Tams, Manischewitz				
American Mato Crackers	(1 oz.)	1½ S	115	(N/A)
Daily Thin Tea Matzos	(1 oz.)	1½ S	103	1
Dietetic Mato Thins	(1 piece)	1 S	91	.30

*Contains concentrated sources of carbohydrates

Food	*Portion*	*Exchanges*	*Calories*	*Sodium* (mg)
Egg 'n' Onion Matzos	(1 oz.)	1½ S	112	180
Garlic Tams	(10)	1 S, 1½ Fat	153	165
Mato Cracker Miniatures	(10–20)	1 S	90	0
Onion Tams	(10)	1 S, 1½ Fat	150	157
Passover Egg Matos	(1 piece)	1½ S	132	0
Passover Egg Matos Crackers	(10)	1½ S	108	< 5
Passover Matos	(1 piece)	1½ S	129	0
Tam Tams	(10)	1 S, 1½ Fat	147	171
Unsalted Matos	(1 oz.)	1½ S	110	< 5
Wheat Mato Crackers	(10)	1 S	90	< 10
Wheat Tams	(10)	1 S, 1½ Fat	150	180
Whole-Wheat Matos w/Bran	(1 piece)	1½ S	110	< 5
Pie Crust & Pastry				
Flako Pie Crust Mix*	(1/6 of a 9″ pie crust)	1 S, 1 Fr, 3 Fat	260	350
General Mills				
Pie Crust Mix	(1/16 package)	½ S, 2 Fat	120	140
Pie Crust Sticks	(1/8 stick)	½ S, 2 Fat	120	140
Pepperidge Farm, Frozen				
Puff Pastry, Patty Shells	(1 shell)	1 S, 3 Fat	210	180
*Puff Pastry Sheets**	(1/4 sheet)	1 S, ½ Fr, 3½ Fat	260	290
Pillsbury				
All Ready Refrigerated Pie Crust	(1/8 of 2-crust pie)	1½ S, 3 Fat	240	310
Pie Crust Sticks & Mix	(1/6 of 2-crust pie)	1½ S, 3½ Fat	270	430
Plain Wiener Wrap	(1 wrap)	½ S, ½ Fat	60	430
Ragu Pizza Quick Mix Crust Mix	(1/12 container)	2 S, ½ Fat	170	360
Taco/Tostada Shells, Ortega	(1 shell)	½ S, ½ Fat	50	5
Wheat Germ, Quaker Oats	(1/4 cup)			
Honey Crunch Kretschmer*		1 S, ½ MFMt	110	0
Regular Kretschmer		1 S, 1 LMt	110	0

■ Pancakes

Food	*Portion*	*Exchanges*	*Calories*	*Sodium* (mg)
Blueberry				
Aunt Jemima frozen	(3 four-inch pancakes)	3 S, ½ Fat	260	1030
Hungry Jack mix	(3 four-inch pancakes)	2 S, ½ Fr, 3 Fat	320	820

*Contains concentrated sources of carbohydrates

Food	Portion	Exchanges	Calories	Sodium (mg)
Buckwheat, Aunt Jemima				
mix	(3 four-inch pancakes)	1½ S, 1½ Fat	200	520
Buttermilk				
Aunt Jemima				
frozen	(3 four-inch pancakes)	2½ S, ½ Fat	210	950
Aunt Jemima mix (3 four-inch pancakes)				
Buttermilk		2½ S, 2 Fat	300	990
*Buttermilk, Complete**		3 S, ½ Fr, ½ Fat	260	960
General Mills mix				
Buttermilk	(⅓ cup)	2½ S, 2 Fat	280	810
Complete Buttermilk	(½ cup)	2½ S, ½ Fat	210	500
Hungry Jack mix (3 four-inch pancakes)				
Buttermilk		2 S, 2 Fat	240	570
*Buttermilk Complete**		2 S, ½ Fr	180	710
Buttermilk Complete Packets		2 S, ½ Fat	180	680
Pillsbury frozen*	(3 pancakes)	2 S, 1½ Fr, ½ Fat	260	590
Complete, Aunt Jemima				
mix*	(3 four-inch pancakes)	3 S, ½ Fr, 1 Fat	280	460
Extra Lights, Hungry Jack				
mix	(3 four-inch pancakes)	2 S, 1 Fat	210	490
Complete		2 S, ½ Fat	190	700
Original				
Aunt Jemima				
frozen	(3 four-inch pancakes)	3 S, 1 Fat	260	1010
Aunt Jemima mix	(3 four-inch pancakes)	2 S, 1½ Fat	227	550
Pillsbury frozen*	(3 pancakes)	2 S, 1 Fr, ½ Fat	240	550
Panshakes, Hungry Jack				
mix	(3 four-inch pancakes)	2½ S, 1 Fat	250	880
Plain				
Aunt Jemima				
frozen	(3 four-inch pancakes)	2½ S, ½ Fat	210	1110
General Mills mix,				
Bisquick	(2 oz.)	2½ S, 1 Fat	230	700
Sweet 'n' Low				
mix	(4 three-inch pancakes)	1½ S, 1 Fat	140	40
Potato, Sweet 'n' Low,				
w/o cooking oil	(2 pancakes)	1 S	76	35
Whole-Wheat, Aunt Jemima				
mix	(3 four-inch pancakes)	2 S, 2 Fat	250	730

*Contains concentrated sources of carbohydrates

Food	Portion	Exchanges	Calories	Sodium (mg)
■ Rice & Rice Mixes				
Apple Pecan, Stouffer's	(½ pkg.)	½ S, 1 Fr, 1 Fat	130	200
Beef, Rice a Roni Rice & Pasta Mixes	(½ cup)			
Beef-Flavored		2 S, 1 Fat	170	910
Microwave, Beef Flavor & Mushroom		1½ S, 1 Fat	150	760
Broccoli				
Green Giant, Rice 'n' Broccoli in Flavored Cheese	(½ cup)	1 S, 1 Fat	120	510
Uncle Ben's Country Inn, Broccoli Rice au Gratin	(½ cup)	1½ S, 1½ Fat	170	420
Brown				
Rice a Roni Brown & Wild Rice mix w/Mushrooms	(½ cup)	1½ S, 1½ Fat	180	840
Riceland Natural Brown	(½ cup)	1½ S	100	0
Uncle Ben's Brown & Wild	(½ cup)	1½ S, 1 Fat	150	500
Uncle Ben's Country Inn Savory Brown	(½ cup)	1½ S, 1 Fat	150	400
Chicken				
Rice a Roni Rice & Pasta Mixes	(½ cup)			
Chicken Flavor		2 S, 1 Fat	170	770
Chicken Flavor/Chicken Broth w/Herb		2 S, 1½ Fat	220	1090
Chicken & Mustard Flavor		1½ S, 1½ Fat	180	840
Rice a Roni Microwave Mixes	(½ cup)			
Chicken Flavor & Mushroom		1½ S, 1 Fat	140	720
Chicken Flavor & Vegetables		1½ S, 1 Fat	140	770
Uncle Ben's Country Inn, Chicken Stock Rice	(½ cup)	½ S, 1 Fat	150	400
Converted, Uncle Ben's	(⅔ cup)	½ S, ½ Fat	140	450
Florentine, Uncle Ben's Country Inn	(½ cup)	1½ S, 1½ Fat	170	490
Fried Rice w/Almonds, Rice a Roni Mix	(½ cup)	1½ S, 1 Fat	140	700
Garden-Style, Uncle Ben's Country Inn	(½ cup)	1½ S, 1 Fat	140	640
Herb				
Green Giant w/Herb Butter Sauce	(½ cup)	1½ S, 1 Fat	150	390
Lipton Herb & Butter	(½ cup)	1½ S, 1 Fat	160	510
Rice a Roni Mix, Herb & Butter	(½ cup)	1½ S, 1 Fat	130	790
Uncle Ben's Country Inn, Herbed Rice	(½ cup)	1½ S, 1½ Fat	170	710

Food	Portion	Exchanges	Calories	Sodium (mg)
Italian				
Green Giant Italian Blend White Rice & Spinach in Cheese Sauce	(½ cup)	1 S, 1 V, 1½ Fat	170	400
Uncle Ben's Country Inn, Italiano Rice	(½ cup)	1½ S, 1 Fat	190	580
Jubilee, Green Giant	(½ cup)	1½ S, 1 Fat	150	340
Long Grain & Wild				
Green Giant	(½ cup)	1½ S	120	550
Rice a Roni w/Herbs & Seasoning	(½ cup)	1½ S, 1 Fat	140	630
Rice a Roni Microwave, Original, w/Herbs & Seasonings	(½ cup)	1½ S, 1 Fat	140	840
Riceland Extra-Long Grain	(½ cup)	1½ S	100	0
Uncle Ben's Long-Grain & Wild (½ cup)				
Beef Stock Sauce		1½ S, 1 Fat	160	660
Beef Stuffing		1½ S, 2 Fat	190	570
Chicken Stock Sauce		1½ S, 1 Fat	160	690
Chicken Stuffing Blend		1½ S, 2 Fat	190	610
Fast Cooking Recipe		1½ S, 1 Fat	130	430
Original Recipe		1½ S, ½ Fat	120	440
Medley, Stouffer's	(½ pkg.)	1 S, ½ V, ½ Fat	110	340
Oriental				
Lipton Rice & Sauce Oriental	(½ cup)	1½ S, 1 Fat	160	540
Uncle Ben's Country Inn, Rice Oriental	(½ cup)	1½ S, 1 Fat	140	480
Pilaf				
Green Giant	(½ cup)	1½ S	120	520
Lipton	(½ cup)	1½ S, 1 Fat	170	490
Rice a Roni	(½ cup)	2 S, 1 Fat	190	1200
Plain				
Chun King	(.5 oz.)	½ S	40	620
Uncle Ben's Boil in Bag	(single serving pkg.)	1 S	90	10
Risotto, Rice a Roni Mix	(¾ cup)	2 S, 1½ Fat	210	1110
Royale, Uncle Ben's Country Inn	(½ cup)	1½ S, 1 Fat	150	560
Spanish				
Lipton	(½ cup)	1½ S, ½ Fat	150	540
Rice a Roni Mix	(½ cup)	1½ S, 1 Fat	140	1050
Uncle Ben's Country Inn	(½ cup)	1½ S, 1 Fat	160	750
Van Camp's	(1 cup)	1½ S, 1 V, ½ Fat	150	1360

Food	Portion	Exchanges	Calories	Sodium (mg)
Vegetable Medley, Uncle Ben's Country Inn	(½ cup)	1½ S, 1 Fat	160	430
Whole-Grain, Uncle Ben's Natural	(⅔ cup)	1½ S, ½ Fat	150	460
Wild, Uncle Ben's Select	(½ cup)	1 S, ½ Fat	120	290
Yellow Rice Dinner, Rice a Roni*	(¾ cup)	2 S, 1 Fr, 1½ Fat	287	1160

■ Snacks

Food	Portion	Exchanges	Calories	Sodium (mg)
Bugles, General Mills	(1 oz.)	1 S, 1½ Fat	150	290
Nacho Cheese		1 S, 2 Fat	160	270
Cheese Snacks				
Cheetos (1 oz.)				
Crunchy		1 S, 2 Fat	160	270
Puffed Balls		1 S, 2 Fat	160	360
Herr's Cheese Curls	(1 oz.)	1 S, 1½ Fat	140	320
Keystone (1 oz.)				
Cheese Curl		1 S, 1½ Fat	150	185
Cheese Curl, Fried		1 S, 1½ Fat	150	200
Lance				
Cheese Balls	(1⅛ oz.)	1 S, 2½ Fat	190	420
Crunchy Cheese Twist	(1½ oz.)	1½ S, 2½ Fat	230	510
Planters (1 oz.)				
Cheez Balls		1 S, 2 Fat	160	270
Cheez Curls		1 S, 2 Fat	160	290
Wise (1 oz.)				
Cheez Doodles, Crunchy		1 S, 2 Fat	160	230
Cheez Doodles, Puffed		1 S, 2 Fat	150	360
Cheez Waffies		1 S, 1½ Fat	140	420
Corn Chips				
Fritos Corn Chips	(1 oz.)	1 S, 2 Fat	150	220
Dip Size		1 S, 2 Fat	150	210
Herr's Corn Chips, Regular	(1 oz.)	1 S, 1½ Fat	140	125
BBQ		1 S, 1½ Fat	150	180
Keystone Corn Chips	(1 oz.)	1 S, 2 Fat	170	85
BBQ		1 S, 2 Fat	170	260
Lance Corn Chips, Regular	(1¾ oz.)	1½ S, 3 Fat	260	350
*BBQ**		1 S, 1 Fr, 3 Fat	280	360

*Contains concentrated sources of carbohydrates

Food	Portion	Exchanges	Calories	Sodium (mg)
Corn Chips, cont.				
Planters Corn Chips	(1 oz.)	1 S, 2 Fat	160	160
Wise (1 oz.)				
Corn Chips		1 S, 2 Fat	160	180
Corn Crunchies		1 S, 2 Fat	160	180
Corn Spirals, Toasted		1 S, 2 Fat	160	125
Corn Spirals, Nacho Cheese Flavor		1 S, 2 Fat	160	190
Crispbreads, Weight Watchers, Harvest Rice, Golden Wheat, Garlic Flavor	(2 wafers)	½ S	30	55
Doo Dads, Nabisco (½ cup)				
Cheddar 'n' Herb		1 S, 1 Fat	140	400
Original		1 S, 1 Fat	140	360
Zesty Cheese		1 S, 1 Fat	140	420
Mix, Guy's Tasty Mix	(1 oz.)	1 S, 1½ Fat	130	510
Popcorn				
General Mills Pop-Secret, Natural Flavor	(3 cups)	1 S, 1½ Fat	140	260
Butter Flavor		1 S, 1½ Fat	140	250
No Salt		1 S, 1½ Fat	140	0
Herr's, Regular	(1 oz.)	½ S, 2 Fat	140	250
Cheese		1 S, 1½ Fat	140	240
Keystone (1 oz.)				
Butter		1 S, 1½ Fat	150	110
*Caramel Corn**		½ S, 1 Fr, ½ Fat	130	115
Cheese		1 S, 1½ Fat	150	145
*Sugar Corn**		½ S, 1 Fr, ½ Fat	130	30
Lance, Plain	(1 oz.)	1 S, 1½ Fat	140	240
Cheese	(⅞ oz.)	1 S, 1½ Fat	130	280
Orville Redenbacher's, popped (4 cups)				
Butter Flavor		1 S, 1 Fat	110	0
Natural Flavor		1 S, 1 Fat	120	0
Oil & Salt		1 S, 1½ Fat	160	700
Gourmet Original Plain		1 S	90	0
Gourmet White, Hot Air		1 S	90	0
Gourmet White, Oil & Salt		1 S, 1½ Fat	160	700
Gourmet White Plain		1 S	90	0
Microwave, Butter Flavor		1 S, 1 Fat	110	200
Microwave, Natural Flavor		1 S, 1 Fat	120	260
Pillsbury Frozen Microwave, popped (3 cups)				
Butter Flavor		1 S, 2 Fat	190	270
Original Flavor		1 S, 2 Fat	190	270

*Contains concentrated sources of carbohydrates

Food	Portion	Exchanges	Calories	Sodium (mg)
Salt-Free		1 S, 1 Fat	140	5
Planters, popped	(2 cups)	½ S	40	0
Microwave, Butter	(3 cups)	1 S, 2 Fat	140	560
Microwave, Plain	(3 cups)	1 S, 2 Fat	140	560
Weight Watchers, popped	(2 cups)	½ S	100	5
Wise (1 oz.)				
White Cheddar Cheese		½ S, 2 Fat	140	340
Tender Eating Baby		½ S, 2 Fat	140	240
Pork Rind, Keystone	(1 oz.)	2½ LMt	140	695
Hot		2½ LMt	140	1045
Potato Chips				
Delta Gold	(1 oz.)	1 S, 2 Fat	160	160
Herr's (1 oz.)				
Bar-B-Q		1 S, 2 Fat	150	200
No-Salt		1 S, 2 Fat	150	10
Old Bay		1 S, 2 Fat	150	360
Red Hot		1 S, 2 Fat	150	300
Regular		1 S, 1½ Fat	140	180
Salt 'n' Vinegar		1 S, 2 Fat	150	340
Sour Cream		1 S, 2 Fat	150	310
Lance				
BBQ	(1⅛ oz.)	1 S, 2½ Fat	190	430
Cajun	(1 oz.)	1 S, 2 Fat	160	220
Regular	(1⅛ oz.)	½ S, 3 Fat	190	220
Ripple	(1⅛ oz.)	½ S, 3 Fat	190	220
Sour Cream & Onion	(1⅛ oz.)	1 S, 2½ Fat	190	390
Lay's	(1 oz.)	1 S, 2 Fat	150	240
Unsalted		1 S, 2 Fat	150	10
Munchos Potato Crisps	(1 oz.)	1 S, 2 Fat	150	290
New York Deli	(1 oz.)	1 S, 2 Fat	160	120
O'Gradys Extra Thick & Crunchy	(1 oz.)	1 S, 2 Fat	150	210
Planters Potato Crunchies	(1.25 oz.)	1½ S, 2 Fat	190	310
Ruffles	(1 oz.)	1 S, 2 Fat	150	250
Weight Watchers Great Snackers (½ oz.)				
*Barbecue**		½ S, ½ Fat	60	170
Cheddar Cheese		½ S, ½ Fat	60	170
Toasted Onion		½ S, ½ Fat	60	120

*Contains concentrated sources of carbohydrates

Food	Portion	Exchanges	Calories	Sodium (mg)
Potato Chips, cont.				
Wise (1 oz.)				
Bravos, Nacho Cheese Flavor		1 S, 1½ Fat	150	180
Natural Flavor		1 S, 2 Fat	160	190
Ridgies, Barbecue Flavor, Rippled		1 S, 2 Fat	150	240
Puffs, Planters, Sour Cream & Onion*	(1 oz.)	½ S, ½ Fr, 2 Fat	160	300
Pretzels				
Herr's (1 oz.)				
Extra Thin		1½ S	110	450
No-Salt		1½ S	110	100
Keystone	(1 oz.)	1½ S	110	435
Mister Salty (portions are listed as number of pretzels)				
Butter-Flavored Rings	(23)	1½ S, ½ Fat	110	570
Butter-Flavored Sticks	(90)	1½ S	110	620
Dutch	(2)	1½ S	110	440
Juniors	(29)	1½ S, ½ Fat	110	500
Mini	(16)	1½ S	110	450
Mini Mix	(23)	1½ S	110	480
Rings	(22)	1½ S, ½ Fat	110	510
Sticks	(90)	1½ S	110	620
Twists	(5)	1½ S, ½ Fat	110	590
Veri-Thin Sticks	(45)	1½ S	110	770
Planters	(1 oz.)	1½ S	110	700
Rold Gold (1 oz.)				
Rods		1½ S, ½ Fat	110	520
Sticks		1½ S	110	780
Tiny Tims		1½ S, ½ Fat	110	590
Twists		1½ S	110	470
Seyfert's Butter Rods	(¾ oz.)	1 S	83	398
Tortilla Chips				
Doritos	(1 oz.)	1 S, 1 Fat	140	230
Nacho Cheese		1 S, 1½ Fat	140	250
Salsa Rio		1½ S, ½ Fat	140	170
Herr's (1 oz.)				
Nacho Cheese		1½ S, ½ Fat	110	230
Toasted		1 S, 1 Fat	140	170
Keystone	(1 oz.)	1 S, 1½ Fat	150	15
Jalapeño		1 S, 1½ Fat	150	80
Nacho		1 S, 1½ Fat	150	180
La Famous	(1 oz.)	1 S, 1½ Fat	140	180

*Contains concentrated sources of carbohydrates

Food	Portion	Exchanges	Calories	Sodium (mg)
No Salt Added		1 S, 1½ Fat	140	5
Lance (1⅛ oz.)				
Jalapeño & Cheese		1 S, 1½ Fat	160	250
Nacho		1 S, 1½ Fat	160	240
Tostitos	(1 oz.)	1 S, 1½ Fat	140	170

■ Stuffing

Food	Portion	Exchanges	Calories	Sodium (mg)
Chicken				
General Mills mix	(⅙ pkg.)	1½ S, 1½ Fat	180	620
Green Giant	(½ cup)	1½ S, 1 Fat	170	670
Rice a Roni mix, Bread/Chicken Flavor w/Rice	(½ cup)	1½ S, 3 Fat	240	780
Corn Bread				
General Mills mix	(⅙ pkg.)	1½ S, 1½ Fat	180	710
Pepperidge Farm	(1 oz.)	1½ S	110	320
Pillsbury	(½ cup)	1½ S, 1 Fat	170	660
Rice a Roni mix, Cornbread w/Rice	(½ cup)	1½ S, 3 Fat	240	910
Cubes, Pepperidge Farm	(1 oz.)	1½ S	110	430
Herb				
General Mills, Traditional Herb	(⅙ pkg.)	1½ S, 1½ Fat	190	640
Pepperidge Farm, Herb-Seasoned	(1 oz.)	1½ S	110	410
Rice a Roni mix, Bread/Herb & Butter & Wild Rice	(½ cup)	1½ S, 3 Fat	240	850
Mushroom, Green Giant	(½ cup)	1 S, 1 V, 1 Fat	150	780
Pork, General Mills, mix	(⅙ pkg.)	1½ S, 1½ Fat	190	640
Wild Rice (½ cup)				
Green Giant		1½ S, 1 Fat	160	540
Rice a Roni mix, Bread w/Wild Rice		1½ S, 3 Fat	240	750

■ Waffles & French Toast (frozen)

Food	Portion	Exchanges	Calories	Sodium (mg)
Apple Waffles				
Aunt Jemima, Apple & Cinnamon	(2 waffles)	2 S, 1 Fat	170	630
Eggo (1 waffle)				
Apple Cinnamon		1 S, 1 Fat	130	300
Apple Homestyle		1 S, 1 Fat	120	300
Blueberry Waffles				
Aunt Jemima	(2 waffles)	2 S, 1 Fat	170	630

Food	Portion	Exchanges	Calories	Sodium (mg)
Blueberry Waffles, cont.				
Eggo, Artificially Flavored	(1 waffle)	1 S, 1 Fat	130	300
Buttermilk Waffles				
Aunt Jemima	(2 waffles)	2 S, 1 Fat	170	700
Eggo	(1 waffle)	1 S, 1 Fat	120	300
French Toast, Aunt Jemima (2 slices)				
Cinnamon Swirl		2 S, 1½ Fat	210	470
Plain		1½ S, 1 Fat	170	560
Raisin		2 S, 1 Fat	190	550
Nutri-Grain, Eggo Waffles	(1 waffle)	1 S, 1 Fat	130	300
Original Waffles, Aunt Jemima	(2 waffles)	2 S, 1 Fat	170	650
Raisin Waffles				
Aunt Jemima	(2 waffles)	2 S, ½ Fr, 1 Fat	200	680
Eggo, Raisin & Bran Nutri-Grain	(1 waffle)	1 S, 1 Fat	130	300
Strawberry Waffles, Eggo, Artificially Flavored	(1 waffle)	1 S, 1 Fat	130	300

8

DAIRY PRODUCTS

So many different types of milk and milk products are available today that you might be confused about which kind to buy. Is high-protein milk needed? How about milk with added calcium or acidophilus culture? It all depends on the individual. Ask your dietitian.

Some cheese manufacturers are making an effort to meet the needs of consumers who want to reduce fat in their diets. Skim milk, cheeses made with skim milk, and "lite cheeses" are good choices. High-fat cheeses should be used only occasionally, depending on your dietitian's advice.

Ask your dietitian whether you should use butter or margarine. The American Diabetic Association and The American Dietetic Association suggest foods that have a fat ratio of 2:1 polyunsaturated to saturated fat.

Ice cream can be an occasional treat, as long as you keep the portion size small. Remember to ask your dietitian for advice.

Food	Portion	Exchanges	Calories	Sodium (mg)
■ Butter & Margarine				
Butter (lightly salted)				
Hotel Bar	(1 tsp.)	1 Fat	35	35
Keller's	(1 tsp.)	1 Fat	35	35
Land O' Lakes (1 tbsp.)				
Sweet Cream		2 Fat	100	115
Sweet Cream, Whipped		1½ Fat	60	75
Butter (unsalted)				
Land O' Lakes (1 tbsp.)				
Sweet Cream		2 Fat	100	2
Sweet Cream, Whipped		1½ Fat	60	1
Margarine (diet & reduced-calorie)				
Blue Bonnet Diet	(1 tbsp.)	1 Fat	50	100
Fleischmann's Diet	(1 tbsp.)	1 Fat	50	100
w/Lite Salt		1 Fat	50	50
Mazola Reduced-Calorie	(1 tbsp.)	1 Fat	50	130
Weight Watchers Reduced-Calorie (1 tbsp.)				
Tubs, regular		1 Fat	50	110
Margarine (salted)				
Blue Bonnet (1 tbsp.)				
Soft		2 Fat	100	95
Soft Butter Blend		2 Fat	90	95
Spread (52% fat)		1½ Fat	80	110
Spread, Light Tasty (52% vegetable oil)		1½ Fat	60	100
Spread Stick (70% fat)		2 Fat	90	95
Spread Stick (75% fat)		2 Fat	90	95
Stick		2 Fat	100	95
Stick, Butter Blend		2 Fat	90	95
Whipped, Soft		1½ Fat	70	70
Whipped, Spread (60% fat)		1 Fat	50	55
Whipped, Stick		1½ Fat	70	70
Country Morning Blend (1 tbsp.)				
Lightly Salted Soft (tub)		2 Fat	90	85
Lightly Salted Stick		2 Fat	100	115
Fleischmann's (1 tbsp.)				
Light Corn Oil Spread, Soft		1½ Fat	80	70
Light Corn Oil Spread, Stick		1½ Fat	80	70
Soft		2 Fat	100	95
Squeeze		2 Fat	100	85
Stick		2 Fat	100	95
Whipped, Lightly Salted		1½ Fat	70	60

Food	Portion	Exchanges	Calories	Sodium (mg)
Land O' Lakes (1 tbsp.)				
Premium Corn Oil Stick		2 Fat	100	115
Regular Soft Tub (soy oil)		2 Fat	100	115
Regular Stick (soy oil)		2 Fat	100	115
Mazola	(1 tbsp.)	2 Fat	100	100
Nucoa	(1 tbsp.)	2 Fat	100	160
Soft		2 Fat	90	150
Weight Watchers Sticks	(1 tbsp.)	1½ Fat	60	110
Margarine (unsalted)				
Blue Bonnet, Unsalted Butter Blend, Stick	(1 tbsp.)	2 Fat	90	0
Country Morning Blend (1 tbsp.)				
Soft Tub		2 Fat	90	1
Stick		2 Fat	100	1
Fleischmann's (1 tbsp.)				
Soft		2 Fat	100	0
Stick		2 Fat	100	0
Whipped		1½ Fat	70	0
Mazola	(1 tbsp.)	2 Fat	100	0
Weight Watchers Tubs	(1 tbsp.)	1 Fat	50	0

■ Cheese (natural)

Food	Portion	Exchanges	Calories	Sodium (mg)
Blue, Frigo	(1 oz.)	1 HFMt	100	400
Brick, Land O' Lakes	(1 oz.)	1 HFMt	110	160
Cheddar				
Frigo	(1 oz.)	1 HFMt	110	200
Land O' Lakes	(1 oz.)	1 HFMt	110	175
Weight Watchers (1 oz.)				
Shredded		1 MFMt	80	150
Shredded, Low-Sodium		1 MFMt	80	70
Colby, Land O' Lakes	(1 oz.)	1 HFMt	110	170
Cottage Cheese				
Borden (½ cup)				
Dry Curd, 5% milkfat		1½ LMt	80	20
4% milkfat		2 LMt	120	400
Unsalted, 4% milkfat		2 LMt	120	40
Land O' Lakes	(4 oz.)	2 LMt	120	460
2% milkfat		2 LMt	100	460
Lite-Line Lowfat, 1.5% milkfat	(½ cup)	1½ LMt	90	400
Weight Watchers Lowfat	(4 oz.)	2 LMt	90	420
Cream Cheese, Weight Watchers Reduced-Calorie	(2 tbsp.)	½ MFMt	35	40

Food	Portion	Exchanges	Calories	Sodium (mg)
Natural Cheese, cont.				
Edam, Land O' Lakes	(1 oz.)	1 HFMt	100	275
Feta, Frigo	(1 oz.)	1 HFMt	100	400
Fontina, Frigo	(1 oz.)	1 HFMt	110	400
Gouda, Land O' Lakes	(1 oz.)	1 HFMt	100	230
Monterey Jack, Land O' Lakes	(1 oz.)	1 HFMt	110	150
Mozzarella				
Frigo Low Moisture (1 oz.)				
Part Skim		1 MFMt	80	190
Whole Milk		1 HFMt	90	190
Land O' Lakes, Low Moisture Part Skim	(1 oz.)	1 MFMt	80	150
Polly-O All Natural (1 oz.)				
Lite		1 MFMt	70	200
Part Skim		1 MFMt	80	280
Whole Milk		1 HFMt	90	280
Polly-O String, Part Skim	(1 oz.)	1 HFMt	90	200
Weight Watchers (1 oz.)				
Shredded		1 MFMt	70	150
Sticks		1 MFMt	70	150
Muenster, Land O' Lakes	(1 oz.)	1 HFMt	100	180
Natural Cheese Sticks, Weight Watchers	(1 oz.)	1 MFMt	80	150
Low-Sodium		1 MFMt	80	70
Parmesan, Frigo (1 oz.)				
Grated, 18% moisture		2 MFMt	130	510
Loaf, 32% moisture		1 HFMt	110	350
Parma Zest		1½ MFMt	120	410
Parma Zest (sold in New York State)		1½ MFMt	120	600
& Romano, Grated, 18% moisture		2 MFMt	130	510
Pizza, Frigo	(1 oz.)	1 HFMt	90	210
Provolone				
Frigo	(1 oz.)	1 HFMt	100	230
Land O' Lakes	(1 oz.)	1 HFMt	100	250
Ricotta				
Frigo (1 oz.)				
Low-Fat		½ LMt	20	20
Part Skim		½ HFMt	45	100
Whole Milk		½ HFMt	50	100
Polly-O All Natural (1 oz.)				
Lite		1 MFMt	80	65

Food	Portion	Exchanges	Calories	Sodium (mg)
No-Salt Part Skim		1 MFMt	90	20
Part Skim Milk		1 HFMt	90	45
Whole Milk		1 HFMt	100	45
Romano, Frigo (1 oz.)				
Grated, 18% moisture		2 MFMt	130	510
Loaf		1 HFMt	110	350
Swiss				
Frigo	(1 oz.)	1 HFMt	110	80
Land O' Lakes	(1 oz.)	1 HFMt	110	75
Weight Watchers, Low-Sodium	(1 oz.)	1 LMt	50	140
Taco, Frigo	(1 oz.)	1 HFMt	110	200

■ Cheese (processed cheese & cheese substitutes)

Food	Portion	Exchanges	Calories	Sodium (mg)
American				
Borden Process (1 oz.)				
Light, 15% milkfat		1 MFMt	70	420
Singles		1 HFMt	90	350
Slices		1 HFMt	110	460
Easy Cheese Pasteurized Process Spread	(1 oz.)	1 MFMt	80	350
Land O' Lakes Processed	(1 oz.)	1 HFMt	110	405
Lite-Line Pasteurized Process	(1 oz.)	1 LMt	50	410
Reduced Sodium, 15% milkfat		1 MFMt	70	90
Sodium Lite, 15% milkfat		1 MFMt	70	200
Weight Watchers, Dijon Flavor, sliced	(1 oz.)	1 LMt	50	400
Cheddar				
Easy Cheese Pasteurized Process Spread	(1 oz.)	1 MFMt	80	370
Sharp		1 MFMt	80	320
Fisher Ched-o-Mate, Shredded Substitute	(1 oz.)	1 HFMt	90	330
Frigo Imitation	(1 oz.)	1 MFMt	70	310
Lite-Line Process, Sharp	(1 oz.)	1 LMt	50	440
Weight Watchers				
Cheddar & Cheddar-Onion Flavor, cups		1 MFMt	70	255
Sharp Flavor, sliced		1 LMt	50	400
Cheese 'n' Bacon, Easy Cheese Spread	(1 oz.)	1 MFMt	80	350
Golden Velvet Spread, Land O' Lakes	(1 oz.)	1 MFMt	80	380

Food	Portion	Exchanges	Calories	Sodium (mg)
Processed Cheese, cont.				
Jalapeño Cheese Food, Land O' Lakes	(1 oz.)	1 HFMt	90	360
LaChedda Cheese Food, Land O' Lakes	(1 oz.)	1 HFMt	90	335
Low-Cholesterol, Lite-Line Pasteurized Cheese Food Substitute	(1 oz.)	1 HFMt	90	430
Mozzarella				
Fisher Pizza-mate Shredded Substitute	(1 oz.)	1 HFMt	90	310
Frigo Imitation	(1 oz.)	1 HFMt	90	240
Lite-Line Process Cheese	(1 oz.)	1 LMt	50	340
Nacho, Easy Cheese Spread	(1 oz.)	1 MFMt	80	340
Onion Cheese Food, Land O' Lakes	(1 oz.)	1 HFMt	90	330
Pepperoni Cheese Food, Land O' Lakes	(1 oz.)	1 HFMt	90	395
Port Wine, Weight Watchers, cup	(1 oz.)	1 MFMt	70	255
Salami Cheese Food, Land O' Lakes	(1 oz.)	1 HFMt	100	400
Swiss				
Land O' Lakes Processed, American/Swiss	(1 oz.)	1 HFMt	100	445
Lite-Line Pasteurized Process	(1 oz.)	1 LMt	50	380

■ Cream & Creamers

Food	Portion	Exchanges	Calories	Sodium (mg)
Cream				
Half & Half, Land O' Lakes	(1 tbsp.)	½ Fat	20	5
Lean Cream, Land O' Lakes	(6 tbsp.)	1 LFMk	120	90
w/Chives	(6 tbsp.)	1 LFMk	120	360
Creamer (dairy), Weight Watchers	(10 pkt.)	1 SMk	100	150
Creamer (non-dairy)				
Carnation Coffee-Mate				
Dry Powder	(1½ pkt.)	½ Fat	24	6
Dry Powder	(2 tsp.)	½ Fat	24	4
Liquid	(1½ fl. oz.)	1 Fat	47	11
Cremora	(2 tsp.)	½ Fat	24	10
Rich, Coffee Rich	(½ oz.)	½ Fat	20	10
Wendy's	(⅝ oz.)	½ Fat	28	20

Food	Portion	Exchanges	Calories	Sodium (mg)
Dips (dairy)				
Buttermilk, Land O' Lakes Lean Cream	(3 tbsp.)	½ S, ½ Fat	60	636
Dill, Land O' Lakes Lean Cream	(3 tbsp.)	½ S, ½ Fat	60	246
Flavored, Land O' Lakes Cultured	(4 oz.)	½ SMk, 2 Fat	140	630
French Onion, Land O' Lakes Lean Cream	(3 tbsp.)	½ S, ½ Fat	60	351
Jalapeño, Land O' Lakes Lean Cream	(3 tbsp.)	½ S, ½ Fat	60	171
Onion & Garlic, Land O' Lakes Lean Cream	(3 tbsp.)	½ S, ½ Fat	60	336
Sour Cream				
Land O' Lakes (1 tbsp.)				
Cultured		½ Fat	25	5
Regular		½ Fat	32	6
Pet Imitation	(2 tbsp.)	1 Fat	50	50
Weight Watchers, Blend	(1½ oz.)	½ LFMk	53	60
Topping, Richwhip nondairy				
Liquid	(¼ oz. or 1 fl. oz., whipped)	½ Fat	20	4
Pressurized	(¼ oz.)	½ Fat	20	5
Prewhipped	(2 tbsp.)	½ Fat	24	10
Whipping Cream, Land O' Lakes	(1 tbsp.)	1 Fat	45	5
Gourmet Heavy		1 Fat	60	5

■ Milk & Milk Drinks

Food	Portion	Exchanges	Calories	Sodium (mg)
Buttermilk				
Borden Golden Churn, Lowfat, 1½% milkfat	(1 cup)	1 LFMk	120	250
Land O' Lakes	(8 fl. oz.)	1 SMk	100	255
Swiss Miss All Purpose Buttermilk Powder, reconstituted	(8 oz.)	½ S, ½ SMk	80	190
Chocolate Milk				
Borden Dutch Chocolate Lowfat*	(1 cup)	1 LFMk, 1 Fr	180	180
Land O' Lakes*	(8 oz.)	1 WMk, 1 Fr	210	150
1%		1 SMk, 1 Fr	160	150
Skim		1 SMk, 1 Fr	140	155
Meadow Gold*	(1 cup)	1 WMk, 1 Fr	210	240
Eggnog				
Borden, canned*	(4 oz.)	½ WMk, ½ Fr, 1 Fat	160	80

*Contains concentrated sources of carbohydrates

Food	Portion	Exchanges	Calories	Sodium (mg)
Egg nog, cont.				
Land O' Lakes*	(8 fl. oz.)	1 LFMk, 1½ Fr, 2 Fat	300	142
Evaporated Milk				
Carnation	(4 oz.)	1 WMk, ½ Fat	170	135
Lowfat		1 LFMk	110	130
Skimmed		1 SMk	100	147
Pet	(½ cup)	1 WMk, ½ Fat	170	140
Pet 99, Skimmed	(½ cup)	1 SMk	100	150
Hot Cocoa Mix				
Butter-Nut*, prepared with water	(6 oz.)	½ S, 1 Fr, ½ Fat	115	107
Carnation Sugar-Free*	(1 env.)	½ SMk	50	160
Swiss Miss Sugar Free (1 env.)				
Milk Chocolate		½ SMk	50	190
Milk Chocolate w/Marshmallow Flavor		½ SMk	50	200
w/Sugar-Free Mini Marshmallows		½ SMk	50	180
Weight Watchers, Chocolate Marshmallow, Milk Chocolate	(1 env.)	1 SMk	60	160
Instant Breakfast, Carnation, No Sugar Added, before adding milk (1 env.)				
Chocolate		1 SMk	70	140
Chocolate Malt		1 SMk	70	150
Strawberry		1 SMk	70	120
Vanilla		1 SMk	70	120
Lowfat Milk				
Borden (1 cup)				
w/L. Acidophilus Culture Added, 1% milkfat		1 SMk	100	130
High-Protein, Protein Fortified		1 LFMk	140	150
Land O' Lakes (8 oz.)				
1%		1 SMk	90	125
2%		1 LFMk	120	120
Viva Homogenized w/extra calcium, 2% milkfat	(1 cup)	1LFMk	120	125
Nonfat Dry Milk, reconstituted				
Carnation	(8 oz.)	1 SMk	80	125
Land O' Lakes, Flash Instant	(8 oz.)	1 SMk	80	125
Skim Milk				
Borden (1 cup)				
Homogenized		1 SMk	90	130
Skim-Line, Protein Fortified Nonfat		1 SMk	100	150

*Contains concentrated sources of carbohydrates

Food	Portion	Exchanges	Calories	Sodium (mg)
Land O' Lakes	(8 oz.)	1 SMk	90	125
Weight Watchers	(8 oz.)	1 SMk	90	140
Whole Milk				
Borden (1 cup)				
Hi-Calcium Homogenized Vitamin D w/Added Calcium		1 WMk	150	13
Homogenized Vitamin D		1 WMk	150	130
Land O' Lakes, Homogenized	(8 oz.)	1 WMk	150	120

■ Yogurt & Yogurt Drinks

Food	Portion	Exchanges	Calories	Sodium (mg)
Amaretto Almond, Yoplait Yo Creme*	(5 oz.)	1 LFMk, 1½ Fr, 1 Fat	240	80
Apple				
Dannon Fruit-on-the-Bottom, Dutch*	(8 oz.)	1 LFMk, 2 Fr	240	120
Yoplait Custard-Style*	(6 oz.)	1 LFMt, 1 Fr	190	95
Yoplait 150, Cinnamon*	(6 oz.)	1 LFMt, 1½ Fr	220	90
Banana				
Dannon Fruit-on-the-Bottom*	(8 oz.)	1 LFMk, 2 Fr	240	120
Yoplait Original*	(6 oz.)	1 LFMk, 1 Fr	190	105
Banana Strawberry, Colombo*	(8 oz.)	1 LFMk, 2 Fr	235	160
Bavarian Chocolate, Yoplait Yo Creme*	(5 oz.)	1 LFMk, 1½ Fr, 1 Fat	270	95
Berries, Yoplait 150*	(6 oz.)	1 LFMk, 2 Fr	230	95
Black Cherry				
Weight Watcher à la Francais Nonfat*	(6 oz.)	1 SMk	90	130
Weight Watcher Nonfat*	(8 oz.)	1 SMk, 1 Fr	150	120
Blueberry				
Colombo*	(8 oz.)	1 LFMk, 2 Fr, ½ Fat	250	160
Dannon Fresh Flavors*	(8 oz.)	1 SMk, 1½ Fr, ½ Fat	200	160
Dannon Fruit-on-the-Bottom*	(8 oz.)	1 LFMk, 2 Fr	240	120
	(4.4 oz.)	½ LFMk, 1 Fr	130	65
Weight Watcher à la Francais Nonfat	(6 oz.)	1 SMK	90	130
Weight Watchers Nonfat	(8 oz.)	1 SMk, 1 Fr	150	120
Yoplait Custard-Style	(6 oz.)	1 LFMk, 1 Fr	190	95
Yoplait 150	(6 oz.)	1 SMk, 1 Fr	150	5
Yoplait Original	(6 oz.)	1 LFMk, 1 Fr	190	105

*Contains concentrated sources of carbohydrates

Food	Portion	Exchanges	Calories	Sodium (mg)
Yogurt, cont.				
Boysenberry				
Dannon Fruit-on-the-Bottom*	(8 oz.)	1 LFMk, 2 Fr	240	120
Yoplait Custard-Style*	(6 oz.)	1 LFMk, 1 Fr	190	95
Breakfast, Lowfat, Yoplait 150				
Cherry				
Dannon Fruit-on-the-Bottom*	(8 oz.)	1 LFMk, 2 Fr	240	120
Yoplait Custard Style*	(6 oz.)	1 LFMk, 1 Fr	190	95
Yoplait 150*	(6 oz.)	1 SMk, 1 Fr	150	5
*w/Almonds**		1 SMk, 1½ Fr, ½ Fat	210	90
Yoplait Yo Creme, Cherries Jubilee*	(5 oz.)	½ LFMk, 2 Fr, 1 Fat	220	80
Coffee, Dannon Fresh Flavors*	(8 oz.)	1 SMk, 1½ Fr, ½ Fat	200	140
Lemon				
Dannon Fresh Flavors*	(8 oz.)	1 SMk, 1½ Fr, ½ Fat	200	140
Weight Watchers à la Francais Nonfat*	(6 oz.)	1 SMK	90	130
Weight Watchers Nonfat*	(8 oz.)	1 SMk, 1 Fr	150	120
Yoplait Custard-Style*	(6 oz.)	1 LFMk, 1 Fr	190	95
Yoplait Original*	(6 oz.)	1 LFMk, 1 Fr	190	105
Mixed Berries				
Dannon Extra Smooth*	(4.4 oz.)	½ LFMk, 1 Fr	130	80
Dannon Fruit-on-the-Bottom*	(8 oz.)	1 LFMk, 2 Fr	240	120
Dannon Hearty Nuts & Raisins*	(8 oz.)	1 LFMk, 2½ Fr	260	120
Weight Watchers à la Francais Nonfat*	(6 oz.)	1 SMk	90	130
Weight Watchers Nonfat*	(8 oz.)	1 SMk, 1 Fr	150	120
Yoplait Custard-Style*	(6 oz.)	1 LFMk, 1 Fr	180	95
Orange, Yoplait Custard-Style*	(6 oz.)	1 LFMk, 1 Fr	190	95
Orchard Fruit, Dannon Hearty Nuts & Raisins*	(8 oz.)	1 LFMk, 2½ Fr	260	120
Peach				
Colombo*	(8 oz.)	1 LFMk, 2 Fr	230	160
Dannon Fruit-on-the-Bottom*	(8 oz.)	1 LFMk, 2 Fr	240	120

*Contains concentrated sources of carbohydrates

Food	Portion	Exchanges	Calories	Sodium (mg)
Weight Watchers à la Francais Nonfat*	(6 oz.)	1 SMk	90	130
Weight Watchers Nonfat*	(8 oz.)	1 SMk, 1 Fr	150	120
Yoplait Custard-Style*	(6 oz.)	1 LFMk, 1 Fr	190	95
Yoplait 150*	(6 oz.)	1 SMk, 1 Fr	150	5
Piña Colada				
Dannon Fruit-on-the-Bottom*	(8 oz.)	1 LFMk, 2 Fr	240	120
Yoplait Custard-Style*	(6 oz.)	1 LFMk, 1 Fr	190	95
Pineapple, Yoplait Custard-Style*	(6 oz.)	1 LFMk, 1 Fr	190	95
Plain				
Colombo, Nonfat Lite	(6 oz.)	1 SMk	83	135
Dannon (8 oz.)				
Low-Fat		1 LFMk	140	160
Non-Fat		1 SMk	110	160
Lite-Line Lowfat, Swiss-Style 1½% milkfat	(1 cup)	1½ SMk	140	150
Meadow Gold Lowfat, 2% milkfat	(1 cup)	1 LFMk, ½ SMk	160	160
Mountain High	(1 cup)	1½ LFMk	200	140
Weight Watchers, Nonfat	(8 oz.)	1 SMk	90	130
Yoplait Original	(6 oz.)	1 LFMk	130	120
Raspberries & Cream, Yoplait Yo Creme*	(5 oz.)	½ LFMk, 2 Fr, 1 Fat	230	80
Raspberry				
Dannon Extra-Smooth*	(4.4 oz.)	½ LFMk, 1 Fr	130	80
Dannon Fresh Flavors*	(8 oz.)	1 SMk, 1½ Fr, ½ Fat	200	160
Dannon Fruit-on-the-Bottom*	(8 oz.)	1 LFMk, 2 Fr	240	120
Weight Watchers à la Francais Nonfat*	(6 oz.)	1 SMk	90	130
Weight Watchers Nonfat*	(8 oz.)	1 SMk, 1 Fr	150	120
Yoplait Custard-Style*	(6 oz.)	1 LFMk, 1 Fr	190	95
Yoplait 150*	(6 oz.)	1 SMk, 1 Fr	150	5
Yoplait Original*	(6 oz.)	1 LFMk, 1 Fr	190	105
Strawberries Romanoff, Yoplait Yo Creme*	(5 oz.)	½ LFMk, 2 Fr, 1 Fat	220	80
Strawberry				
Colombo*	(8 oz.)	1 LFMk, 2 Fr	230	160
*Nonfat Lite**		1 SMk, 2 Fr	200	110

*Contains concentrated sources of carbohydrates

Food	Portion	Exchanges	Calories	Sodium (mg)
Yogurt, cont.				
Dannon Extra-Smooth*	(4.4 oz.)	½ LFMk, 1 Fr	130	80
Dannon Fresh Flavors*	(8 oz.)	1 SMk, 1½ Fr, ½ Fat	200	160
Dannon Fruit-on-the-Bottom*	(8 oz.)	1 LFMk, 2 Fr	240	120
Weight Watchers à la Francais Nonfat*	(6 oz.)	1 SMk	90	130
Weight Watchers Nonfat*	(8 oz.)	1 SMk, 1 Fr	150	120
Yoplait Custard-Style*	(6 oz.)	1 LFMk, 1 Fr	190	95
Yoplait 150*	(6 oz.)	1 SMk, 1 Fr	150	5
Yoplait Original*	(6 oz.)	1 LFMk, 1 Fr	190	105
Strawberry w/Almonds, Yoplait 150*	(6 oz.)	1 SMk, 1½ Fr, ½ Fat	210	90
Strawberry Banana				
Dannon Fresh Flavors*	(8 oz.)	1 SMk, 1½ Fr, ½ Fat	200	160
Dannon Fruit-on-the-Bottom*	(8 oz.)	1 LFMk, 2 Fr	240	120
Weight Watchers à la Francais Nonfat*	(6 oz.)	1 SMk	90	130
Weight Watchers Nonfat*	(8 oz.)	1 SMk, 1 Fr	150	120
Yoplait Custard-Style*	(6 oz.)	1 LFMk, 1 Fr	190	95
Yoplait 150*	(6 oz.)	1 LFMk, 2 Fr	240	90
Strawberry Vanilla, Colombo*	(8 oz.)	1 LFMk, 2½ Fr	260	160
Tropical Fruits, Yoplait 150*	(6 oz.)	1 LFMk, 2 Fr	230	90
Vanilla				
Colombo (8 oz.)				
*French**		1 LFMk, 1 Fr, ½ Fat	210	140
*Nonfat Lite**		1 SMk, 1 Fr	160	130
Dannon Fresh Flavors*	(8 oz.)	1 SMk, 1½ Fr, ½ Fat	200	140
	(4.4 oz.)	½ LFMk, 1 Fr	110	90
Dannon Hearty Nuts & Raisins*	(8 oz.)	1 LFMk, 2½ Fr	270	120
Weight Watchers à la Francais Nonfat*	(6 oz.)	1 SMk	90	130
Weight Watchers Nonfat	(8 oz.)	1 SMk, 1 Fr	150	120
Yoplait Custard-Style*	(6 oz.)	1 LFMk, 1 Fr	180	110
Yogurt Drinks, Dan'up*	(8 oz.)	1 LFMk, 1 Fr	190	110

*Contains concentrated sources of carbohydrates

9

CONDIMENTS, SALAD DRESSINGS, SAUCES, OILS, & GRAVIES

Many condiments are free exchanges, but remember to discuss with your dietitian the number of servings allowed per day. Many condiments contain oils, so condiments should always be considered in calculating exchange values.

It's believed that saturated fat in the diet raises blood cholesterol levels. Polyunsaturated fat helps lower blood cholesterol levels (but only by half as much as saturated fats raise it). The American Heart Association recommends that no more than 30% of calories in your diet should be from fat sources. Choose your fats wisely.

Compare these common fats and oils before you use them. The information below is provided by the U.S. National Heart, Lung, and Blood Institute.

Type of Oil or Fat	*Percent of Polyunsaturated Fat*	*Percent of Saturated Fat*
Safflower Oil	74%	9%
Sunflower Oil	64%	10%
Corn Oil	58%	13%
Average vegetable oil (soybean plus cottonseed)	40%	13%
Olive oil	9%	14%
Peanut oil	30%	19%
Chicken fat (Schmaltz)	26%	29%
Average vegetable shortening	20%	32%
Lard	12%	40%
Beef fat	4%	48%
Butter	4%	61%
Palm oil	2%	81%
Coconut oil	2%	86%

Consider using reduced-calorie condiments if you want more spread with less fat. Some gravies also are high in fat, so use them sparingly.

Food	Portion	Exchanges	Calories	Sodium (mg)
■ Condiments				
Apple Butter, Bama	(2 tbsp.)	½ F	25	5
Bacon Bits, General Mills, Bac Os	(3 tbsp.)	1 V, 1 LMT	90	390
Dip (non-dairy)				
Ortega, Acapulco Dip	(1 oz.)	free	8	0
Wise				
Jalapeño Flavored Bean	(3 tbsp.)	½ S	38	150
Taco	(2 tbsp.)	½ V	12	115
Ketchup (1 tbsp.)				
Hunt's No Salt Added		free	20	5
Weight Watchers		free	8	110
Mayonnaise (1 tbsp.)				
Bama		2 Fat	100	65
Bennett's Real		2½ Fat	110	65
Best Foods Real		2 Fat	100	80
Hellmann's Real		2 Fat	100	80
Mayonnaise & Spreads (reduced-calorie) (1 tbsp.)				
Best Foods				
Mayonnaise		1 Fat	50	120
Sandwich spread		1 Fat	50	170
Hellmann's				
Light Mayonnaise		1 Fat	50	120
Sandwich spread		1 Fat	50	170
Weight Watchers				
Cholesterol Free		1 Fat	40	80
Low Sodium		1 Fat	40	35
Regular		1 Fat	40	80
Mustard (1 tsp.)				
Chun King		free	4	65
French's				
Bold 'n' Spicy		free	6	50
Dijon		free	8	140
Prepared Yellow		free	4	60
Grey Poupon Dijon		free	18	450
La Choy Chinese Hot		free	8	130
Peppers & Chiles				
Ortega (1 oz.)				
Green Chiles (whole, diced, strips, sliced)		free	10	20
Hot Peppers (whole, diced)		free	8	0
Jalapeño Peppers (whole, diced)		free	10	20
Tomatoes & Jalapeños		free	8	120

Food	Portion	Exchanges	Calories	Sodium (mg)
Vlasic (1 oz.)				
Hot Banana Pepper Rings		free	4	465
Mexican Jalapeño Peppers		free	8	380
Mild Cherry Peppers		free	8	410
Mild Greek Pepperoncini		free	4	450
Pickles				
Vlasic (1 oz.)				
Hot & Spicy Garlic Mix		free	4	380
Kosher Baby Dills; Kosher Crunchy Dills; Kosher Dill Gherkins		free	4	210
Kosher Dill Spears		free	4	175
Lightly Spiced Cocktail Onions		free	4	365
No Garlic Dills		free	4	210
Original Dills		free	2	375
Zesty Crunchy Dills		free	4	250
Zesty Dill Spears		free	4	230
Vlasic Bread & Butter				
*Old Fashioned Chunks**	(2 oz.)	1 Fr	50	220
*Sweet Butter Chips**	(2 oz.)	1 Fr	60	320
*Sweet Butter Stix**	(3 oz.)	1 Fr	54	330
Vlasic Refrigerated Pickles				
*Deli Bread & Butter Chunks**	(2 oz.)	1 Fr	50	240
Half-The-Salt Kosher Crunchy Dills	(1 oz.)	free	4	125
Hamburger Dill Chips	(1 oz.)	free	2	175
Kosher Deli Dills	(1 oz.)	free	4	290
Kosher Dill Spears	(1 oz.)	free	4	120
*Sweet Butter Chips**	(2 oz.)	1 Fr	60	160
Relish				
Vlasic (1 oz.)				
Dill		free	2	415
*Hamburger**		½ Fr	40	255
*Hot Dog**		½ Fr	40	255
*Sweet**		½ Fr	30	220
Syrup				
Aunt Jemima (1 fl. oz.)				
*Butter Lite**		1 Fr	50	65
*Lite**		1 Fr	60	65
Weight Watchers Reduced Calorie*	(1 tbsp.)	1 Fr	60	60

*Contains concentrated sources of carbohydrates

Food	Portion	Exchanges	Calories	Sodium (mg)
Vinegar (1 fl. oz.)				
Regina Red Wine; Red Wine/Garlic; White Wine		free	4	0

■ Salad Dressings

Food	Portion	Exchanges	Calories	Sodium (mg)
Blue Cheese, Weight Watchers Dry Mix	(1 tbsp.)	free	8	110
Caesar, Weight Watchers	(1 tbsp.)	free	4	195
Creamy Italian (1 tbsp.)				
Weight Watchers		1 Fat	50	80
Weight Watchers Dry Mix		free	4	180
French (1 tbsp.)				
Weight Watchers		free	10	170
Weight Watchers Dry Mix		free	4	150
Italian (1 tbsp.)				
Weight Watchers		free	6	310
Weight Watchers Dry Mix		free	8	140
Weight Watchers Reduced-Calorie, Whipped	(1 tbsp.)	1 Fat	35	80
Regular, Bama	(1 tbsp.)	1 Fat	50	105
Russian (1 tbsp.)				
Weight Watchers		1 Fat	50	80
Weight Watchers Dry Mix		free	4	120
Thousand Island (1 tbsp.)				
Weight Watchers		1 Fat	50	80
Weight Watchers Dry Mix		free	4	140
Tomato Vinaigrette, Weight Watchers	(1 tbsp.)	free	8	150

■ Sauces

Food	Portion	Exchanges	Calories	Sodium (mg)
Barbeque Sauce, French's, Cattlemen's Mild*	(1 tbsp.)	½ Fr	25	260
Berry Sauce, Ocean Spray, Whole	(2 oz.)	1½ Fr	90	15
Bolognese Sauce, Fresh Chef	(4 oz.)	1 S, 1 Fat	130	590
Cheese Sauce, Snow's, Welsh Rarebit	(½ cup)	1 HFMt, ½ S, ½ Fat	170	460
Chili Hot Dog Sauce, Wolf	(about ⅙ cup)	1 V, ½ Fat	40	200
Clam Sauce				
Fresh Chef (4 oz.)				
Red		½ S, 1 Fat	90	560

*Contains concentrated sources of carbohydrates

Food	Portion	Exchanges	Calories	Sodium (mg)
White		½ S, 2 Fat	130	640
Cranberry Sauce, Ocean Spray, Jellied	(2 oz.)	1½ Fr	90	15
Diable Sauce, Escoffier	(1 tbsp.)	free	20	160
Enchilada Sauce				
El Molino Hot	(2 tbsp.)	½ V	16	100
Ortega (1 oz.)				
Hot		free	12	280
Mild		free	12	280
Green Chili Sauce				
El Molino Mild	(2 tbsp.)	½ V	10	210
Ortega (1 oz.)				
Hot		free	10	180
Medium		free	8	180
Mild		free	8	180
Lemon Butter Sauce, Weight Watchers, Dry Mix	(1 tbsp.)	free	6	90
Newburg Sauce, Snow's w/Sherry	(⅓ cup)	½ WMk, 1 Fat	120	520
Pesto Sauce, Fresh Chef	(4 oz.)	1 S, 1 MFMt, 1 Fat	630	1020
Picante Sauce				
Ortega	(1 oz.)	free	10	300
Wise	(2 tbsp.)	½ V	12	130
Pizza Sauce				
Contadina (¼ cup)				
w/Cheese		1 V, ½ Fat	40	350
Original Quick & Easy		1 V, ½ Fat	40	350
w/Pepperoni		1V, ½ Fat	45	340
w/Tomato Chunks		1 V	25	280
Ragu (3 tbsp.)				
Extra Tomatoes		1 V	25	190
Quick Chunky		1 V, ½ Fat	45	320
Quick Mushroom		½ V, ½ Fat	40	300
Quick Pepperoni		1 V, ½ Fat	50	330
Quick Sausage		½ V, ½ Fat	40	300
Quick Traditional		½ V, ½ Fat	40	300
Ranchera Salsa, Ortega	(1 oz.)	free	12	250
Sauce Robert, Escoffier	(1 tbsp.)	free	20	70
Soy Sauce, Chun King	(1 tsp.)	free	6	430
Spaghetti Sauce				
Al Fresco Garden	(4 oz.)	½ S, ½ Fr, 1 Fat	100	630
w/Mushrooms		½ S, ½ Fr,1 Fat	100	560

Food	Portion	Exchanges	Calories	Sodium (mg)
Spaghetti Sauce, cont.				
w/Peppers		½ S, ½ Fr, 1 Fat	100	560
Prego	(4 oz.)	½ S, 1 Fr, 1 Fat	140	670
Meat Flavored		½ S, 1 Fr, 1 Fat	150	920
w/Mushrooms		½ S, 1 Fr, 1 Fat	140	640
No Salt Added		½ S, ½ Fr, 1 Fat	100	25
Prego Plus (4 oz.)				
w/Beef Sirloin & Onion		½ S, 1 Fr, ½ LMt, 1 Fat	160	420
w/Sausage & Green Pepper		½ S, 1 Fr, ½ MFMt, 1 Fat	170	480
w/Veal & Sliced Mushrooms		½ S, 1 Fr, ½ MFMt, ½ Fat	150	380
Ragu	(4 oz.)	½ S, ½ V, ½ Fat	80	740
w/Extra Cheese		½ S, ½ V, ½ Fat	80	570
w/Extra Garlic		½ S, ½ V, ½ Fat	80	640
Flavored w/Meat		½ S, ½ V, ½ Fat	80	740
w/Mushrooms		½ S, ½ V, ½ Fat	80	740
Ragu Chunky Gardenstyle (4 oz.)				
Extra Tomatoes, Garlic & Onions		½ S, 1 V, ½ Fat	80	400
Green Peppers & Mushrooms		½ S, 1 V, ½ Fat	80	400
Italian Garden Combinations		½ S, 1 V, ½ Fat	80	400
Mushrooms & Onions		½ S, 1 V, ½ Fat	80	400
Sweet Green & Red Bell Peppers		½ S, 1 V, ½ Fat	80	400
Ragu Extra Thick & Zesty	(4 oz.)	½ S, 1 V, 1 Fat	100	740
Flavored w/Meat		½ S, 1 V, 1 Fat	100	740
w/Mushrooms		½ S, 1 V, 1 Fat	110	740
Ragu Homestyle	(4 oz.)	½ S, ½ V, ½ Fat	70	390
Flavored w/Meat		½ S, ½ V, ½ Fat	70	390
w/Mushrooms		½ S, ½ V, ½ Fat	70	390
Ragu Marinara	(4 oz.)	½ S, 1 V, ½ Fat	90	740
Ragu Thick & Hearty (4 oz.)				
Flavored w/Leaner Ground Beef		½ S, 1½ V, 1 Fat	120	520
w/Mushrooms & Marinara		½ S, 1 V, 1 Fat	110	520
Weight Watchers (⅓ cup)				
Flavored w/Meat		2 V	50	440
w/Mushrooms		2 V	40	430
Steak Sauce (1 tbsp.)				
A.1.		free	12	280
French's*		½ Fr	25	150
Steak Supreme		free	20	25

*Contains concentrated sources of carbohydrates

Food	Portion	Exchanges	Calories	Sodium (mg)
Sweet 'n' Sour Sauce				
Chun King				
*Sauce/Glaze Mix for Sweet 'n' Sour Entree**	(3.8 oz.)	6½ Fr	370	40
*Sweet/Sour Sauce**	(1.8 oz.)	1 Fr	60	420
Contadina, Sweet 'n' Sour International Sauce*	(4 oz.)	2 Fr, ½ Fat	150	430
La Choy Sweet & Sour Sauce	(1 tbsp.)	½ Fr	30	320
Taco Sauce				
El Molino Red Taco Sauce	(2 tbsp.)	½ V	10	170
Ortega (1/10 of pkt.)				
Mild Taco Meat Seasoning		free	9	197
Taco Salsa, Hot		free	10	300
Taco Salsa, Mild		free	10	290
Taco Sauce, Hot		free	12	210
Taco Sauce, Mild		free	12	220
Western-Style Taco Sauce		free	8	180
Tartar Sauce (1 tbsp.)				
Best Foods		1½ Fat	70	220
Hellmann's		1½ Fat	70	220
Weight Watchers		1 Fat	35	80
Tomato Sauce				
Contadina	(½ cup)	2 V	45	520
Italian-Style		1½ V	40	760
Fresh Chef Sauces	(4 oz.)	1 S, 2 Fat	160	690
Hunt's				
w/Bits	(4 oz.)	1 V	30	690
w/Cheese	(4 oz.)	½ LMt, 1 V	45	800
w/Mushrooms	(4 oz.)	1 V	25	710
No Salt Added	(3 oz.)	1 V	26	19
Tomato Paste (2 oz.)				
Contadina		2 V	48	37
Italian		2½ V	70	710
Hunt's		2 V	45	150
Italian-Style		2 V	50	520
No Salt Added		2 V	45	25
Tomato Purée				
Contadina	(½ cup)	2 V	50	80
Hunt's	(2 oz.)	1 V	23	90

*Contains concentrated sources of carbohydrates

Food	Portion	Exchanges	Calories	Sodium (mg)
Tomato Sandwich Sauce				
Hunt's Manwich				
Mexican Flavor	(2.5 oz.)	1 V	35	460
Mexican Flavor, w/Ground Beef on Enriched Hamburger Roll	(5.8 oz.)	1½ S, 1½ MFMt, 1 V, 1 Fat	310	690
Original Flavor	(2.5 oz.)	1 V	35	400
Original Flavor w/Ground Beef on Enriched Hamburger Roll	(5.8 oz.)	1½ S, 1½ MFMt, 1 V, 1 Fat	310	630
Sloppy Joe, Dry Mix	(.25 oz.)	1 V	20	350
Sloppy Joe, Dry Mix w/Tomato Paste, Water, & Ground Beef on Enriched Hamburger Roll	(5.9 oz.)	1½ S, 1½ MFMt, 1½ V, 1 Fat	320	590
Ragu Joe Sauce for Sloppy Joe	(3.5 oz.)	2 V	50	650
Worcestershire Sauce, French's	(1 tbsp.)	free	10	160

■ Oil

Food	Portion	Exchanges	Calories	Sodium (mg)
Buttery Flavor, Wesson	(1 tbsp.)	3 Fat	120	0
Cooking Spray				
Mazola No-Stick	(1-second spray)	free	3	0
Weight Watchers	(1-second spray)	free	2	0
Corn (1 tbsp.)				
Mazola		3 Fat	120	0
Wesson		3 Fat	120	0
Peanut, Planters	(1 tbsp.)	3 Fat	120	0
Popcorn, Planters	(1 tbsp.)	3 Fat	120	0
Vegetable, Wesson	(1 tbsp.)	3 Fat	120	0

■ Gravy

Food	Portion	Exchanges	Calories	Sodium (mg)
Au Jus, Franco-American, canned	(2 oz.)	free	5	290
Beef, Franco-American, canned	(2 oz.)	½ Fat	25	310
Brown				
Franco-American, Brown w/Onions, canned	(2 oz.)	½ Fat	25	340
Pillsbury, Brown, mix	(½ cup)	½ S	30	600
Weight Watchers, Dry Mix	(¼ cup)	free	10	360
w/Mushrooms		free	10	270
w/Onions		free	10	310

Food	Portion	Exchanges	Calories	Sodium (mg)
Chicken				
Franco-American, canned (2 oz.)				
Chicken		1 Fat	50	310
Chicken Giblet		½ Fat	30	300
Pillsbury, Chicken, mix.	(½ cup)	½ S	50	460
Weight Watchers, Chicken, Dry Mix	(½ cup)	free	10	410
Home-Style, Pillsbury, mix	(½ cup)	½ S	30	600
Mushroom, Franco-American, canned	(2 oz.)	½ Fat	25	310
Pork, Franco-American, canned	(2 oz.)	1 Fat	40	350
Turkey, Franco-American, canned	(2 oz.)	½ Fat	30	290

10

NUTS, NUT PRODUCTS, & SEEDS

Nuts are very high in fat, so be sure to measure the amount you consume. An extra handful of nuts can make a big difference.

Peanut butter is not a complete protein source, so eat it with milk and a wheat source such as bread. Ask your dietitian how to balance proteins in your diet.

Food	Portion	Exchanges	Calories	Sodium (mg)
Almonds (1 oz.)				
Fisher Honey Roasted		1 HFMt, 1 Fat	150	75
Planters				
Blanched, Slivered, Whole, or Sliced		½ S, ½ HFMt, 2 Fat	170	0
Dry Roasted		½ S, ½ HFMt, 2 Fat	170	200
Honey Roasted		½ S, ½ HFMt, 2 Fat	170	180
Bars				
Lance				
*Chocolaty Peanut Bar**	(2 oz.)	½ S, 1½ Fr, 1 HFMt, 2 Fat	320	40
*Nut-O-Lunch**	(1 oz.)	½ S, ½ Fr, ½ HFMt, ½ Fat	140	110
*Peanut Bar**	(1¾ oz.)	½ S, 1 Fr, 1 HFMt, 1 Fat	260	80
Planters (1.6 oz.)				
*Honey Roasted Peanut Bar**		½ S, 1 Fr, ½ HFMt, 2 Fat	230	145
*Peanut Bar**		½ S, 1 Fr, 1 HFMt, ½ Fat	230	70
*Sweet 'n' Crunchy Peanut Bar**		½ S, 1 Fr, 1 HFMt, 1 Fat	250	110
Cashews				
Fisher (1 oz.)				
Dry Roasted		1 HFMt, 1 Fat	160	160
Honey Roasted		1 HFMt, 1 Fat	150	70
Oil Roasted Halves		1 HFMt, 1 Fat	160	160
Oil Roasted Lightly Salted		1 HFMt, 1 Fat	160	40
Oil Roasted Whole		1 HFMt, 1 Fat	160	140
Guy's Salted Whole	(1 oz.)	1 MFMt, 2 Fat	170	140
Lance				
Cashews	(1⅛ oz.)	½ S, ½ HFMt, 2 Fat	190	95
*Honey Toasted**	(1⅛ oz.)	½ S, ½ Fr, ½ HFMt, 2 Fat	200	160
*Honey Toasted, Long Tube**	(1⅛ oz.)	½ S, ½ Fr, ½ HFMt, 2 Fat	200	150
Long Tube	(1¼ oz.)	½ S, ½ HFMt, 2½ Fat	200	105
Planters (1 oz.)				
Dry Roasted		½ S, ½ HFMt, 2 Fat	160	230
Dry Roasted Unsalted		½ S, ½ HFMt, 2 Fat	160	0
*Honey Roasted**		1 Fr, ½ HFMt, 1½ Fat	170	170
Oil Roasted, Fancy		½ S, ½ HFMt, 2 Fat	170	135
Oil Roasted Halves		½ S, ½ HFMt, 2 Fat	170	135
Oil Roasted Unsalted Halves		½ S, ½ HFMt, 2 Fat	170	0
Mixed Nuts				
Fisher (1 oz.)				
Dry Roasted		1 HFMt, 1½ Fat	170	110
Honey Roasted Peanut/Cashew Mix		1 HFMt, 1 Fat	150	90
Oil Roasted Cashews & Almonds		1 HFMt, 1½ Fat	170	140
Oil Roasted Lightly Salted		1 HFMt, 1½ Fat	170	35

*Contains concentrated sources of carbohydrates

Food	Portion	Exchanges	Calories	Sodium (mg)
Mixed Nuts, cont.				
Oil Roasted Lightly Salted Cashews & Almonds		1 HFMt, 1½ Fat	170	40
Oil Roasted, No Peanuts		1 HFMt, 1½ Fat	170	115
Guy's, Mixed w/Peanuts	(1 oz.)	1 HFMt, 2 Fat	180	140
Planters (1 oz.)				
Dry Roasted		½ S, ½ HFMt, 2 Fat	160	250
Dry Roasted Unsalted		½ S, ½ HFMt, 2 Fat	170	0
Fruit 'n' Nut Mix		1 Fr, ½ HFMt, 1 Fat	150	90
Honey Roasted Cashews & Peanuts		½ S, ½ HFMt, 2 Fat	170	170
Oil Roasted		½ S, ½ HFMt, 2½ Fat	180	130
Oil Roasted Deluxe		½ S, ½ HFMt, 2½ Fat	180	135
Oil Roasted Unsalted		½ S, ½ HFMt, 2½ Fat	180	0
Tavern Nuts		½ S, ½ HFMt, 2 Fat	170	65
Peanut Butter (2 tbsp.)				
Bama				
Creamy		1 HFMt, 2 Fat	200	140
Crunchy		1 HFMt, 2 Fat	200	115
Skippy				
Creamy		2 HFMt	190	150
Super Chunk		2 HFMt	190	130
Peanuts				
Fisher (1 oz.)				
Dry Roasted		1 HFMt, 1 Fat	160	230
Dry Roasted, Lightly Salted		1 HFMt, 1 Fat	160	85
Dry Roasted, Unsalted		1 HFMt, 1 Fat	160	0
Honey Roasted		1 HFMt, 1 Fat	150	100
Honey Roasted, Dry Roasted		1 HFMt, 1 Fat	150	90
Oil Roasted Lightly Salted, Party		1 HFMt, 1½ Fat	170	35
Oil Roasted Lightly Salted, Spanish		1 HFMt, 1½ Fat	170	55
Oil Roasted, Spanish		1 HFMt, 1½ Fat	170	120
Guy's (1 oz.)				
Dry Roasted		1 MFMt, 2 Fat	170	310
Salted Spanish		1 MFMt, 2 Fat	170	170
Lance				
Dry Roasted	(1⅛ oz.)	½ S, 1 HFMt, 1 Fat	190	160
*Honey Toasted**	(1¼ oz.)	½ Fr, 1 HFMt, 1½ Fat	210	220
Redskin	(1⅛ oz.)	½ S, 1 HFMt, 2 Fat	192	90
Roasted, in shell	(1¾ oz.)	½ S, 1 HFMt, 1 Fat	190	0
Salted	(1⅛ oz.)	½ S, 1 HFMt, 1 Fat	190	95
Salted, Long Tube	(3 oz.)	½ S, 1½ HFMt, 1½ Fat	240	120

*Contains concentrated sources of carbohydrates

Food	Portion	Exchanges	Calories	Sodium (mg)
Planters (1 oz.)				
Dry Roasted		½ S, ½ HFMt, 2 Fat	160	250
Dry Roasted Spanish		½ S, ½ HFMt, 2 Fat	160	200
Dry Roasted Unsalted		½ S, ½ HFMt, 2 Fat	170	0
Honey Roasted		½ S, ½ HFMt, 2 Fat	170	180
Honey Roasted, Dry Roasted		½ S, ½ HFMt, 2 Fat	160	90
Oil Roasted Cocktail		½ S, ½ HFMt, 2 Fat	170	160
Oil Roasted Cocktail, Unsalted		½ S, ½ HFMt, 2 Fat	170	0
Oil Roasted Salted		½ S, ½ HFMt, 2 Fat	170	160
Oil Roasted Spanish		½ S, ½ HFMt, 2 Fat	170	150
Raw Spanish		½ S, ½ HFMt, 1½ Fat	150	0
Roasted-In-Shell, Salted		½ S, ½ HFMt, 2 Fat	160	160
Roasted-In-Shell, Unsalted		½ S, ½ HFMt, 2 Fat	160	0
*Sweet 'n' Crunchy**		1 Fr, ½ HFMt, 1 Fat	140	20
Weight Watchers	(1 pouch)	1 HFMt	100	5
Pecans (1-oz. edible portion)				
Diamond		4 Fat	182	(N/A)
Fisher, Honey Roasted		4 Fat	170	100
Planters, Chips, Halves, Pieces		4 Fat	190	0
Pistachios				
Lance	(1⅛ oz.)	½ S, ½ HFMt, 2 Fat	180	230
Planters, Dry Roasted; and Planters, Red	(1 oz.)	½ S, ½ HFMt, 2 Fat	170	250
Walnuts (1-oz. edible portion)				
Diamond		½ HFMt, 3 Fat	192	(N/A)
Planters				
Black		1 HFMt, 2 Fat	180	0
English, Whole, Halves & Pieces		½ HFMt, 3 Fat	190	0
Sesame Seeds				
Planters (1 oz.)				
Dry Roasted Mix		½ S, ½ HFMt, 1½ Fat	160	330
Oil Roasted Mix		½ S, ½ HFMt, 2 Fat	160	220
Sunflower Nuts				
Fisher (1 oz.)				
Dry Roasted		1 HFMt, 1½ Fat	170	110
Dry Roasted Unsalted		1 HFMt, 1½ Fat	170	0
Planters (1 oz.)				
Dry Roasted		½ S, ½ HFMt, 2 Fat	160	260
Dry Roasted Unsalted		½ S, ½ HFMt, 2 Fat	170	0
Oil Roasted		½ S, ½ HFMt, 2 Fat	170	130
Sunflower Seeds, Planters	(1 oz.)	½ S, ½ HFMt, 2 Fat	160	30

*Contains concentrated sources of carbohydrates

11

SUGAR-FREE SWEETS

You need not give up sweets if you choose sweets without sucrose. Sweeteners such as aspartame, saccharine, fructose, and sorbitol can be used. Ask your dietitian to explain the differences between these products and to describe any problems that these items might cause. Your dietitian also should discuss limitations on free exchanges for sugar-free foods and beverages.

Enjoy the products that are allowed by your dietitian; sugar-free sweets will let you enjoy many foods and snacks that you might not otherwise be able to choose. Here is just a sampling of the many sugar-free treats that are available.

Food	Portion	Exchanges	Calories	Sodium (mg)
Beverages				
Coffee, Instant	(1 tsp.)	free	2	< 5
Diet Coke	(12 oz.)	free	1	8
Diet Pepsi	(12 oz.)	free	1	2
Fruit Drinks, Sweet 'n' Low: Cherry, Fruit Punch, Grape Drink, Lemonade	(8 oz.)	½ Fr	30	19
Shake Mix				
Chocolate, Diet-Trim	(12–14 oz.)	1 SMk	70	145
Chocolate, Shapely Shake	(12 oz.)	1 SMk	60	140
Vanilla, Diet-Trim	(12–14 oz.)	1 SMk	70	180
Vanilla, Shapely Shake	(12 oz.)	1 SMk	60	124
Cake, Sweet 'n' Low mix (1/10 cake)				
Banana		1 S, ½ Fat	90	40
Chocolate		1 S, ½ Fat	90	40
Gingerbread		1 S, ½ Fat	90	20
Lemon		1 S, ½ Fat	90	40
Mint Chocolate		1 S, ½ Fat	90	40
White		1 S, ½ Fat	90	40
Yellow		1 S, ½ Fat	90	40
Candy & Mints				
Mints, Breath Savers	(1 piece)	free	8	0
Custard, Mousse, & Pudding (½ cup)				
Butterscotch Pudding, Royal Instant (prepared w/ 2% low-fat milk)		½ LFMk, ½ S	100	470
Cheesecake Mousse, Sans Sucre		½ SMk, ½ Fat	73	180
Chocolate Custard, Sweet 'n' Low Mix (prepared w/ skim milk)		1 SMk	70	115
Chocolate Mousse, Sans Sucre		1 LFMk	75	77
Chocolate Pudding, Royal Instant (prepared w/ 2% low-fat milk)		½ LFMk, ½ S	110	480
Lemon Custard Mix, Sweet 'n' Low (prepared w/ skim milk)		1 SMK	70	145
Lemon Mousse, Sans Sucre		½ LFMk	70	49
Strawberry Mousse, Sans Sucre		½ LFMk	70	49
Vanilla Custard Mix, Sweet 'n' Low (prepared w/ skim milk)		1 SMk	70	145
Vanilla Pudding, Royal Instant (prepared w/ 2% low-fat milk)		½ LFMk, ½ S	100	470
Frostings & Toppings, Sweet 'n' Low (1 tbsp.)				
Chocolate Frosting & Fudge Topping Mix		1 Fat	60	20
White Frosting Mix		1 Fat	60	20

Food	Portion	Exchanges	Calories	Sodium (mg)
Gelatin, Royal Desserts				
Cherry, Lime, Orange, Raspberry, Strawberry	(½ cup)	free	6	70–75
Gum (1 piece)				
Carefree Bubblegum				
Fruit, Strawberry, Wintergreen		free	10	0
Carefree Gum				
Cinnamon, Fruit, Peppermint, Spearmint		free	8	0
Sweeteners				
Pillsbury				
Sprinkle Sweet	(1 tsp.)	free	2	1
*Sweet *10*	(⅛ tsp.)	free	0	1½
Sweet 'n' Low	(1 pkt.)	free	4	5
Weight Watchers	(1 pkt.)	free	4	30

12

DESSERTS & SWEETS

When diabetes is under very good control, an occasional sweet might be allowed by your dietitian. But if you eat sweets without proper guidance, you could upset your body's metabolism. It's best to share all information with your dietitian before making a decision.

For cakes, shakes, and other foods made from mixes, exchanges are based upon preparing each food according to package directions.

The products listed here represent a few of the many once-in-a-while treats on the market.

Food	Portion	Exchanges	Calories	Sodium (mg)
■ Brownies & Gingerbread (made from mixes)				
Brownie Mix, Pillsbury (one 2″ square)				
Black Forest*		1 S, ½ Fr, 1 Fat	160	100
Double Fudge*		1 S, ½ Fr, 1 Fat	160	105
Family-Size Fudge*		½ S, 1 Fr, 1 Fat	150	95
Family-Size Walnut*		1 S, 1½ Fat	150	90
Fudge*		1 S, ½ Fr, 1 Fat	150	100
Rocky Road Fudge*		1 S, ½ Fr, 1½ Fat	170	100
Fudge Jumbles, Pillsbury (1 bar)				
Chocolate Chip Oatmeal*		½ S, ½ Fr, ½ Fat	100	55
Peanut Butter Oatmeal*		½ S, ½ Fr, ½ Fat	100	55
Gingerbread				
Nabisco, Dromedary*	(one 2″ square)	½ S, 1 Fr, ½ Fat	100	190
Pillsbury*	(one 3″ square)	1 S, 1½ Fr, ½ Fat	190	310
■ Bars, Brownies, & Snack Cakes (prepared)				
Angel Food Break Cake	(1 oz.)	1 S	70	100
Apple Sandwich Break Cake*	(.83 oz.)	½ S, ½ Fr, ½ Fat	90	70
Banana, Hostess Suzy Q's*	(2.25 oz.)	½ S, 2 Fr, 1½ Fat	240	230
Blueberry Sandwich Break Cake*	(.83 oz.)	½ S, ½ Fr, ½ Fat	100	85
Brownie				
Break Cake, Fudge*	(2.8 oz.)	1 S, 2 Fr, 3½ Fat	370	260
Fudge, Plantation*	(3 oz.)	1 S, 2½ Fr, 3 Fat	370	(N/A)
Butterscotch Chocolate Chip Bar, Kellogg's Rice Krispies*	(1 bar)	½ S, 1 Fr, ½ Fat	120	60
Carrot Break Cake*	(3.5 oz.)	1 S, 3 Fr, 2½ Fat	370	380
Chocolate				
Break Cake Chocolate Cupcakes*	(2 cupcakes)	1 S, 3 Fr, 2 Fat	350	330
Figurines 100 Diet Bar (1 bar)				
*Chocolate**		½ S, ½ Fr, 1 Fat	100	45
*Chocolate Caramel**		½ S, ½ Fr, 1 Fat	100	55
*Chocolate Peanut Butter**		½ S, ½ Fr, 1 Fat	100	45
*S'Mores**		½ S, ½ Fr, 1 Fat	100	45
Hostess				
*Choco Bliss**	(1.75 oz.)	½ S, 1½ Fr, 1½ Fat	200	130
*Choco-Diles**	(2 oz.)	½ S, 2 Fr, 2 Fat	240	180
*Cup Cakes, Chocolate**	(1.75 oz.)	½ S, 1½ Fr, 1½ Fat	170	250

*Contains concentrated sources of carbohydrates

Food	Portion	Exchanges	Calories	Sodium (mg)
*Ding/Dongs/King Dongs**	(1.33 oz.)	½ S, 1 Fr, 1½ Fat	170	130
*Suzy Q's, Chocolate**	(2.25 oz.)	½ S, 2½ Fr, 1½ Fat	250	260
Kellogg's Rice Krispies Bars (1 bar)				
*Chocolate Chip**		½ S, 1 Fr, ½ Fat	120	110
*Cocoa Krispies Chocolate Chip**		½ S, 1 Fr, ½ Fat	120	110
Crumb Cake, Hostess*	(1.5 oz.)	½ S, 1½ Fr, 1 Fat	160	100
Dessert Cup, Hostess*	(1 oz.)	½ S, 1 Fr	90	190
Filled Twins, Break Cake*	(2 twins)	1 S, 2½ Fr, 1½ Fat	300	240
Fruit				
Break Cake				
*Fruit 'n' Honey Bar**	(.83 oz.)	½ S, ½ Fr, ½ Fat	90	65
*Supreme Fruit Cake**	(1 oz.)	1 Fr, 1 Fat	110	(N/A)
Fleetwood, Fruit & Honey Bars	(2 units)	1 S, 1 Fr, 1 Fat	180	390
Hostess, Fruit Loaf*	(5 oz.)	1½ S, 3½ Fr, 1½ Fat	400	520
Fudge Bar, Fleetwood*	(2 bars)	1 S, 1 Fr, 1½ Fat	210	240
HoHo's, Hostess*	(1 oz.)	½ S, ½ Fr, 1 Fat	120	70
Hoot 'n' Toots Break Cake*	(3.25 oz.)	1 S, 4 Fr, 3 Fat	450	260
Hostess O's*	(2.25 oz.)	1 S, 1 Fr, 1½ Fat	220	250
Lil' Angels, Hostess*	(1 oz.)	½ S, 1 Fr	90	120
Oatmeal Creme Cake, Coosa*	(1⅛ oz.)	½ S, 1 Fr, 1 Fat	140	180
Orange Cup Cake, Hostess*	(1.5 oz.)	½ S, 1 Fr, 1 Fat	150	140
Peanut				
Kellogg's Rice Krispies Bar (1 bar)				
*Peanut Butter**		1 S, 1 Fat	130	115
*Peanut Chocolate Chip**		1 S, 1 Fat	130	60
Pecan Twirls, Pet*	(1 oz.)	½ S, ½ Fr, 1 Fat	110	75
Pudding Cake*	(1.75 oz.)	½ S, 1½ Fr, 1 Fat	170	200
Raisin, Kellogg's Rice Krispies Bar*	(1 bar)	½ S, 1 Fr, ½ Fat	120	110
Raspberry Sandwich Break Cake*	(.83 oz.)	½ S, ½ Fr, ½ Fat	100	90
Sno Balls, Hostess*	(1.5 oz.)	1 Fr, ½ Fat	80	90
Tiger Tail, Hostess*	(1.5 oz.)	½ S, 1½ Fr, ½ Fat	140	160
Twinkies, Hostess*	(1.5 oz.)	½ S, 1½ Fr, ½ Fat	140	180
Vanilla, Figurines 100 Diet Bar*	(1 bar)	½ S, ½ Fr, 1 Fat	100	45

*Contains concentrated sources of carbohydrates

Food	Portion	Exchanges	Calories	Sodium (mg)
■ Cakes (made from mixes)				
Angel Food, Traditional, General Mills*	(1/12 pkg.)	2 S	130	170
Apple				
General Mills Snackin', Applesauce Raisin*	(1/9 pkg.)	1 S, 1 Fr, 1 Fat	190	260
General Mills Supermoist, Apple Cinnamon*	(1/12 cake)	1 S, 1½ Fr, 2 Fat	250	280
Pillsbury Coffee Cake, Apple Cinnamon*	(1/8 cake)	1 S, 1½ Fr, 1½ Fat	240	160
Pillsbury Streusel Swirl, Dutch Apple*	(1/16 cake)	1 S, 1½ Fr, 2 Fat	260	200
Banana				
General Mills Snackin', Banana Walnut*	(1/9 pkg.)	1 S, 1 Fr, 1½ Fat	200	260
Pillsbury Plus*	(1/12 cake)	1 S, 1½ Fr, 2 Fat	250	290
Boston Cream, Pillsbury Bundt*	(1/16 cake)	1 S, 1½ Fr, 2 Fat	270	310
Butter				
General Mills Snackin', Butter Recipe Chocolate*	(1/12 pkg.)	1 S, 1½ Fr, 2½ Fat	270	450
General Mills Supermoist (1/12 cake)				
*Butter Brickle**		1 S, 1½ Fr, 2 Fat	260	280
*Butter Pecan**		1 S, 1½ Fr, 2 Fat	250	320
*Butter Recipe Yellow**		1 S, 1½ Fr, 2 Fat	260	350
Carrot				
General Mills Supermoist*	(1/12 cake)	1 S, 1 Fr, 2½ Fat	260	280
Pillsbury Plus Carrot 'n' Spice*	(1/12 cake)	1 S, 1½ Fr, 2 Fat	260	330
Cheesecake, Nabisco Royal No-Bake (1/8 cake)				
Lite*		½ S, ½ Fr, ½ LFMk, 1½ Fat	210	380
Real*		½ S, 1 Fr, ½ WMk, 1 Fat	280	370
Cherry				
General Mills Supermoist, Cherry Chip*	(1/12 cake)	1 S, 1½ Fr, ½ Fat	190	270
Pillsbury Bundt, Black Forest Cherry*	(1/16 cake)	1 S, 1½ Fr, 1½ Fat	240	310
Chocolate				
General Mills Angel Food*	(1/12 pkg.)	2 S	150	300

*Contains concentrated sources of carbohydrates

Food	Portion	Exchanges	Calories	Sodium (mg)
General Mills Snackin' (1/9 pkg.)				
*German Chocolate Coconut Pecan**		1 S, 1 Fr, 1 Fat	190	260
*Golden Chocolate Chip**		1 S, 1 Fr, 1 Fat	190	260
General Mills Supermoist (1/12 cake)				
*Chocolate Chip**		1 S, 1½ Fr, 2½ Fat	280	300
*Chocolate Chocolate Chip**		1 S, 1½ Fr, 2 Fat	250	400
*Chocolate Fudge**		1 S, 1 Fr, 2½ Fat	260	450
*German Chocolate**		1 S, 1 Fr, 2½ Fat	260	420
*Milk Chocolate**		1 S, 1 Fr, 2½ Fat	260	350
*Sour Cream Chocolate**		1 S, 1 Fr, 2½ Fat	260	430
Pillsbury Bundt (1/16 cake)				
*Chocolate Macaroon**		1 S, 1½ Fr, 2 Fat	250	300
*Chocolate Mousse**		1 S, 1½ Fr, 1½ Fat	230	310
Pillsbury Plus (1/12 cake)				
*Chocolate Chip**		1 S, 1 Fr, 3 Fat	270	290
*Chocolate Mint**		1 S, 1 Fr, 2½ Fat	250	370
*Dark Chocolate**		1 S, 1 Fr, 2½ Fat	250	380
*German Chocolate**		1 S, 1½ Fr, 2 Fat	250	340
Cinnamon, Pillsbury Streusel Swirl*	(1/16 cake)	1 S, 1½ Fr, 2 Fat	260	200
Coffee Cake, Aunt Jemima Easy Mix*	(1/8 cake)	1 S, 1 Fr, 1 Fat	170	270
Date Nut Roll, Nabisco Dromedary	(½″ slice)	½ S, ½ Fr, ½ Fat	80	160
Devil's Food, General Mills Supermoist*	(1/12 cake)	1 S, 1½ Fr, 2½ Fat	270	430
Fudge, Pillsbury Bundt, Tunnel of*	(1/16 cake)	1 S, 1½ Fr, 2 Fat	270	310
Lemon				
General Mills Angel Food, Lemon Custard*	(1/12 pkg.)	2 S	150	300
General Mills Supermoist	(1/12 cake)	1 S, 1½ Fr, 2 Fat	260	280
Pillsbury Bundt (1/16 cake)				
Lemon Blueberry		1 S, 1 Fr, 1½ Fat	200	270
Tunnel of Lemon		1 S, 2 Fr, 1½ Fat	270	300
Pillsbury Streusel Swirl	(1/16 cake)	1 S, 1½ Fr, 2 Fat	270	340
Marble, General Mills Supermoist*	(1/12 cake)	1 S, 1½ Fr, 2 Fat	260	300
Mocha, Pillsbury Plus*	(1/12 cake)	1 S, 1 Fr, 2½ Fat	250	380

*Contains concentrated sources of carbohydrates

Food	Portion	Exchanges	Calories	Sodium (mg)
Cakes (made from mixes), cont.				
Oats 'n' Brown Sugar, Pillsbury Plus*	(1/12 cake)	1 S, 1½ Fr, 2 Fat	260	310
Pecan Brown Sugar, Pillsbury Streusel Swirl*	(1/16 cake)	1 S, 1½ Fr, 2 Fat	260	200
Pineapple Cream, Pillsbury Bundt*	(1/16 cake)	1 S, 1½ Fr, 2 Fat	260	300
Pound				
Nabisco Dromedary*	(½″ slice)	1 S, ½ Fr, 1 Fat	150	160
Pillsbury Bundt*	(1/16 cake)	1 S, 1 Fr, 2 Fat	230	260
Spice, General Mills Supermoist*	(1/12 cake)	1 S, 1½ Fr, 2 Fat	250	320
Strawberry				
General Mills Angel Food*	(½ pkg.)	2 S	150	260
Pillsbury Plus*	(1/12 cake)	1 S, 1½ Fr, 2 Fat	260	300
Vanilla, Golden, General Mills Snackin'*	(1/12 pkg.)	1 S, 1 Fr, 3 Fat	280	280
White				
General Mills Angel Food*	(1/12 pkg.)	2 S	150	300
General Mills Supermoist, Sour Cream*	(1/12 cake)	1 S, 1½ Fr, ½ Fat	180	300
Yellow, General Mills Supermoist*	(1/12 cake)	1 S, 1½ Fr, 2 Fat	250	30

■ Cakes (prepared)

Food	Portion	Exchanges	Calories	Sodium (mg)
Black Forest, Weight Watchers*	(3 oz.)	1 S, 1 Fr, 1 Fat	180	270
Blueberry Pound, Weight Watchers*	(2.5 oz.)	1 S, 1 Fr, 1 Fat	180	105
Boston Cream, Pepperidge Farm Supreme*	(2⅞ oz.)	1 S, 1½ Fr, 2½ Fat	290	190
Butter Pound, Pepperidge Farm Old-Fashioned	(1 oz.)	1 S, 1 Fat	120	140
Butterscotch Pecan, Pepperidge Farm Layer*	(1⅝ oz.)	1½ Fr, 1½ Fat	160	110
Carrot				
Pepperidge Farm Old Fashioned, w/Cream Cheese Icing*	(1⅜ oz.)	1 Fr, 1½ Fat	130	140
Weight Watchers*	(3 oz.)	1 S, ½ Fr, 1½ Fat	180	340
Cheesecake, Weight Watchers*	(3.9 oz.)	½ S, 1 Fr, ½ LMt, ½ SMk, 1 Fat	210	220

*Contains concentrated sources of carbohydrates

Food	Portion	Exchanges	Calories	Sodium (mg)
Strawberry		1½ Fr, ½ LMt, ½ SMk, ½ Fat	180	220
Chocolate				
Pepperidge Farm Layer (1⅝ oz.)				
*Chocolate Fudge**		1½ Fr, 2 Fat	180	140
*Chocolate Mint**		1½ Fr, 2 Fat	170	140
*German Chocolate**		1½ Fr, 2 Fat	180	170
Pepperidge Farm Supreme				
*Chocolate**	(2⅞ oz.)	1 S, 1½ Fr, 3 Fat	300	140
*Dutch Chocolate**	(1¾ oz.)	1½ Fr, 2 Fat	190	115
Weight Watchers (2.5 oz.)				
*Chocolate**		1 S, 1 Fr, 1 Fat	180	290
*German Chocolate**		1 S, 1 Fr, 1½ Fat	190	350
Coconut, Pepperidge Farm Layer*	(1⅝ oz.)	1½ Fr, 2 Fat	180	140
Devil's Food, Pepperidge Farm Layer*	(1⅝ oz.)	1½ Fr, 2 Fat	170	120
Golden, Pepperidge Farm Layer*	(1⅝ oz.)	1½ Fr, 2 Fat	180	110
Lemon Coconut, Pepperidge Farm Supreme*	(3 oz.)	1 S, 1½ Fr, 2½ Fat	280	220
Peach Melba, Pepperidge Farm Supreme*	(3⅛ oz.)	1 S, 2 Fr, 1½ Fat	270	135
Pineapple Creme, Pepperidge Farm Supreme*	(2 oz.)	1 S, 1 Fr, 1½ Fat	190	130
Raspberry Mocha, Pepperidge Farm Supreme*	(3⅛ oz.)	1 S, 1½ Fr, 3 Fat	310	170
Strawberry				
Pepperidge Farm Supreme, Strawberry Cream*	(2 oz.)	2 Fr, 1½ Fat	190	120
Weight Watchers Strawberry Shortcake*	(3 oz.)	1 S, 1 Fr, 1 Fat	160	165
Vanilla, Pepperidge Farm Layer*	(1⅝ oz.)	1½ Fr, 2 Fat	170	115

■ Cookies

Unless otherwise noted, the number in parentheses indicates the number of whole cookies per portion.

Food	Portion	Exchanges	Calories	Sodium (mg)
Animal Crackers				
Barnum's*	(11)	1 S, ½ Fr, ½ Fat	130	120
Sunshine*	(14)	½ S, 1 Fr, ½ Fat	120	180
Almond Supreme, Pepperidge Farm Special Collection*	(2)	½ S, ½ Fr, 2 Fat	140	45

*Contains concentrated sources of carbohydrates

Food	Portion	Exchanges	Calories	Sodium (mg)
Cookies, cont.				
Apple				
Lance Apple Cinnamon*	(1 oz.)	½ S, 1 Fr, ½ Fat	120	90
Nabisco Apple Newtons*	(1)	½ S, 1 Fr, ½ Fat	110	45
Nabisco Almost Home Family Style, Iced Dutch Apple Fruit Sticks*	(1)	1 Fr	70	40
Apricot-Raspberry, Pepperidge Farm Fruit	(3)	½ S, 1 Fr, 1 Fat	150	85
Arrowroot, Nabisco National Biscuit*	(6)	1 S, ½ Fr, 1 Fat	130	80
Banana Creme Break Cake*	(2 oz.)	1 S, 1½ Fr, 1½ Fat	240	200
Blueberry				
Lance*	(1 oz.)	½ S, 1 Fr, ½ Fat	120	90
Nabisco Blueberry Newton*	(1)	½ S, 1 Fr, ½ Fat	110	80
Bonnie, Lance*	(1 3/16 oz.)	1 S, ½ Fr, 1 Fat	160	125
Brown Edge, Nabisco Wafers*	(5)	½ S, 1 Fr, 1 Fat	140	80
Brownie				
Break Cake Brownie Creme*	(2 oz.)	1 S, 1½ Fr, 1½ Fat	240	150
Pepperidge Farm Old-Fashioned, Brownie Chocolate Nut*	(3)	½ S, ½ Fr, 2 Fat	170	80
Butter Flavored, Nabisco Famous Assortment*	(6)	1 S, ½ Fr, 1 Fat	130	140
Cherry Newton, Nabisco*	(1)	½ S, 1 Fr, ½ Fat	110	80
Chocolate				
Break Cake, Chocolate Sugar Wafer*	(1.25 oz.)	½ S, 1½ Fr, 2 Fat	200	95
Lance				
*Choc-O-Lunch**	(1 5/16 oz.)	1 S, ½ Fr, 1½ Fat	180	150
*Choc-O-Lunch**	(1 oz.)	½ S, 1 Fr, 1 Fat	130	115
*Choc-O-Mint**	(1¼ oz.)	½ S, 1 Fr, 2 Fat	180	90
Nabisco				
*Chocolate Grahams**	(3)	1 S, ½ Fr, 1½ Fat	150	70
*Chocolate Snaps**	(7)	1 S, ½ Fr, 1 Fat	130	140
*Famous Chocolate Wafers**	(5)	1 S, ½ Fr, 1 Fat	130	200
*Oreo Big Stuff Chocolate Sandwich**	(1)	1 S, 1 Fr, 2½ Fat	250	220
*Oreo Chocolate Sandwich**	(3)	½ S, 1 Fr, 1 Fat	140	170
*Oreo Double Stuff Chocolate Sandwich**	(2)	½ S, 1 Fr, 1½ Fat	140	120

*Contains concentrated sources of carbohydrates

Food	Portion	Exchanges	Calories	Sodium (mg)
*Oreo Fudge Covered Chocolate Sandwich**	(2)	½ S, 1 Fr, 1½ Fat	150	100
*Oreo Mint Creme Chocolate Sandwich**	(2)	½ S, 1 Fr, 1 Fat	140	160
*Pinwheels Chocolate & Marshmallow Cakes**	(1)	½ S, 1 Fr, 1 Fat	130	35
*Pure Chocolate Middles**	(2)	1 S, 1½ Fat	150	65
Nabisco Famous Assortment				
*Giggles Sandwich, Chocolate**	(2)	½ S, ½ Fr, 1 Fat	140	70
*Ideal Bars, Chocolate Peanut**	(2)	1 S, 1½ Fat	150	130
*I Screams Double Dip Creme Sandwich, Chocolate**	(2)	½ S, 1 Fr, 1½ Fat	150	70
*Oreo Chocolate Sandwich**	(3)	½ S, 1 Fr, 1 Fat	140	170
Pepperidge Farm Special Collection (2)				
*Chocolate Chunk Pecan**		½ S, ½ Fr, 1 Fat	130	50
*Milk Chocolate Macadamia**		½ S, 1 Fr, 1½ Fat	140	75
Sunshine				
*Chocolate Fudge Sandwich**	(2)	½ S, ½ Fr, 1½ Fat	150	110
*Hydrox Creme Filled Chocolate Sandwich**	(3)	½ S, 1 Fr, 1½ Fat	160	140
Chocolate Chip				
Break Cake*	(2.5 oz.)	1 S, 2 Fr, 2½ Fat	310	330
Keebler Chips Deluxe*	(1)	1 Fr, 1 Fat	90	75
Lance*	(1 oz.)	½ S, ½ Fr, 1½ Fat	135	70
Nabisco				
*Chewy Chips Ahoy! Chocolate Chip**	(2)	1 S, 1 Fat	130	110
*Chips Ahoy! Pure Chocolate Chip**	(3)	1 S, 1½ Fat	140	95
*Chips 'n' More Coconut Chocolate Chip**	(2)	½ S, ½ Fr, 1½ Fat	150	95
*Chips 'n' More Fudge Chocolate Chip**	(3)	1 S, ½ Fr, 1 Fat	140	90
*Chips 'n' More Original Chocolate Chip**	(2)	1 S, 1½ Fat	150	70
*Chocolate Chip Snaps**	(6)	1 S, ½ Fr, 1 Fat	130	100
*Cookies 'n' Fudge Striped Chocolate Chip**	(3)	½ S, ½ Fr, 1½ Fat	150	80
Nabisco Almost Home Real Chocolate Chip*	(2)	½ S, 1 Fr, 1 Fat	130	100
Pepperidge Farm Old-Fashioned (3)				
*Chocolate Chip**		½ S, ½ Fr, 1½ Fat	150	95

*Contains concentrated sources of carbohydrates

Food	Portion	Exchanges	Calories	Sodium (mg)
Cookies, cont.				
*Chocolate Chocolate Chip**		½ S, ½ Fr, 2 Fat	160	70
Pillsbury Refrigerated*	(3)	1 S, 1 Fr, 2 Fat	210	150
Sunshine Chip-a-Roos*	(2)	½ S, ½ Fr, 1½ Fat	130	100
Coconut Break Cake (2 oz.)				
Coconut Macaroons*		1 S, 1 Fr, 3 Fat	270	160
Frosty Coconut Macaroons*		1 S, 1 Fr, 2½ Fat	260	170
Creme, Nabisco				
Baronet Creme Sandwich*	(3)	½ S, 1 Fr, 1 Fat	140	75
Biscos Waffle Cremes*	(3)	½ S, 1 Fr, 1½ Fat	150	30
Cameo Creme Sandwich*	(2)	½ S, 1 Fr, 1 Fat	140	80
Custard Cup, Sunshine*	(2)	½ S, ½ Fr, 1 Fat	130	160
Danish, Nabisco Famous Assortment, Imported*	(5)	½ S, ½ Fr, 1½ Fat	150	70
Date, Pepperidge Farm Kitchen Hearth (3)				
Date Nut Granola*		½ S, 1 Fr, 1½ Fat	170	100
Date Pecan*		½ S, 1 Fr, 1½ Fat	170	65
Devil's Food				
Break Cake, Devil's Food Creme*	(2 oz.)	1 S, 1½ Fr, 1½ Fat	230	75
Nabisco, Devil's Food Cakes*	(1)	½ S, 1 Fr	110	70
Fig				
Lance				
*Fig Bar**	(1½ oz.)	1 S, 1 Fr, ½ Fat	150	85
*Fig Cake**	(2⅛ oz.)	1 S, 2 Fr, ½ Fat	210	90
Nabisco Famous Cookie Assortment, Fig Newton*	(2)	½ S, 1 Fr, ½ Fat	100	100
Progressive, Fig Bars*	(1 oz.)	½ S, ½ Fr, ½ Fat	110	140
Sunshine, Fig Bars*	(2)	½ S, 1 Fr, ½ Fat	90	60
Fudge				
Lance, Fudge Chocolate Chip*	(1 oz.)	½ S, 1 Fr, 1 Fat	130	130
Nabisco Almost Home				
*Fudge Chocolate Chip**	(2)	½ S, 1 Fr, 1 Fat	130	130
*Fudge Chocolate Chip Raisin**	(2)	½ S, ½ Fr, 1 Fat	130	85
*Fudge & Peanut Butter Chip**	(2)	1 S, 1 Fat	130	100
*Fudge 'n' Nut Brownies**	(1)	½ S, 1 Fr, 1½ Fat	160	75
*Fudge 'n' Vanilla Creme Sandwiches**	(1)	½ S, 1 Fr, 1 Fat	140	110

*Contains concentrated sources of carbohydrates

Food	Portion	Exchanges	Calories	Sodium (mg)
Nabisco Famous Assortment Heyday Bars: Fudge, Caramel, & Peanut*	(1)	1 S, 1½ Fat	140	45
Pillsbury Refrigerated Fudge Brownies*	(1)	½ S, 1 Fr, 1 Fat	140	115
Sunshine Chips 'n' Middles Fudge Sandwich*	(2)	½ S, 1 Fr, 1 Fat	140	130
Ginger				
Nabisco Old-Fashioned Ginger Snaps*	(4)	1 S, ½ Fr, ½ Fat	120	200
Pepperidge Farm Old-Fashioned Gingerman*	(3)	½ S, ½ Fr, 1 Fat	100	80
Sunshine Ginger Snaps*	(5)	½ S, ½ Fr, ½ Fat	100	120
Golden Fruit Raisin Biscuits, Sunshine*	(2)	½ S, 1½ Fr, ½ Fat	150	80
Graham, Nabisco				
Bugs Bunny*	(9)	1 S, ½ Fr, 1 Fat	120	130
Cookies 'n' Fudge Party*	(3)	½ S, 1 Fr, 1½ Fat	140	100
Hazelnut, Pepperidge Farm Old-Fashioned*	(3)	½ S, 1 Fr, 1½ Fat	170	105
Health, Fleetwood, Original	(2)	1 S, 1 Fat	130	205
Hermit, Break Cake*	(2 oz.)	1 S, 1½ Fr, 1½ Fat	230	280
Kettle, Nabisco Famous Assortment*	(4)	1 S, ½ Fr, 1 Fat	130	115
Lemon				
Pepperidge Farm Old-Fashioned Lemon Nut Crunch*	(3)	½ S, 1 Fr, 2 Fat	180	80
Sunshine Lemon Coolers*	(5)	½ S, 1 Fr, 1 Fat	140	115
Marshmallow				
Nabisco				
*Mallomars Chocolate Cakes**	(2)	½ S, ½ Fr, 1 Fat	130	35
*Marshmallow Puffs**	(1)	½ S, 1 Fr, 1 Fat	120	55
*Marshmallow Sandwich**	(4)	½ S, 1 Fr, ½ Fat	120	80
*Marshmallow Twirl Cakes**	(1)	½ S, 1 Fr, 1 Fat	130	55
Sunshine Mallopuffs*	(2)	½ S, 1 Fr, 1 Fat	140	100
Mint, Nabisco, Mystic Mint Sandwich*	(2)	½ S, 1 Fr, 1½ Fat	150	95
Molasses				
Fleetwood*	(2)	1 S, 1 Fr, 1 Fat	190	380
Nabisco Pantry Molasses*	(2)	1 S, ½ Fr, 1 Fat	130	130
Pepperidge Farm Old-Fashioned Molasses Crisps*	(3)	½ S, ½ Fr, 1 Fat	100	75

*Contains concentrated sources of carbohydrates

Food	Portion	Exchanges	Calories	Sodium (mg)
Cookies, cont.				
Oatmeal				
Break Cake, Oatmeal Creme*	(2 oz.)	1 S, 1½ Fr, 1½ Fat	240	250
Fleetwood (2)				
*Date Filled Oatmeal**		½ S, 1½ Fr, 1½ Fat	200	270
*Oatmeal**		1 S, 1 Fr, 2 Fat	220	305
Keebler Old-Fashioned*	(1)	½ S, ½ Fr, ½ Fat	80	50
Lance*	(1 oz.)	½ S, 1 Fr, 1 Fat	130	70
Nabisco Bakers Bonus Oatmeal*	(2)	1 S, ½ Fr, 1 Fat	130	90
Nabisco Almost Home (2)				
*Oatmeal Chocolate Chip**		1 S, ½ Fr, 1 Fat	130	90
*Oatmeal Raisin**		1 S, ½ Fr, 1 Fat	130	100
Pepperidge Farm Old-Fashioned (3)				
*Irish Oatmeal**		½ S, 1 Fr, 1 Fat	150	125
*Oatmeal Raisin**		½ S, 1 Fr, 1½ Fat	170	170
Pillsbury Oatmeal Raisin*	(3)	1 S, 1 Fr, 1½ Fat	200	190
Sunshine (2)				
*Country Style Oatmeal**		½ S, ½ Fr, 1 Fat	110	125
*Oatmeal Peanut Sandwich**		½ S, ½ Fr, 1 Fat	140	130
Peanut, Fleetwood Jumbles*	(2)	1 S, ½ Fr, 2 Fat	200	165
Peanut Butter				
Break Cake				
*Peanut Butter Creme**	(2 oz.)	1 S, 1½ Fr, 1½ Fat	240	220
*Peanut Butter Wafer**	(1.25 oz.)	½ S, 1 Fr, 2 Fat	180	75
Nabisco				
*Nutter Butter Peanut Butter Sandwich**	(2)	1 S, 1 Fat	140	100
*Nutter Butter Peanut Creme Patties**	(4)	1 S, 1½ Fat	150	95
Nabisco Almost Home (2)				
*Peanut Butter Chocolate Chip**		1 S, 1 Fat	140	100
*Peanut Butter Fudge**		1 S, 1½ Fat	140	90
Pillsbury Refrigerated*	(3)	1 S, 1 Fr, 1½ Fat	200	190
Sunshine Peanut Butter Wafers*	(3)	½ S, ½ Fr, 1 Fat	120	55
Pecan				
Keebler Sandies*	(1)	½ Fr, 1 Fat	80	75
Nabisco Shortbread*	(2)	1 S, 2 Fat	150	80

*Contains concentrated sources of carbohydrates

Food	Portion	Exchanges	Calories	Sodium (mg)
Raisin				
Break Cake, Raisin Creme*	(2 oz.)	1 S, 1½ Fr, 1½ Fat	240	210
Pepperidge Farm Kitchen Hearth Raisin Bran*	(3)	½ S, 1 Fr, 1½ Fat	160	85
Shortbread				
Nabisco Cookies 'n' Fudge Striped*	(3)	½ S, 1 Fr, 1½ Fat	150	110
Nabisco Famous Assortment Lorna Doone*	(4)	1 S, 1½ Fat	140	130
Pepperidge Farm Old-Fashioned*	(3)	½ S, ½ Fr, 1½ Fat	130	75
Spice Bar, Break Cake*	(2 oz.)	1 S, 1½ Fr, 1½ Fat	230	220
Sprinkles, Sunshine Biscuits*	(2)	½ S, 1 Fr, ½ Fat	130	130
Strawberry				
Break Cake, Strawberry Wafer*	(1.5 oz.)	½ S, 1½ Fr, 2 Fat	220	100
Lance*	(1 oz.)	½ S, 1 Fr, ½ Fat	120	100
Pepperidge Farm Fruit*	(3)	½ S, 1 Fr, 1 Fat	160	70
Nabisco Strawberry Newtons*	(1)	½ S, 1 Fr, ½ Fat	110	85
Sugar				
Nabisco Biscos Sugar Wafers*	(8)	½ S, 1 Fr, 1½ Fat	150	35
Nabisco Almost Home Old-Fashioned*	(2)	1 S, ½ Fr, 1 Fat	130	150
Nabisco Famous Assortment Biscos Sugar Wafers*	(8)	½ S, 1 Fr, 1½ Fat	150	50
Pepperidge Farm Old-Fashioned*	(3)	½ S, 1 Fr, 1 Fat	150	120
Pillsbury Refrigerated*	(3)	1 S, 1 Fr, 1½ Fat	200	190
Sunshine Biscuits*	(3)	½ S, ½ Fr, 1 Fat	130	40
Tea Biscuit, Social, Nabisco*	(6)	1 S, ½ Fr, 1 Fat	130	105
Toy, Sunshine Biscuits*	(10)	½ S, 1 Fr, ½ Fat	120	180
Vanilla				
Break Cake, Vanilla Sugar Wafer*	(1.5 oz.)	½ S, 1½ Fr, 2 Fat	220	105
Lance Van-O-Lunch*	(1 5/16 oz.)	½ S, 1½ Fr, 1 Fat	180	150
	(1 oz.)	½ S, 1 Fr, 1 Fat	140	115

*Contains concentrated sources of carbohydrates

Food	Portion	Exchanges	Calories	Sodium (mg)
Cookies, cont.				
Nabisco				
*Cookie Break Artificially Flavored Creme Sandwiches**	(3)	½ S, 1 Fr, 1 Fat	140	95
*Nilla Wafers**	(7)	½ S, 1 Fr, 1 Fat	130	95
Nabisco Famous Assortment Giggles Sandwich*	(2)	½ S, ½ Fr, 1 Fat	140	50
Sunshine				
*Dixie**	(2)	½ S, ½ Fr, 1 Fat	130	110
*Wafers**	(6)	½ S, ½ Fr, 1 Fat	130	105
Vienna Finger Sandwich, Sunshine*	(2)	½ S, 1 Fr, 1 Fat	140	125

■ Ice Cream, Ice Milk, & Frozen Diet Bars

Food	Portion	Exchanges	Calories	Sodium (mg)
Buttered Pecan, Lady Borden Ice Cream*	(½ cup)	1 S, 2 Fat	180	65
Chocolate				
Borden Ice Cream, Chocolate Swirl*	(½ cup)	1 S, 1 Fat	130	65
Borden Ice Milk*	(½ cup)	1 S, ½ Fat	100	80
Olde-Fashioned Recipe Ice Cream, Dutch Chocolate*	(½ cup)	1 S, 1 Fat	130	65
Weight Watchers Frozen Bars				
*Chocolate Dip**	(1.7 fl. oz.)	½ S, 1½ Fat	110	35
*Chocolate Mint Treat**	(1.75 fl. oz.)	1 S	60	50
*Chocolate Mousse**	(1.75 fl. oz.)	½ S	35	30
*Chocolate Treat**	(2.75 fl. oz.)	1½ S	100	75
Weight Watchers Ice Milk*	(4 fl. oz.)	1 S, ½ Fat	110	75
Fudge				
Weight Watchers Frozen Bar, Double Fudge Treat*	(1.75 fl. oz.)	1 S	60	50
Weight Watchers Ice Milk, Fudge Marble*	(4 fl. oz.)	1 S, ½ Fr, ½ Fat	120	75
Neapolitan, Weight Watchers Ice Milk	(4 fl. oz.)	1 S, ½ Fat	110	75
Orange Vanilla Treat, Weight Watchers Frozen Bar*	(1.75 fl. oz.)	1 S	60	50
Oreo Cookies 'n' Cream, Nabisco				
Chocolate, Mint, Vanilla*	(3 fl. oz.)	1 S, 1½ Fat	140	100
Sandwich*	(1 sand.)	1½ S, ½ Fr, 2 Fat	240	300

*Contains concentrated sources of carbohydrates

Food	Portion	Exchanges	Calories	Sodium (mg)
Snackwich*	(1 sand.)	½ S, ½ Fat	60	80
on a Stick*	(1 bar)	1 S, 3 Fat	220	100
Peaches 'n' Creme, Weight Watchers Ice Milk*	(4 fl. oz.)	1 S, ½ Fr, ½ Fat	120	75
Strawberry				
Borden Ice Cream*	(½ cup)	1 S, 1 Fat	130	55
Borden Ice Milk*	(½ cup)	1 S, ½ Fat	90	65
Olde-Fashioned Recipe Ice Cream, Strawberries 'n' Cream*	(½ cup)	1 S, 1 Fat	130	55
Weight Watchers Ice Milk, Strawberries 'n' Creme*	(4 fl. oz.)	1 S, ½ Fr, ½ Fat	120	75
Vanilla				
Borden Ice Milk*	(½ cup)	1 S, ½ Fat	90	65
Ice Cream, Homestyle Vanilla*	(½ cup)	1 S, 2 Fat	150	55
Land O' Lakes Ice Cream*	(4 fl. oz.)	1 S, 1½ Fat	140	60
Land O' Lakes Ice Milk*	(4 fl. oz.)	1 S, ½ Fat	90	50
Weight Watchers Frozen Bar, Ice Milk Sandwich*	(1 sand.)	1 S, 1 Fr, ½ Fat	150	170
Weight Watchers Ice Milk*	(4 fl. oz.)	1 S, ½ Fat	100	75
Yogurt, Colombo (frozen)				
Lite Nonfat*	(4 oz.)	1 Fr, ½ SMk	95	70
Lowfat*	(4 oz.)	½ Fr, ½ LFMk	99	35

■ Pastry

Food	Portion	Exchanges	Calories	Sodium (mg)
Cinnamon Roll				
Break Cake Cinnamon Nut Roll*	(2 rolls)	1½ S, 2 Fr, 2 Fat	330	220
Pillsbury Best Quick Cinnamon Rolls w/Icing*	(1 roll)	1 S, 1 Fr, 1½ Fat	210	260
Criss Cross, Pepperidge Farms Puff Pastry, Apple (frozen)	(2 oz.)	1 S, ½ Fr, 1½ Fat	170	140
Danish				
Earth Grain (2 oz.)				
*Apple**		1 S, ½ Fr, 2½ Fat	230	(N/A)
*Cherry**		1 S, ½ Fr, 2½ Fat	230	(N/A)
*Cinnamon**		1 S, 1 Fr, 2 Fat	220	(N/A)
Hostess				
*Apple**	(3.50 oz.)	1 S, 1½ Fr, 4 Fat	360	410
*Butterhorn**	(2.85 oz.)	1½ S, 1 Fr, 3½ Fat	330	520
*Raspberry**	(2.85 oz.)	2 S, 1 Fr, 1 Fat	270	295

*Contains concentrated sources of carbohydrates

Food	Portion	Exchanges	Calories	Sodium (mg)
Danish, cont.				
Pillsbury				
*Best Apple w/Icing**	(1 roll)	1 S, 1 Fr, 2 Fat	240	260
*Caramel w/Nuts**	(2 rolls)	1½ S, 1 Fr, 3 Fat	310	490
*Orange w/Icing**	(2 rolls)	1 S, 1½ Fr, 3 Fat	290	450
Donuts				
Break Cake, Sugar Gem*	(6 donuts)	1 S, 1½ Fr, 3 Fat	310	(N/A)
Earth Grain				
*Bear Claw**	(2 oz.)	1 S, ½ Fr, 3 Fat	250	(N/A)
*Cinnamon Apple**	(2.5 oz.)	1 S, 1½ Fr, 3½ Fat	310	270
*Devil's Food**	(2.6 oz.)	1 S, 1 Fr, 4 Fat	330	320
*Old-Fashioned Glazed**	(2.5 oz.)	1 S, 1½ Fr, 3½ Fat	310	270
*Old-Fashioned Powdered**	(2.16 oz.)	1 S, 1 Fr, 3½ Fat	290	260
Hostess				
*Chocolate Coated**	(1 oz.)	½ S, ½ Fr, 1½ Fat	130	100
*Cinnamon**	(1 oz.)	½ S, ½ Fr, 1 Fat	110	140
*Krunch**	(1 oz.)	½ S, ½ Fr, 1 Fat	110	130
*Old-Fashioned**	(1.5 oz.)	½ S, 1 Fr, 2 Fat	180	220
*Old-Fashioned Glazed**	(2 oz.)	½ S, 1½ Fr, 2½ Fat	230	200
*Plain**	(1 oz.)	½ S, 1½ Fat	110	135
*Powdered Sugar**	(1 oz.)	½ S, ½ Fr, 1 Fat	110	118
Hostess Donettes				
*Chocolate Coated**	(.9 oz. or 2 units)	½ S, ½ Fr, 1 Fat	120	100
*Powdered**	(1 oz. or 3 units)	1 S, 1 Fat	120	120
Dumpling, Pepperidge Farms Puff Pastry				
Apple (frozen)*	(3 oz.)	1 S, 1 Fr, 2½ Fat	260	230
Flips, Fleetwood (2 units)				
Apple Filled*		½ S, 1½ Fr, 1½ Fat	200	290
Apricot Filled*		½ S, 1½ Fr, 1½ Fat	210	140
Banana Fudge*		½ S, 1½ Fr, 1½ Fat	200	140
Blueberry*		½ S, 1½ Fr, 1½ Fat	200	165
Fruit Squares, Pepperidge Farm (1 square)				
Apple*		1 S, 1 Fr, 2 Fat	220	170
Blueberry*		1 S, 1 Fr, 2 Fat	220	190
Cherry**		1 S, 1 Fr, 2 Fat	230	180
Honey Buns				
Break Cake	(1 bun)	1 S, 1½ Fr, 4½ Fat	380	140
Wonder Glazed*	(3.75 oz.)	1½ S, 1 Fr, 4 Fat	370	250
Wonder Iced*	(3.75 oz.)	2 S, 1½ Fr, 4 Fat	410	210
Popover, Flako (mix)	(1 popover)	1½ S, 1 Fat	170	360

*Contains concentrated sources of carbohydrates

Food	Portion	Exchanges	Calories	Sodium (mg)
Pop-Tarts, Kellogg's (1 pastry)				
Blueberry*		1½ S, 1 Fr, 1 Fat	210	220
*Frosted Blueberry**		1 S, 1½ Fr, 1 Fat	200	220
Brown Sugar Cinnamon*		1 S, 1 Fr, 1½ Fat	210	210
*Frosted Brown Sugar Cinnamon**		1 S, 1 Fr, 1½ Fat	210	200
Cherry*		1½ S, 1 Fr, 1 Fat	210	230
*Frosted Cherry**		1 S, 1½ Fr, 1 Fat	210	230
Dutch Apple, Frosted*		1 S, 1½ Fr, 1 Fat	210	210
Strawberry*		1 S, 1½ Fr, 1 Fat	200	220
*Frosted Strawberry**		1 S, 1½ Fr, 1 Fat	200	210
Strudel				
Pepperidge Farm Apple (frozen)*	(3 oz.)	1 S, 1 Fr, 2 Fat	240	210
Pillsbury Toaster Strudel (1 unit)				
*Apple Spice**		½ S, 1½ Fr, 1½ Fat	190	190
*Blueberry**		½ S, 1½ Fr, 1½ Fat	190	200
*Cherry**		½ S, 1½ Fr, 1½ Fat	190	200
*Cinnamon**		½ S, 1½ Fr, 1½ Fat	190	200
*Raspberry**		½ S, 1½ Fr, 1½ Fat	190	200
*Strawberry**		½ S, 1½ Fr, 1½ Fat	190	200
Sweet Rolls				
Hungry Jack Butter Tastin' w/Icing*	(2 rolls)	1 S, 1½ Fr, 3 Fat	290	570
Pillsbury Cinnamon w/Icing*	(2 rolls)	1 S, 1 Fr, 2 Fat	230	520
Weight Watchers Apple*	(2.5 oz.)	1 S, 1½ Fr, 1 Fat	180	95
Toastettes, Nabisco (1 unit)				
Apple*		1 S, 1½ Fr, 1 Fat	200	170
Blueberry*		1 S, 1½ Fr, 1 Fat	200	200
*Frosted Blueberry**		1 S, 1½ Fr, 1 Fat	200	200
Brown Sugar Cinnamon, Frosted*		1 S, 1½ Fr, 1 Fat	200	170
Cherry*		1 S, 1½ Fr, 1 Fat	200	200
*Frosted Cherry**		1 S, 1½ Fr, 1 Fat	200	200
Fudge, Frosted*		1 S, 1½ Fr, 1 Fat	200	220
Strawberry*		1 S, 1½ Fr, 1 Fat	200	200
*Frosted Strawberry**		1 S, 1½ Fr, 1 Fat	200	200
Turnovers (1 turnover)				
Pepperidge Farm (frozen)				
*Apple**		1 S, 1 Fr, 3½ Fat	300	210
*Blueberry**		1 S, 1 Fr, 4 Fat	310	230
*Cherry**		1 S, 1 Fr, 4 Fat	310	280

*Contains concentrated sources of carbohydrates

Food	Portion	Exchanges	Calories	Sodium (mg)
Turnovers, cont.				
*Peach**		1 S, 1 Fr, 3½ Fat	310	260
*Raspberry**		1 S, 1½ Fr, 3 Fat	310	260
Pillsbury (frozen)				
*Apple**		1 S, ½ Fr, 1½ Fat	170	320
*Blueberry**		1 S, ½ Fr, 1½ Fat	170	320
*Cherry**		1 S, ½ Fr, 1½ Fat	170	320

■ Pies

Food	Portion	Exchanges	Calories	Sodium (mg)
Apple				
Hostess Fruit*	(4.5 oz.)	1 S, 2½ Fr, 4 Fat	390	490
Weight Watchers*	(3.5 oz.)	½ S, 2 Fr, 1 Fat	180	300
Banana Marshmallow, Break Cake*	(1 pie)	½ S, 1 Fr, 1 Fat	150	80
Blackberry, Hostess Fruit*	(4.5 oz.)	1 S, 2½ Fr, 3 Fat	380	360
Blueberry, Hostess Fruit*	(4.5 oz.)	1 S, 3 Fr, 3½ Fat	410	450
Boston Cream, Weight Watchers*	(3 oz.)	½ S, 1½ Fr, ½ SMk, 1 Fat	180	320
Cherry				
Hostess Fruit*	(4.5 oz.)	1 S, 3 Fr, 3½ Fat	410	450
Weight Watchers*	(3.5 oz.)	½ S, 2 Fr, 1 Fat	200	160
Chocolate				
Break Cake (1 pie)				
*Chocolate Marshmallow**		½ S, 1 Fr, 1 Fat	150	70
*Double Decker Chocolate Marshmallow**		1 S, 3 Fr, 2 Fat	360	170
Hostess Pudding*	(5 oz.)	1 S, 4 Fr, 4 Fat	490	439
Nabisco Royal No-Bake Mix (⅛ pie)				
*Chocolate Mint**		½ S, 1 Fr, ½ WMk, 2 Fat	260	280
*Chocolate Mousse**		1½ Fr, ½ WMk, 1½ Fat	230	260
Devil's Food Marshmallow, Break Cake*	(1 pie)	½ S, 1 Fr, 1 Fat	140	85
Fried, Break Cake*	(1 pie)	1½ S, 2 Fr, 4 Fat	410	(N/A)
Lemon				
Hostess Fruit*	(4.5 oz.)	1 S, 2½ Fr, 4 Fat	400	430
Nabisco Royal No-Bake Mix, Lemon Meringue*	(⅛ pie)	1 S, 2 Fr, 2 Fat	290	310
Peach, Hostess Fruit*	(4.5 oz.)	1 S, 2½ Fr, 3 Fat	380	380
Pecan, Progressive*	(3 oz.)	2 S, 2 Fr, 1½ Fat	330	(N/A)
Strawberry, Hostess Fruit*	(4.5 oz.)	1 S, 2½ Fr, 3 Fat	340	400
Vanilla				
*Hostess Pudding**	(5 oz.)	1 S, 4 Fr, 3½ Fat	470	400

*Contains concentrated sources of carbohydrates

Food	Portion	Exchanges	Calories	Sodium (mg)
*Break Cake, Double Decker Vanilla Marshmallow**	(1 pie)	1 S, 3 Fr, 2 Fat	360	210

■ Pudding & Mousse

Food	Portion	Exchanges	Calories	Sodium (mg)
Butterscotch, Weight Watchers Dry Dessert Pudding (mix)*	(½ cup)	½ S, ½ SMk	90	460
Cheesecake, Weight Watchers Dry Dessert Mousse (mix)*	(½ cup)	½ Fr, ½ SMk, ½ Fat	60	75
Chocolate				
Weight Watchers Dry Dessert (mix)	(½ cup)			
*Mousse**		½ SMk, ½ Fat	60	45
*Pudding**		½ S, ½ SMk	90	420
Weight Watchers Specialty Desserts, Mousse*	(2.5 oz.)	1 S, ½ Fr, ½ SMk, 1 Fat	170	190
Raspberry, Weight Watchers Dry Dessert Mousse (mix)*	(½ cup)	½ Fr, ½ SMk, ½ Fat	60	75
Vanilla, Weight Watchers Dry Dessert, Pudding (mix)*	(½ cup)	½ S, ½ Fr, ½ SMk	90	510

■ Shake Mix, Weight Watchers

Food	Portion	Exchanges	Calories	Sodium (mg)
Chocolate Fudge	(1 env.)	1 SMk	70	170
Orange Sherbert	(1 env.)	1 SMk	70	210

■ Sherbert, Sorbet, & Sweetened Pops

Food	Portion	Exchanges	Calories	Sodium (mg)
Fruit Flavors Sherbert, Land O' Lakes*	(4 fl. oz.)	½ S, 1½ Fr	130	25
Mandarin Orange Sorbet, Dole	(4 oz.)	2 Fr	110	9
Orange Sherbert, Borden*	(½ cup)	2 S	110	40
Peach Sorbet, Dole	(4 oz.)	2 Fr	120	10½
Pineapple Sorbet, Dole	(4 oz.)	2 Fr	120	10½
Raspberry Sorbet, Dole	(4 oz.)	2 Fr	110	12
Strawberry Sorbet, Dole	(4 oz.)	2 Fr	110	11
Sweetened Pops, Life Savers*				
Lime, Orange, Pineapple, Wild Cherry, Flavor Pops	(1 pop)	1 Fr	40	0

13

FAST FOODS

For many people, the hurried pace of life makes fast-food restaurants an attractive alternative to home cooking. Choices can be made at most fast-food restaurants that will fit a diabetic's food plan. You need to be selective when you place your order, but you needn't rule out these restaurants.

Look for restaurants that have salad bars, with condiments offered on the side.

It's surprising how much fat and sodium are contained in some of these foods. Look at breakfast foods as closely as lunch and supper items, because some of these foods are alarmingly fatty.

Unless otherwise noted, all food values in this chapter are calculated based on a serving size of one item (one burger, for example) or one serving (one order of fries, for example).

Food	Portion	Exchanges	Calories	Sodium (mg)

■ Arby's

Manufacturer suggests that diabetics avoid items such as Arby's sauce and ranch-style dressing.

Food	Portion	Exchanges	Calories	Sodium (mg)
Bac'n Cheddar Deluxe		2 S, 3 HFMt, 2½ Fat	526	1672
Beef 'n' Cheddar		2 S, 3 HFMt, ½ Fat	455	955
Chicken Breast Sandwich		2½ S, 2½ LMt, 4 Fat	509	1082
Fish Fillet Sandwich		3½ S, 1½ MFMt, 5 Fat	580	928
French Fries*		1 S, 1 Fr, 2 Fat	215	114
Hot Ham 'n' Cheese		1½ S, 2½ LMt, 1 Fat	292	1350
Philly Beef 'n' Swiss		2 S, 2½ HFMt, 1½ Fat	460	1300
Potato Cakes*		1 S, ½ Fr, 2½ Fat	201	397
Roast Beef Sandwich				
Giant		3 S, 4 MFMt, ½ Fat	531	908
Junior		1½ S, 1 MFMt, ½ Fat	218	345
King		3 S, 3 MFMt, 1 Fat	467	766
Regular		2 S, 2½ MFMt, ½ Fat	353	588
Super		3½ S, 2 MFMt, 2½ Fat	501	798
Turkey Deluxe		2 S, 2½ LMt, 2 Fat	375	1047
Turnover				
Apple		1 S, 1 Fr, 3½ Fat	303	178
Cherry		1 S, 1 Fr, 3 Fat	280	200

■ Burger Chef

Food	Portion	Exchanges	Calories	Sodium (mg)
Biscuit Sandwich w/Sausage		2 S, 1½ MFMt, 3½ Fat	418	1313
Burger				
Cheeseburger		1½ S, 1½ MFMt, 1 Fat	278	641
Double Cheeseburger		1½ S, 3 MFMt, 1½ Fat	402	835
Hamburger		1½ S, 1 MFMt, 1 Fat	235	480
Mushroom Burger		2 S, 3 MFMt, 1 V, 3 Fat	520	744
Chicken Club		2 S, 4 LMt, 1 V, 2½ Fat	521	(N/A)
Fisherman's Filet		2½ S, 2½ LMt, ½ V, 5 Fat	534	(N/A)
French Fries				
large		2 S, 3 Fat	285	456
reg.		1½ S, 2 Fat	204	327
Hash Rounds*		1 S, 1 Fr, 3 Fat	235	349
Lettuce Salad		free	11	8
Scrambled Eggs & Bacon Platter		3 S, 1½ MFMt, 4½ Fat	567	1108
Scrambled Eggs & Sausage Platter		3 S, 2½ MFMt, 5½ Fat	668	1411
Shef				
Big		2 S, 2 MFMt, 1 V, 5 Fat	556	840
Super		2 S, 3 MFMt, 1 V, 4½ Fat	604	1088

*Contains concentrated sources of carbohydrates

Food	Portion	Exchanges	Calories	Sodium (mg)
Burger Chef, cont.				
Top		2 S, 3½ MFMt, 3 Fat	541	1007
Sunrise w/Bacon		2 S, 1 MFMt, 3½ Fat	392	978
Sunrise w/Sausage		2 S, 3 MFMt, 3½ Fat	526	1412

■ Burger King

Food	Portion	Exchanges	Calories	Sodium (mg)
Apple Pie		1 S, 2 Fr, 2½ Fat	305	412
Breakfast Croissan'wich				
Plain		1½ S, 1 MFMt, 3 Fat	304	637
w/Bacon		1½ S, 1 MFMt, ½ HFMt, 3 Fat	355	762
w/Ham		1½ S, 2 MFMt, 2 Fat	335	987
w/Sausage		1½ S, 2 MFMt, 6 Fat	538	1042
Burger. *See also* **Whopper**				
Bacon Double		2 S, 4 MFMt, 2 Fat	510	728
Cheeseburger		2 S, 1½ HFMt, ½ MFMt	317	651
Hamburger		2 S, 1½ HFMt	275	509
Chicken Specialty Sandwich		3½ S, 2 MFMt, 1 V, 6 Fat	688	1423
Chicken Tenders (6)		½ S, 2½ LMt, ½ Fat	204	636
French Fries, reg.		1½ S, 2½ Fat	227	160
French Toast Sticks		3 S, 6 Fat	499	498
Ham & Cheese Specialty Sandwich		3 S, 2 MFMt, 2½ Fat	471	1534
Onion Rings		1½ S, 1 V, 3 Fat	274	665
Scrambled Egg Platter		2 S, 1½ MFMt, 4½ Fat	468	808
w/Bacon		2 S, 2 MFMt, 5½ Fat	536	975
w/Sausage		2 S, 2½ MFMt, 8 Fat	702	1213
Whaler Fish Sandwich		3 S, 1½ MFMt, 4 Fat	488	592
Whopper Sandwich		2½ S, 3 MFMT, 1 V, 4 Fat	628	880
w/Cheese		2½ S, 3 MFMt, 1 V, 4 Fat	711	1164
Jr.		2 S, 1½ MFMt, 2 Fat	322	486
Jr. plus Cheese		2 S, 2 MFMt, 2 Fat	364	628

■ Dairy Queen

Food	Portion	Exchanges	Calories	Sodium (mg)
Banana Split*		3 S, 3½ Fr, 2 Fat	540	150
Burger				
Single Hamburger		2 S, 2 MFMt, 1 Fat	360	630
w/Cheese		2 S, 3 MFMt, 1 Fat	410	790
Double Hamburger		2 S, 4½ MFMT, 1 Fat	530	660
w/Cheese		2 S, 5½ MFMt, 2 Fat	650	980
Triple Hamburger		2 S, 7 MFMt, 2 Fat	710	690
w/Cheese		2 S, 7½ MFMt, 2½ Fat	820	1010
Buster Bar*		1½ S, 2 Fr, 1 LMt, 5 Fat	460	175

*Contains concentrated sources of carbohydrates

Food	Portion	Exchanges	Calories	Sodium (mg)
Chicken Sandwich		3 S, 3 MFMt, 5 Fat	670	870
Chipper Sandwich*		1½ S, 2 Fr, 1½ Fat	318	170
Chocolate Malt				
*large**		7 S, 5½ Fr, 5 Fat	1060	360
*reg.**		5 S, 4 Fr, 3½ Fat	760	260
*small**		3 S, 3 Fr, 2½ Fat	520	180
Chocolate Shake				
*large**		6 S, 5 Fr, 5 Fat	990	360
*reg.**		4½ S, 3½ Fr	710	260
*small**		3 S, 2½ Fr, 2 Fat	490	180
Chocolate Sundae				
*reg.**		2 S, 2 Fr, 1½ Fat	310	120
*large**		3 S, 2 Fr, 2 Fat	440	165
*small**		1 S, 1 Fr, 1 Fat	190	75
Cone				
*Dipped, large**		3 S, 1½ Fr, 5 Fat	570	145
*Dipped, reg.**		2 S, 1 Fr, 3 Fat	340	100
*Dipped, small**		1 S, ½ Fr, 2 Fat	190	55
*large**		2 S, 1 Fr, 2 Fat	340	110
*Queen's Choice Chocolate**		1½ S, 1 Fr, 3 Fat	326	84
*Queen's Choice Vanilla**		1 S, 1½ Fr, 3 Fat	322	71
*reg.**		2 S, ½ Fr, 1 Fat	240	80
*small**		1 S, ½ Fr, 1 Fat	140	45
Dilly Bar*		1 S, ½ Fr, 3 Fat	210	50
Double Delight*		3 S, 1½ Fr, 4 Fat	490	150
DQ Sandwich*		1 S, ½ Fr, 1 Fat	140	40
Fish Sandwich		3 S, 1½ MFMt, 2 Fat	400	875
w/Cheese		2½ S, 2 MFMt, 2 Fat	440	1035
Float*		3½ S, 3 Fr, 1½ Fat	410	85
Freeze*		3 S, 3 Fr, 2½ Fat	500	180
French Fries				
large		2½ S, 3 Fat	320	185
reg.		1½ S, 2 Fat	200	115
Frozen Dessert*	(4 oz.)	1 S, 1 Fr, 1 Fat	180	65
Fudge Nut Bar*		2½ S, 5 Fat	406	167
Heath Blizzard*	(16 oz.)	5 S, 3 Fr, 5 Fat	800	325
Hot Dog		1½ S, 1 MFMt, 2 Fat	280	830
w/Cheese		1½ S, 1½ MFMt, 2½ Fat	330	990
w/Chili		1½ S, 1½ MFMt, 2½ Fat	320	985
Super		3 S, 1 MFMt, 4½ Fat	520	1365
Super w/Cheese		3 S, 2 MFMt, 5 Fat	580	1605

*Contains concentrated sources of carbohydrates

Food	Portion	Exchanges	Calories	Sodium (mg)
Dairy Queen, cont.				
Super w/Chili		3 S, 2 MFMt, 4 Fat	570	1595
Hot Fudge "Brownie Delight" Sundae*		3 S, 2½ Fr, 5 Fat	600	225
Mr. Misty				
*large**		5½ Fr	340	10
*reg.**		4 Fr	250	10
*small**		3 Fr	190	10
Mr. Misty Float*		1½ S, 3½ Fr, 1½ Fat	390	95
Mr. Misty Freeze*		3 S, 3 Fr, 2½ Fat	500	140
Onion Rings		2 S, 3 Fat	280	140
Parfait*		3 S, 2 Fr, 1½ Fat	430	140
*Peanut Buster**		5 S, 1 Fr, 6½ Fat	740	250
Strawberry Shortcake*		3 S, 3½ Fr, 2 Fat	540	215
Dairy Queen Brazier				
All-White Chicken Nuggets		1 S, 2 MFMt, 1½ Fat	276	505
BBQ Nugget Sauces*		1 Fr	41	130
Chicken Breast Fillet		3 S, 2½ MFMt, 4 Fat	608	725
w/Cheese		3 S, 3 MFMt, 4½ Fat	661	921
DQ Biggie		1½ S, 1½ HFMt, 5 Fat	480	1192
w/Cheese		1½ S, 2 HFMt, 5 Fat	533	1995
w/Chili		1½ S, 2½ HFMt, 4 Fat	575	1900
Fish Fillet		3 S, 1½ MFMt, 2 Fat	430	674
w/Cheese		3 S, 2 MFMt, 2 Fat	483	870

■ Dunkin' Donuts

Food	Portion	Exchanges	Calories	Sodium (mg)
Biscuit		1½ S, 4½ Fat	332	438
Brownie*		1 S, 1½ Fr, 2½ Fat	280	170
Cake Ring				
*Plain**		1 S, 1 Fr, 4 Fat	319	348
*Chocolate w/Glaze**		1 S, 1 Fr, 4 Fat	324	383
*Coconut Coated**		1½ S, 1 Fr, 5½ Fat	417	332
Chocolate Chip Cookie*		½ S, ½ Fr, 1½ Fat	129	103
Chocolate Frosted Yeast Ring*		1 S, 1 Fr, 2½ Fat	246	194
Croissant				
Almond		2 S, 6 Fat	435	521
*Chocolate**		2 S, ½ Fr, 7 Fat	502	311
Filled Donut				
*Apple, w/Cinnamon Sugar**		1 S, ½ Fr, 2½ Fat	219	200
*Bavarian w/Chocolate Frosting**		1 S, 2 Fr, 2 Fat	231	237
*Bavarian Cream**		1 S, ½ Fr, 3 Fat	226	184
*Blueberry**		1 S, ½ Fr, 2 Fat	196	175

*Contains concentrated sources of carbohydrates

Food	Portion	Exchanges	Calories	Sodium (mg)
*Jelly**		1 S, 4½ Fat	274	272
*Lemon**		1 S, 1 Fr, 2 Fat	221	216
French Cruller w/Glaze*		½ S, ½ Fr, 3 Fat	201	163
Honey Dipped Coffee Roll*		2 S, 1 Fr, 3 Fat	348	278
Honey Dipped Cruller*		1½ S, 1 Fr, 4½ Fat	370	356
Honey Dipped Yeast Ring*		1 S, ½ Fr, 2 Fat	208	180
Macaroon*		1½ S, 1½ Fr, 3½ Fat	351	183
Muffin				
Apple Spice		3 S, 2 Fat	327	382
Banana Nut		3 S, 2 Fat	327	357
Blueberry		2½ S, 2 Fat	263	347
Bran		3 S, 2½ Fat	353	591
Cherry		3 S, 2 Fat	317	382
Corn		3 S, 2½ Fat	347	577
Munchkins (3)				
*Cake w/Powdered Sugar**		1 S, ½ Fr, 2 Fat	207	234
Chocolate w/Glaze		1 S, ½ Fr, 3½ Fat	264	267
Yeast w/Glaze		1 S, 1 Fat	129	108
Sugared Jelly Stick*		1 S, 1½ Fr, 3½ Fat	332	302

■ Hardee's

Food	Portion	Exchanges	Calories	Sodium (mg)
American Cheese Slice		½ HFMt	47	219
Apple Turnover*		1 S, 1½ Fr, 2½ Fat	271	204
Big Cookie Treat*		1 S, 1 Fr, 3 Fat	278	258
Big Country Breakfast w/Ham		3½ S, 2½ HFMt, 3½ Fat	665	2263
Big Country Breakfast w/Sausage		1½ S, 4 HFMt, 7½ Fat	849	1820
Biscuit				
Bacon & Egg		2 S, 1½ HFMt, 2½ Fat	410	1175
Canadian Sunrise		2 S, 2 HFMt, 2½ Fat	482	1121
Cheese		2 S, ½ HFMt, 2 Fat	304	740
Cinnamon 'n' Raisin		1½ S, ½ Fr, 3 Fat	276	346
Country Ham		2 S, 1 HFMt, 2 Fat	323	1038
Egg		2 S, ½ MFMt, 3 Fat	336	575
Ham		2 S, 1 HFMt, 1 Fat	300	1112
Rise 'n' Shine		2 S, 2½ Fat	257	521
Sausage		2 S, 1 HFMt, 4 Fat	426	831
Sausage & Egg		2 S, 2 HFMt, 3½ Fat	503	885
Steak		3 S, 1 HFMt, 4 Fat	491	1108
Biscuit, Gravy only	(4 oz.)	½ S, ½ HFMt, 1 Fat	144	440
Burger				
Bacon Cheeseburger		2 S, ½ V, 3½ HFMt, 1 Fat	556	2042

*Contains concentrated sources of carbohydrates

Food	Portion	Exchanges	Calories	Sodium (mg)
Hardee's, cont.				
Big Deluxe Burger		2 S, ½ V, 3 MFMt, 2½ Fat	503	868
Cheeseburger		2 S, 1½ MFMt, 1½ Fat	327	745
Hamburger		2 S, 1 MFMt, ½ Fat	244	548
Mushroom 'n' Swiss Burger		2½ S, 1 V, 3½ MFMt, 1 Fat	509	1051
¼-lb. Cheeseburger		2 S, 1 V, 3 MFMt, 2½ Fat	511	1095
Chicken Fillet		2 S, 2 MFMt, 1½ Fat	446	1242
Cool Twist Cone*		1½ S, 1 Fat	164	111
Egg		1 MFMt	79	54
Fisherman's Fillet		3 S, 2 MFMt, 2 Fat	469	1013
French Fries				
*large**		1½ S, 2 Fr, 4½ Fat	438	170
*reg.**		1 S, 1 Fr, 2½ Fat	252	88
Hash Rounds Potatoes		1½ S, 3 Fat	249	304
Hot Dog		1½ S, 1½ HFMt, ½ Fat	285	796
Hot Ham 'n' Cheese		2 S, 2½ LMt	316	1833
Roast Beef				
big		2 S, 3 MFMt, 1 Fat	440	1434
reg.		2 S, 2 MFMt, ½ Fat	312	966
Salad				
Chef		5½ V, 1½ MFMt, 1 Fat	309	788
Side		4 V	90	43
Turkey Club		2 S, 2½ MFMt, 2 Fat	426	1185

■ McDonald's

Food	Portion	Exchanges	Calories	Sodium (mg)
Apple Pie*		1 S, 1 Fr, 3 Fat	260	240
Biscuits				
w/Bacon, Egg & Cheese		2 S, 1 MFMt, ½ HFMt, 4 Fat	449	1230
w/Biscuit Spread		2 S, 2½ Fat	260	730
w/Sausage		2 S, 1½ HFMt, 3½ Fat	440	1080
w/Sausage & Egg		2 S, 1 MFMt, 1½ HFMt, 4 Fat	529	1250
Burger				
Big Mac		2½ S, 2½ MFMt, ½ HFMt, 3 Fat	565	950
Cheeseburger		1½ S, 1 MFMt, ½ HFMt, 1 Fat	307	750
Hamburger		1½ S, 1 MFMt, 1 Fat	255	460
McD.L.T.		2½ S, 3 MFMt, ½ HFMt, 1 V, 4 Fat	678	1170
Quarter Pounder		2 S, 2½ MFMt, 1 V, 1½ Fat	417	660

*Contains concentrated sources of carbohydrates

Food	Portion	Exchanges	Calories	Sodium (mg)
Quarter Pounder w/Cheese		2 S, 2½ MFMt, 1 HFMt, 1 V, 1½ Fat	517	1150
Chicken McNuggets	(6 pieces)	1 S, 2½ MFMt, ½ Fat	288	520
Chicken McNugget Sauce (1 pkt.)				
*Barbeque**		1 Fr	53	340
*Hot Mustard**		½ Fr, 1 Fat	66	250
*Sweet & Sour**		1 Fr	57	190
Chow Mein Noodles (¼ cup)		½ S, ½ Fat	45	60
Cookies (one box)				
*Chocoaty Chip**		1 S, 2 Fr, 3 Fat	325	280
*McDonaldland**		1 S, 2 Fr, 2 Fat	288	300
Croutons (½ oz.)		½ S, ½ Fat	52	140
Danish				
*Apple**		2½ S, 1 Fr, 2½ Fat	389	370
*Cinnamon Raisin**		2 S, 2 Fr, 4 Fat	445	430
*Iced Cheese**		1½ S, 1½ Fr, ½ HFMt, 3½ Fat	395	420
*Raspberry**		2 S, 2 Fr, 3 Fat	414	310
English Muffin		2 S	140	(N/A)
w/butter		2 S, 1 Fat	169	270
French Fries				
large		2½ S, 3 Fat	312	155
reg.		2 S, 2 Fat	220	110
Hash Browns		2 S, 1½ Fat	131	330
Hot Cakes				
no butter or syrup		3½ S	246	(N/A)
w/butter, no syrup		3½ S, 1 Fat	301	(N/A)
Filet-O-Fish		2 S, 1 MFMt, ½ HFMt, 4 Fat	442	1030
McMuffin				
Egg McMuffin		2 S, ½ LMt, 1 MFMt, ½ HFMt	293	740
Sausage McMuffin		2 S, 2 HFMt, 1 Fat	372	830
Sausage McMuffin w/Egg		2 S, 1 MFMt, 2 HFMt, 1 Fat	451	980
Milk Shake				
*Chocolate**		3½ Fr, 1 WMk, ½ Fat	388	240
*Strawberry**		3½ Fr, 1 WMk, ½ Fat	384	170
*Vanilla**		3 Fr, 1 WMk, ½ Fat	354	170
Pork Sausage Patty		1 HFMt, 1½ Fat	180	350
Salad				
Chef		2 LMt, ½ MFMt, ½ HFMt, 1½ V	231	490

*Contains concentrated sources of carbohydrates

Food	Portion	Exchanges	Calories	Sodium (mg)
McDonald's, cont.				
Chicken Oriental		3 LMt, 1 V	141	230
Garden		½ MFMt, ½ HFMt, 1 V	112	160
Shrimp		2 LMt, 1 V	104	480
Side		½ HFMt, ½ V	57	85
Salad Dressing (full pkt.)				
Bleu Cheese		½ S, 7 Fat	345	750
*French**		½ Fr, 4 Fat	232	720
*Lite Vinaigrette**		½ Fr	60	240
*Oriental**		1½ Fr	96	720
*Ranch**		½ Fr, 7 Fat	332	520
*Thousand Island**		1 Fr, 7½ Fat	390	500
Scrambled Eggs		2 MFMt	157	290
Soft Serve w/Cake Cone*		1½ S, 1 Fat	144	70

■ Roy Rogers

(You may also find Roy Rogers brand foods served at some Hardee's restaurants.)

Food	Portion	Exchanges	Calories	Sodium (mg)
Biscuit		1½ S, 2½ Fat	231	575
Breakfast Crescent Sandwich				
Plain		1½ S, 1 MFMt, 4½ Fat	401	867
w/Bacon		1½ S, 1 MFMt, 5 Fat	431	1035
w/Ham		1½ S, 2 MFMt, 6 Fat	557	1192
w/Sausage		1½ S, 2 MFMt, 4 Fat	449	1289
Brownie*		2 S, 1½ Fr, 2 Fat	264	150
Burger				
Bacon Cheeseburger		2 S, 2½ MFMt, 1 HFMt, 3½ Fat	581	1535
Cheeseburger		2 S, 2½ MFMt, 1 HFMt, 3 Fat	563	1404
Hamburger		2 S, 2½ MFMt, 3 Fat	456	495
RR Bar Burger		2 S, 2½ MFMt, 1 HFMt, 1 LMt, 3 Fat	611	1826
Cole Slaw*		½ Fr, 1 V, 1 Fat	110	261
Crescent Roll		1½ S, 3½ Fat	287	547
Danish				
*Apple**		1½ S, ½ Fr, 2 Fat	249	255
*Cheese**		1½ S, ½ Fr, 2½ Fat	254	260
*Cherry**		1½ S, ½ Fr, 3 Fat	271	242
Egg & Biscuit Platter		1½ S, 2 MFMt, 3 Fat	394	734
w/Bacon		1½ S, 2 MFMt, 4 Fat	435	957
w/Ham		1½ S, 2 MFMt, 1 LMt, 3 Fat	442	1156

*Contains concentrated sources of carbohydrates

Food	Portion	Exchanges	Calories	Sodium (mg)
w/Sausage		1½ S, 2 MFMt, 1 HFMt, 4 Fat	550	1059
French Fries				
large		3 S, 3½ Fat	357	220
reg.		2 S, 2½ Fat	268	165
Fried Chicken				
Breast		1 S, 4 MFMt, ½ Fat	412	609
Drumstick/leg		½ S, 1½ MFMt	140	190
Thigh		1 S, 2 MFMt, 2 Fat	296	406
Wing		½ S, 1½ MFMt, 1 Fat	192	528
Hot Topped Potato				
Plain		3 S	211	10
w/Broccoli 'n' Cheese		2½ S, ½ V, ½ HFMt, 1 Fat	376	523
w/Oleo		3 S, 1½ Fat	274	106
w/Sour Cream 'n' Chives		3 S, 4 Fat	408	138
w/Taco Beef 'n' Cheese		3 S, 2 HFMt, 1 Fat	463	726
Macaroni		1 S, 2 Fat	186	603
Pancake Platter w/Syrup & Butter		2½ S, 2 Fr, 3 Fat	452	842
*w/Bacon**		2½ S, 2 Fr, 4 Fat	493	1065
*w/Ham**		2½ S, 2 Fr, 1 LMt, 3 Fat	506	1264
*w/Sausage**		2½ S, 2 Fr, 1 HFMt, 4 Fat	608	1167
Potato Salad		1 S, 1 Fat	107	696
Roast Beef		2 S, 3 LMt	317	785
w/Cheese		2 S, 3 LMt, 1 HFMt	424	1694
Large		2 S, 4 LMt	360	1044
Large w/Cheese		2 S, 4 LMt, 1 HFMt	467	1953

Salad Bar

The following items are free exchanges and contain fewer than 11 calories and fewer than 11 mg of sodium per serving: cucumbers (5–6 slices); green peppers (2 tbsp.); lettuce (1 cup); mushrooms (¼ cup).

Food	Portion	Exchanges	Calories	Sodium (mg)
Bacon Bits	(1 tbsp.)	½ LMt	33	210
Beets, sliced	(½ cup)	1 V	32	200
Broccoli	(½ cup)	1 V	20	7
Carrots, shredded	(⅛ cup)	1 V	22	4
Cheddar Cheese	(¼ cup)	1 HFMt	112	195
Chinese Noodles	(¼ cup)	½ S, ½ Fat	55	100
Croutons	(2 tbsp.)	1 S	70	260
Egg, chopped	(2 tbsp.)	½ MFMt	55	41
Macaroni Salad	(2 tbsp.)	½ S, ½ Fat	60	301
Potato Salad	(2 tbsp.)	½ S, ½ Fat	50	350
Sunflower Seeds	(2 tbsp.)	½ HFMt, 2 Fat	157	8

*Contains concentrated sources of carbohydrates

Food	Portion	Exchanges	Calories	Sodium (mg)
Roy Rogers, cont.				
Tomatoes	(3 slices)	free	20	3
Salad Dressing (2 tbsp.)				
*Bacon 'n' Tomato**		½ Fr, 2½ Fat	136	150
Blue Cheese		3 Fat	150	153
Lo-cal Italian		1½ Fat	70	100
*Ranch**		½ Fr, 3 Fat	155	100
*Thousand Island**		½ Fr, 3 Fat	160	150
Shake				
*Chocolate**		3 Fr, 1 WMk, ½ Fat	358	290
*Strawberry**		2½ Fr, 1 WMk, ½ Fat	315	261
*Vanilla**		2 Fr, 1 WMk, ½ Fat	306	282
Strawberry Shortcake*		3 S, 1 Fr, 4 Fat	447	674
Sundae				
*Caramel**		2½ Fr, 1 WMk	293	193
*Hot Fudge**		3 Fr, 1 WMk, 1 Fat	337	186
*Strawberry**		2 Fr, ½ WMk, ½ Fat	216	99

■ Wendy's

Food	Portion	Exchanges	Calories	Sodium (mg)
Bacon	(1 strip)	½ Fat	30	125
Breakfast Potatoes		2½ S, 4 Fat	360	745
Breakfast Sandwich		2 S, 1½ MFMt, 2 Fat	370	770
Burger				
Big Classic		2 S, 1 V, 2½ MFMt, 2½ Fat	470	900
¼ lb. Single Hamburger		2 S, 3½ MFMt, 3½ Fat	588	1165
Buttermilk Biscuit*		2 S, ½ Fr, 3 Fat	320	860
Chicken Filet		2½ S, 3 LMt, ½ MFMt, 3½ Fat	578	1475
Chicken Fried Steak		1½ S, 3½ MFMt, 4½ Fat	580	1040
Chili, reg.		1 S, 2 V, 1½ MFMt	240	990
Chocolate Chip Cookie*		1 S, 1½ Fr, 3½ Fat	320	235
Condiments				
Half & Half	(⅝ oz.)	½ Fat	28	10
Hot Chili Seasoning	(1 pkt.)	free	6	270
Ketchup	(1 pkt.)	free	12	115
Saltines	(4 each)	½ S	50	140
*Strawberry Jam**	(1 pkt.)	½ Fr	40	trace
Taco Sauce	(1 pkt.)	free	10	105
Tartar Sauce	(1 tbsp.)	2 Fat	80	75

*Contains concentrated sources of carbohydrates

Food	Portion	Exchanges	Calories	Sodium (mg)
Crispy Chicken Nuggets				
(6 pieces, cooked in veg. oil)		1 S, 2 MFMt, 2 Fat	310	660
(6 pieces, cooked in animal/veg. oil)		1 S, 2 MFMt, 2 Fat	290	615
Crispy Chicken Nugget Sauce				
*Barbecue**	(1 pkt.)	1 Fr	50	100
Cheese	(2 oz.)	1 HFMt, 1 Fat	140	415
Chives	(1 tsp.)	½ V	16	(N/A)
Margarine, liquid	(½ oz.)	2 Fat	100	100
Margarine, whipped	(1 tbsp.)	1½ Fat	70	60
Sour Cream	(2 tsp.)	½ Fat	20	5
*Sweet Mustard**	(1 pkt.)	1 Fr	50	140
*Sweet & Sour**	(1 pkt.)	1 Fr	45	55
Danish				
*Apple**		2 S, 1½ Fr, 2½ Fat	360	380
*Cheese**		2 S, 1½ Fr, ½ HFMt, 3 Fat	430	500
*Cinnamon Raisin**		2½ S, 1 Fr, 3½ Fat	410	430
Egg, Fried	(1)	1 MFMt	90	95
Eggs, Scrambled	(2 eggs)	2 MFMt, ½ Fat	190	160
Fish Fillet		3 S, 2 MFMt, 4 Fat	588	1640
French Fries				
(reg., cooked in veg. oil)		2 S, 3 Fat	300	135
(reg., cooked in animal/veg. oil)		2 S, 3 Fat	310	105
French Toast (2 slices)		3 S, 3½ Fat	400	850
*Apple Topping**	(1 pkt.)	2 Fr	130	120
*Blueberry Topping**	(1 pkt.)	1 Fr	60	65
Frosty Dairy Dessert,* small		1½ S, 1½ Fr, 1½ LFMk	400	220
Hot Stuffed Baked Potato		3½ S	250	60
Bacon & Cheese		3½ S, 1 MFMt, 5 Fat	570	1180
Broccoli & Cheese		3½ S, ½ V, ½ MFMt, 4½ Fat	500	430
Cheese		3½ S, 1 MFMt, 5½ Fat	590	450
Chili & Cheese		4 S, 1½ MFMt, 2½ Fat	510	610
Sour Cream & Chives		3½ S, 4½ Fat	460	230
Multi-Grain Bread	(1 slice)	1½ S, ½ Fat	140	215
Omelet				
*#1**		½ Fr, 2½ HFMt	290	570
#2		1 V, 2 HFMt	250	405
#3		1 V, 2½ HFMt	280	485
#4		1 V, 2 MFMt, 1 Fat	210	200

*Contains concentrated sources of carbohydrates

Food	Portion	Exchanges	Calories	Sodium (mg)

Wendy's, cont.

Salad Bar, Garden Spot

The following items are free exchanges and contain fewer than 11 calories and fewer than 11 mg of sodium per serving: alfalfa sprouts (1 oz.); red cabbage (¼ cup); celery (1 tbsp.); cucumbers (4 slices); iceburg lettuce (1 cup); romaine lettuce (1 cup); mushrooms (¼ cup); radishes (½ oz.); red onions (3 rings).

The following items equal ½ Fruit exchange and contain fewer than 40 calories and fewer than 13 mg of sodium per serving: cantaloupe (4 pieces); grapefruit (6 oz.); grapes (¼ cup); honeydew melon (3 pieces); jalapeño peppers (3 tbsp.); oranges (2 oz.); peaches (4 pieces); strawberries (4 oz.).

The following items equal ½ Vegetable exchange and contain fewer than 20 calories and fewer than 16 mg of sodium per serving: broccoli (½ cup); carrots (¼ cup); cauliflower (½ cup); green pepper (½ cup); tomatoes (2 oz.).

Food	Portion	Exchanges	Calories	Sodium (mg)
American Cheese, imitation	(1 oz.)	1 HFMt	90	365
Breadsticks	(2 breadsticks)	½ S	35	60
Cheddar Cheese, imitation	(1 oz.)	1 MFMt	80	310
Cherry Peppers	(1 tbsp.)	free	6	180
Chow Mein Noodles	(½ oz.)	½ S, 1 Fat	70	105
*Cole Slaw**	(¼ cup)	½ Fr, 1 Fat	80	165
Cottage Cheese	(½ cup)	2 LMt	110	425
Croutons	(½ oz.)	½ S, ½ Fat	60	155
Eggs	(1 tbsp.)	½ MFMt	30	25
Green Peas	(2 oz.)	½ S	50	70
Mozzarella Cheese, imitation	(1 oz.)	1 HFMt	90	335
Parmesan Cheese, grated	(1 oz.)	2 MFMt	130	510
Pasta Salad	(¼ cup)	1 S, 1 Fat	130	190
Pepper Rings	(1 tbsp.)	free	2	200
Pineapple Chunks	(½ cup)	1 Fr	70	0
Provolone Cheese, imitation	(1 oz.)	1 HFMt	90	335
Sunflower Seeds & Raisins	(1 oz.)	½ Fr, ½ HFMt, 1 Fat	140	5
Swiss Cheese, imitation	(1 oz.)	1 HFMt	90	365
Turkey Ham	(¼ cup)	1 LMt	50	(N/A)
Watermelon	(4 pieces)	½ Fr	36	trace
Salad Dressing (1 tbsp.)				
Blue Cheese		1½ Fat	60	85

*Contains concentrated sources of carbohydrates

Food	Portion	Exchanges	Calories	Sodium (mg)
Celery Seed		1½ Fat	70	65
*French Style**		½ Fr, 1 Fat	70	130
Golden Italian		1 Fat	50	260
Oil		3 Fat	120	0
Ranch		1 Fat	50	95
*Reduced Calorie Bacon/Tomato**		1 Fat	45	180
*Reduced Calorie Creamy Cucumber**		1 Fat	50	140
*Reduced Calorie Italian**		½ Fat	25	180
*Reduced Calorie Thousand Island**		1 Fat	45	125
*Thousand Island**		1½ Fat	70	115
Wine Vinegar		free	2	5
Sausage Gravy	(6 oz.)	1 S, 2 LMt, 6 Fat	440	1300
Sausage Patty		1 HFMt, 2 Fat	200	405
Wheat Toast, w/Margarine	(2 slices)	1½ S, 1½ Fat	190	315
White Toast, w/Margarine	(2 slices)	2 S, 2 Fat	250	410

*Contains concentrated sources of carbohydrates

14
BABY FOODS

Baby foods are used by persons of all ages—very young children with diabetes as well as adults who have dental problems or who follow special diets.

Exchanges are easily measured when using baby foods. If you use baby juices and foods extensively in your diet, discuss fluoride supplements with your physician.

In planning a diet for children, much guidance should be given by the family dietitian. The stages of baby food should be discussed, as well as the timetable for adding new foods. The physician might have to adjust the insulin dose. Great care should be taken to understand the diet, and monitoring is extremely important when introducing new foods.

A wide variety of commercial baby food is available. The brand included here, randomly chosen, represents a sampling of some of the choices.

Food	Portion	Exchanges	Calories	Sodium (mg)
■ Beechnut Stage 1				
Cereal (¾ oz. dry)				
Barley		1 S	75	22.5
Oatmeal		1 S	75	22.5
Rice		1 S	90	22.5
Fruit (4½-oz. jar)				
Applesauce, Golden Delicious		1 Fr	60	0
Bananas, Chiquita		1½ Fr	100	0
Peaches, Yellow Cling		1 Fr	60	0
Pears, Bartlett		1 Fr	60	0
Prunes		2 Fr	130	0
Juice (4.2-fl.-oz. jar)				
Apple		1 Fr	60	5
Pear		1 Fr	60	5
White Grape		1 Fr	80	10
Meat (3½-oz. jar)				
Beef & Beef Broth		2 LMt	120	75
Chicken & Chicken Broth		2 LMt	110	70
Lamb & Lamb Broth		2 LMt	130	80
Veal & Veal Broth		2 LMt	120	70
Turkey & Turkey Broth		2 LMt	120	60
Vegetables (4½-oz. jar)				
Carrots, Regal Imperial		1½ V	40	130
Green Beans		1½ V	40	0
Peas, Tender Sweet		1 S	70	0
Squash, Butternut		1½ V	40	0
Sweet Potatoes		1 S	70	60
Yellow Wax Beans		1 V	30	0
■ Beechnut Stage 2				
Cereal				
Mixed	(.5 oz. dry)	½ S	50	15
Mixed w/Applesauce & Bananas	(4½-oz. jar)	1 S	80	5
Oatmeal w/Applesauce & Bananas	(4½-oz. jar)	1 S	90	5
Oatmeal w/Bananas	(.5 oz. dry)	½ S	50	15
Rice & Apples	(.5 oz. dry)	1 S	60	15
Rice w/Applesauce & Bananas	(4½-oz. jar)	1 S, ½ Fr	100	25
Rice & Bananas	(.5 oz. dry)	1 S	60	15

Food	Portion	Exchanges	Calories	Sodium (mg)
Dessert (4½-oz. jar)				
Banana Custard Pudding*		2 Fr	120	30
Banana Pineapple*		1½ Fr	100	15
Cottage Cheese w/Pineapple*		1 Fr, ½ S	110	15
Dutch Apple*		1½ Fr	80	20
Guava Tropical Fruit*		1½ Fr	100	10
Mango Tropical Fruit*		1½ Fr	90	15
Mixed Fruit & Yogurt*		2 Fr	110	20
Papaya Tropical Fruit*		1½ Fr	80	15
Peaches & Yogurt*		2 Fr	110	25
Vanilla Custard Pudding*		½ S, 1 Fr, ½ Fat	130	60
Dinner (4½-oz. jar)				
Beef & Egg Noodle		½ S, 1 V, 1 Fat	90	30
Chicken Noodle w/Vegetables		½ S, 1 V, ½ Fat	90	30
Chicken & Rice w/Vegetables		½ S, 1 V, ½ Fat	80	35
Macaroni, Tomato & Beef		½ S, 1 V, ½ Fat	90	40
Turkey Rice w/Vegetables		½ S, 1 V, ½ Fat	70	35
Vegetable Beef		½ S, 1 V, ½ Fat	90	35
Vegetable Chicken		½ S, 1 V, ½ Fat	90	55
Vegetable Ham		½ S, 1 V, ½ Fat	90	30
Vegetable Lamb		½ S, 1 V, ½ Fat	90	40
Dinner Supreme (4½-oz. jar)				
Beef		½ S, ½ MFMt, 1 Fat	120	50
Turkey		½ S, ½ MFMt, ½ Fat	110	45
Fruit (4½-oz. jar)				
Applesauce & Apricots		1 Fr	60	5
Applesauce & Bananas		1 Fr	60	5
Applesauce & Cherries		1 Fr	70	5
Apricots w/Pears & Applesauce		1 Fr	70	0
Bananas w/Pears and Applesauce		1½ Fr	90	0
Bartlett Pears & Pineapple		1½ Fr	80	5
Fruit Dessert		1½ Fr	80	0
Pears & Applesauce		1 Fr	70	0
Plums w/Rice*		2 Fr	110	10
Prunes w/Pears		2 Fr	120	0
Fruit Supreme Dessert (4½-oz. jar)				
Apples & Grapes		1½ Fr	90	5
Apples, Mandarin Oranges & Bananas*		1½ Fr	90	5
Apples, Peaches & Strawberries*		1½ Fr	100	0
Apples, Pears & Bananas		1½ Fr	90	0

*Contains concentrated sources of carbohydrates

Food	Portion	Exchanges	Calories	Sodium (mg)
Apples & Strawberries		1½ Fr	90	0
Vegetables (4½-oz. jar)				
Creamed Corn		1 S	90	25
Garden		2 V	60	25
Mixed		2 V	50	30
Peas & Carrots		½ S, ½ V	60	50

■ Beechnut Stage 3

Food	Portion	Exchanges	Calories	Sodium (mg)
Dessert (7½-oz. jar)				
Cottage Cheese w/Pineapple*		½ LMt, 3 Fr	190	25
Mixed Fruit & Yogurt*		½ SMk, 2 Fr	170	35
Peaches & Yogurt*		½ LFMk, 2 Fr	190	50
Vanilla Custard Pudding*		½ WMk, 2 Fr	210	100
Dinner (7½-oz. jar)				
Beef and Egg Noodle w/Vegetables		1 S, 1 V, 1 Fat	150	60
Chicken Noodle w/Vegetables		1 S, 1 V, 1 Fat	140	50
Macaroni, Tomato & Beef		1 S, 1 V, 1 Fat	150	85
Spaghetti, Tomato & Beef		1 S, 2 V, 1 Fat	170	75
Turkey Rice w/Vegetables		1 S, 1 V, 1 Fat	130	50
Vegetable Bacon		1 S, 1 V, 2 Fat	180	200
Vegetable Beef		1 S, 1 V, 1 Fat	150	80
Vegetable Chicken		1 S, 1 V, 1 Fat	140	70
Vegetable Lamb		1 S, 1 V, 1 Fat	140	50
Fruit (7½-oz. jar)				
Applesauce		1½ Fr	100	10
Applesauce & Bananas		2 Fr	110	10
Applesauce & Cherries		2 Fr	110	10
Apples, Mandarin Oranges & Bananas*		2½ Fr	150	0
Apples, Peaches & Strawberries*		2½ Fr	160	0
Apples, Pears & Bananas*		2½ Fr	160	10
Apples & Strawberries*		2½ Fr	160	0
Apricots w/Pears & Apples		2 Fr	120	10
Bananas w/Pears & Apples		2½ Fr	160	0
Bartlett Pears		2 Fr	110	5
Bartlett Pears & Pineapple		2 Fr	120	5
Fruit Dessert		2 Fr	130	0
Peaches*		2½ Fr	150	0
Vegetables (7½-oz. jar)				
Carrots		2 V	60	220
Green Beans		2 V	60	0
Sweet Potatoes		1½ S	120	100

*Contains concentrated sources of carbohydrates

Food	Portion	Exchanges	Calories	Sodium (mg)
Beechnut Table Time (6 oz.)				
Beef Stew		½ S, 1 MFMt, 1 V	140	380
Hearty Chicken w/Stars Soup		½ S, 1 MFMt, 1 V, 1 Fat	180	350
Spaghetti Rings in Meat Sauce		1 S, ½ HFMt, 1 V	160	390
Vegetable Stew w/Chicken		1 S, 1½ V, 1½ Fat	190	340
Beechnut Unstaged Juices (Unstaged Juices are sold in various sizes)				
Apple	(4 oz.)	1 Fr	60	5
Apple Banana	(4.2 oz.)	1 Fr	60	5
Apple Cherry	(4 oz.)	1 Fr	50	5
Apple Cranberry	(4.2 oz.)	1 Fr	60	5
Apple Grape	(4 oz.)	1 Fr	60	5
Apple Pear	(4.2 oz.)	1 Fr	60	5
Mixed Fruit	(4 oz.)	1 Fr	60	5
Orange	(4 oz.)	1 Fr	60	5
Pear	(4 oz.)	1 Fr	60	5
Tropical Blend	(4 oz.)	1 Fr	70	10

15

ALCOHOL

A diabetic should discuss alcohol consumption with a dietitian or physician. The American Diabetes Association and The American Dietetic Association recommend in *Nutrition Guide for Professionals* that alcohol be taken only in moderation: "not more than 1 to 2 alcohol equivalents once or twice a week.

"One alcohol equivalent is equal to:

—a 1½-ounce shot of distilled beverage (dry brandy, gin, rum, scotch, vodka, whiskey); or

—4 ounces of wine; or

—12 ounches of beer."

These important warnings about alcohol were given by J. McDonald in his article, "Whiskey or Water," published in *Diabetes Forecast*:

1. Avoid alcohol if you have gastritis (inflammation of the stomach) or pancreatitis (inflammation of the pancreas). Persons with certain forms of heart or kidney disease also should avoid alcohol.

2. Avoid alcohol if you are prone to hypertriglyceridemia and atherosclerosis.

3. Avoid drinking on an empty stomach. This can lead to hypoglycemia (low blood sugar).

4. For diabetics taking oral glucose-lowering agents, alcohol can lower blood sugar and cause dizziness, flushness, and nausea.

5. Light beer is less harmful than regular beer, and dry wine is less harmful than sweet.

You can see how important it is to discuss alcohol with a dietitian. A registered dietitian should be able to determine how to calculate alcohol into a diabetic's diet. Alcohol should not take the place of foods for diabetics taking insulin because of the risk of alcohol-induced hypoglycemia. The discussion should center on whether alcohol can be included, and whether calories are a concern. Of course, alcohol should be discouraged during pregnancy.

Alcohol is usually calculated as fat exchanges, but can be calculated as fats and starch/breads, depending upon the carbohydrate content of the beverage.

Here is a small sampling of exchanges for a few domestic light and dark beers.

Food	Portion	Exchanges	Calories	Sodium (mg)
Beer				
Anheuser Busch (12 oz.)				
Bud Light*		½ S, 1½ Fat	108	(trace)
Budweiser*		1 S, 1½ Fat	144	(trace)
Busch*		1 S, 1½ Fat	144	(trace)
King Cobra*		½ S, 2½ Fat	160	(trace)
LA*		1 S, 1 Fat	112	(trace)
Michelob*		1 S, 2 Fat	160	(trace)
Michelob Classic Dark*		1 S, 2 Fat	164	(trace)
Michelob Light*		1 S, 1½ Fat	134	(trace)
Natural Light*		½ S, 1½ Fat	110	(trace)
Miller Brewing Company,				
Miller Lite*	(12 oz.)	2 Fat	96	(N/A)

*Contains concentrated sources of carbohydrates

EXCHANGE LISTS

The following information is reprinted with permission from *Exchange Lists for Meal Planning,* published by The American Diabetes Association, Inc., and The American Dietetic Association. For more information, see "Resources," p. 182.

The reason for dividing food into six different groups is that foods vary in their carbohydrate, protein, fat, and calorie content. Each exchange list contains foods that are alike—each choice contains about the same amount of carbohydrate, protein, fat, and calories.

The following chart shows the amount of these nutrients in one serving from each exchange list.

Exchange List	Carbohydrate (grams)	Protein (grams)	Fat (grams)	Calories
Starch/Bread	15	3	trace	80
Meat—Lean	—	7	3	55
—Medium-Fat	—	7	5	75
—High-Fat	—	7	8	100
Vegetable	5	2	—	25
Fruit	15	—	—	60
Milk—Skim	12	8	trace	90
—Low-Fat	12	8	5	120
—Whole	12	8	8	150
Fat	—	—	5	45

As you read the exchange lists, you will notice that one choice often is a larger amount of food than another choice from the same list. Because foods are so different, each food is measured or weighed so the amount of carbohydrate, protein, fat, and calories is the same in each choice.

If you have a favorite food that is not included in any of these groups, ask your dietitian about it. That food can probably be worked into your meal plan, at least now and then.

The Exchange Lists are the basis of a meal planning system designed by a committee of The American Diabetes Association and The American Dietetic Association. While designed primarily for people with diabetes and others who must follow special diets, the Exchange Lists are based on principles of good nutrition that apply to everyone.

RESOURCES

American Association of Diabetes Educators
500 N. Michigan
Suite 1400
Chicago, IL 60611
(312) 661-1700

Promotes diabetes education, supports research, and provides guidance in establishing local chapters of diabetes educators. Its journal, *The Diabetes Educator,* is published bimonthly.

American Diabetes Association
505 8th Ave.
New York, NY 10018
(212) 947-9707

This association of physicians, health professionals, and lay people has affiliate organizations across the country. Its goals are to promote the search for a cure for diabetes and to improve the health and well-being of persons with diabetes and their families by distributing information to the public, offering a wide variety of patient education and family services, and providing the names of diabetes specialists in your area.

Exchange Lists for Meal Planning is available through local ADA affiliates. *Diabetes Forecast,* a magazine for diabetics and their families, is published monthly; a one-year subscription is $24. *Diabetes '91,* a quarterly patient newsletter, is free. The ADA also published *Diabetes Care,* a bimonthly journal for health professionals.

The American Dietetic Association
216 West Jackson Blvd.
Suite 800
Chicago, IL 60606
(312) 899-0040

This professional organization of dietitians sets standards for education and experience and can provide lists of qualified dietitians in your area.

Canadian Diabetes Association
National Office
89 Bond Street
Toronto, Ontario M5B 2J8
Canada
(416) 362-4440

In Canada, persons with diabetes use

a Food Group System, which uses "Choices" rather than exchanges to simplify meal planning. The CDA's leaflet, "Good Health Eating Guide," is available through local divisions and branches. Contact the National Office for phone numbers of local branches.

Diabetes in the News
P.O. Box 3105
Elkhart, IN 46515

A magazine published by The Ames Center for Diabetes Education. Stories include easy-to-read, up-to-date news and information on diabetes research, management, diet, and recipes. A one-year (six-issue) subscription costs $9.00.

Juvenile Diabetes Foundation International
432 Park Ave. South
New York, NY 10016
(212) 889-7575

The Juvenile Diabetes Foundation was founded by parents of diabetic children who were convinced that, through research, diabetes could be cured. There are 150 chapters worldwide. Phone 1-800-JDF-CURE for information about diabetes research and to request pamphlets about diabetes.

National Diabetes Information Clearinghouse
P.O. Box NDIC
9000 Rockville Pike
Bethesda, MD 20205
(301) 496-7433 or (202) 842-7630

The NDIC responds to all requests for information about diabetes and can provide information about available health-care supplies and instruments, statistics on diabetes, teaching manuals, bibliographies, and the names and addresses of diabetes organizations and professional groups in your area.

Publications include *Diabetes Dateline,* a bimonthly newsletter for health professionals; *Resource Directory,* a list of state and federal programs offering services and financial assistance to people with diabetes; and topical bibliographies that provide full ordering and price information, such as *Cookbooks for People with Diabetes* and *Sports and Exercise for People with Diabetes.*

Sugarfree Center, Inc.
P.O. Box 114
Van Nuys, California 91408
(818) 994-1093

Mail-order source for diabetes self-care products, books, and information. Write for a free copy of its newsletter, *Health-O-Gram.*

BIBLIOGRAPHY

1. The American Diabetes Association, Inc., and The American Dietetic Association. *Exchange Lists for Meal Planning.* Alexandria, VA: The American Diabetes Association, Inc., and Chicago: The American Dietetic Association, 1986.

2. The American Diabetes Association, Inc., and The American Dietetic Association. *Nutrition Guide for Professionals.* Alexandria, VA: The American Diabetes Association, Inc., and Chicago: The American Dietetic Association, 1988.

3. The American Diabetes Association, Inc. "Nutritional Recommendations and Principles for Individuals with Diabetes Mellitus: 1986." *Diabetes Care* (Alexandria, VA) *10* (1987): 126–132.

4. Brink, S.J. *Pedriatric and Adolescent Diabetes Mellitus.* Chicago: Yearbook Medical Publishers Inc., 1987.

5. *Code of Federal Regulations, Parts 100–169.* Washington, D.C.: U.S. Government Printing Office, 1987.

6. Lipson, L. G. "Diabetes and Hypertension." *Diabetes Forecast* (May–June, 1985).

7. McDonald, J. "Whiskey or Water." *Diabetes Forecast* (Nov.–Dec., 1980, updated 1987).

8. National Heart, Lung, and Blood Institute, ''Facts About Blood Cholesterol.'' Bethesda, MD: U.S. Department of Health and Human Services, Public Health Service, National Institutes of Health.

9. National High Blood Pressure Education Program. *Hypertension in Diabetes: Final Report of the Working Group on Hypertension in Diabetes.* Bethesda, MD: U.S. Department of Health and Human Services, Public Health Service, National Institutes of Health, 1987.

10. Powers, M. A., "Historical Review of Diabetes Nutritional Management," *Handbook of Diabetes Nutritional Management.* Rockville, MD: Aspen Publishers, Inc., 1987.

11. Robinson, C. H. and Lawier, M. R. *Normal and Therapeutic Nutrition, 15th ed.* New York: Macmillian Publishing Co., 1977.

INDEX